# PICKING
# THE RIGHT
# UNIT TRUST

*With PEP Secrets*

21.99

# PICKING THE RIGHT UNIT TRUST

## With PEP Secrets

Bruce G. McWilliams

FT
PITMAN
PUBLISHING

London · Hong Kong · Johannesburg
Melbourne · Singapore · Washington DC

PITMAN PUBLISHING
128 Long Acre, London WC2E 9AN
Tel: +44 (0)171 447 2000
Fax: +44 (0)171 240 5771

A Division of Pearson Professional Limited

First published in Great Britain in 1997

ISBN 0 273 62415 6

*British Library Cataloguing in Publication Data*
A CIP catalogue record for this book can be obtained from
the British Library.

1 3 5 7 9 10 8 6 4 2

Typeset by Phoenix Photosetting, Chatham, Kent
Printed and bound in Great Britain by
Biddles Ltd, Guildford and King's Lynn

*The Publishers' policy is to use paper manufactured
from sustainable forests.*

# ABOUT THE AUTHOR

**Bruce G. McWilliams** puts his money where his mouth is: he has invested for 16 years in British, European and American unit trusts. His investment returns have consistently beaten the bank's appalling interest rates. He conducts investor conferences, writes about financial matters, and enjoys the rewards of a diversified unit trust portfolio.

Born in Hollywood, California, Bruce G. McWilliams has had nothing to do with the movie business, though his parents met working as extras on the Alfred Hitchcock classic, *Strangers on a Train*.

A noted financial how-to book author, his two financial books have sold repeatedly in the United States. His last book, *The Bruce G. McWilliams Under-33 Financial Plan* charted a clear strategy for young investors that centred on US unit trusts.

His first book, *Penny Stocks* explained in simple terms how to invest in low-priced shares. *The New York Times* said, 'Bruce G. McWilliams explains how investors of modest means can reap big profits ... and how they can hedge their bets in case they don't win big'.

He previously worked as a Citibank vice-president in London and Zürich, the home of private banking, and on Wall Street in New York City.

He understands the academic and technical side of investing as well as the realities, and holds an MBA in finance and a second masters degree in business economics from The Wharton School in the United States.

# CONTENTS

**Part 4**
**THE EASY YET SOPHISTICATED WAY TO INVEST**

**Part 5**
**GETTING IT RIGHT**

It is of course one of the known facts of investments that a Fixed Investment [unit trust] Fund, provided it is reasonably well spread to start with, will show an extraordinary capacity of survival, both as regards capital value and income, over long periods of years.

from *Unit Trusts and How They Work*, Rosenheim and Merriman, Sir Isaac Pitman & Sons, 1937

# FOREWORD

I really had great fun writing this book. I have invested in unit trusts and their American and European counterparts, mutual funds, for 16 years. My work for the book was personal: I wanted to know myself how to pick the right unit trust. The book gives the investor a complete picture.

As part of my effort, I spoke to as many people in the unit trust and PEP business as possible. Each has been willing to help in the greater cause of showing timid savers that risk can be reduced while returns enhanced with unit trusts. I asked these professionals, 'What should investors look for?' and 'How do you yourself invest?'. I learned the latest technique which I call BRUT (Buying the Right Unit Trust) technique. I spoke with investors. I spoke with journalists. I spoke with regulators. I spoke with financial advisors. I have included their perspectives in the book.

My publisher, Richard Stagg, counselled me about the tone for the book; 'Assume your reader is intelligent, but knows nothing about unit trust and PEP investing.' I took his advice. I go through the basics and give you the tools to employ the BRUT technique. The concepts are used by professionals themselves to choose unit trusts. The secret? – You can do it easily at home, once you know how.

The other great secret of this book: *Ring 'em Up*. If you don't understand a unit trust or PEP brochure you've received, ring up the company to ask your question. If you don't understand the price you received, ring 'em up. If you want more information about a fund's results or objectives, ring up the fund manager. If you don't understand the charges, ring them up. This is what I do and I'll give you several examples in the book. If the fund management company doesn't spell your name right, don't use them. If they don't send the information promptly, go somewhere else. You're the investor, you're the customer.

By the same philosophy, if you have more questions about unit trust and PEP investing, write or call me care of my publisher:

Bruce G. McWilliams
Author: Picking the Right Unit Trust: with PEP Secrets
Publisher: Richard Stagg
Pitman Publishing
128 Long Acre
London WC2 9AN
Tel: 0171-447 2215.

I plan to publish an unbiased, independent newsletter, after receiving regulatory approval, using the techniques highlighted in this book. If you would like to receive a sample copy, send me a note at the above address.

Thank you for buying my book, and I hope you have as much fun reading it as I had writing it.

Go out there, invest smartly, and watch your garden grow.

*Bruce G. McWilliams*

# ACKNOWLEDGEMENTS

The first person I met in the UK unit trust business was Clive Boothman, managing director of Schroders' Unit Trusts and chairman of the Association of Unit Trusts and Investment Funds. I wrote him a letter asking if I could talk with him about the unit trust business. He welcomed our discussion and over the years, I've found his helpfulness and openness charming. He read a draft of this manuscript, and provided a thoughtful and incredibly thorough response and I thank him for this.

Richard Stagg, my publisher at Pitman, and Amelia Lakin, his assistant, have provided the best publishing support I've received on either side of the Atlantic.

I asked several private investors and industry experts to read an early draft, and I appreciated their efforts: Richard Royds at Mercury gave me a laugh and several lengthy opportunities to discuss unit trusts; Roger Cornick at Perpetual; Mary Blair at Threadneedle Asset Management, Sandra Newman, and Louise Newman. Harry Nash at S. G. Warburg guided me helpfully through the maze of unit trust accounting. Gary Smith at Gartmore and Tony Woods at Virgin Direct offered me useful insights into the details of index tracking. Both Roger Jennings of M&G and Stephen C. Abbott at Legal & General met with me on several occasions to discuss an individual's requirements. Giles Kidd-Mays of Jupiter provided many useful sources of information and was most helpful. Eric Swats at Citibank gave me useful comments about his profession, bond investment. Chris Poll provided me with stacks of data and the opportunity to reprint *Micropal*'s useful unit trust summary sheets, which I hope gives you a real-life view on unit trust evaluation.

I discussed unit trust investments with the following people, and I appreciate their willingness to set aside some time for me, usually at a moment's notice:

| Name | Company |
|------|---------|
| Claire Rayner | Agony Aunt |
| Bob Hale | Association of Unit Trusts and Investment Funds (AUTIF) |
| Philip Warland | Association of Unit Trusts and Investment Funds (AUTIF) |
| Emma Weiss | Association of Unit Trusts and Investment Funds (AUTIF) |
| Grant Phillips | Barclays Unicorn |
| Jamie Berry | Berry Investments |
| Jason D. Hollands | BESt Investment |
| Paul Calkin | Calkin & Associates |
| Graham Hooper | Chase de Vere |
| Anthony Barnes | Chelsea Financial Service |
| Dr Bill Mott | Credit Suisse |
| Jeff Prestridge | *Financial Mail on Sunday* |
| Anne Davis | Fidelity Investments |
| Fiona Price | Fiona Price & Partners |
| Duncan Byatt | Gartmore |
| Brian O'Neill | Gartmore |
| Duncan Trinder | Gartmore |
| Jeremy Soutter | Henderson Touche Remnant |
| Andrew Beagley | Investment Management Regulatory Organisation (IMRO) |
| Philip Robinson | Investment Management Regulatory Organisation (IMRO) |
| Jamie Campbell | Jupiter Asset Management |
| William Littlewood | Jupiter Asset Management |
| Paul Donachie | Martin Currie |
| Trevor Mitchell | M. D. H. Hughes Ltd |
| Andrew Brittel | Mercury Asset Management |
| Harry Nash | Mercury Asset Management |
| Paul Barnes | *Micropal* |
| Tim Miller | Portfolio Fund Management |

| Name | Company |
| --- | --- |
| Richard Timberlake | Portfolio Fund Management |
| Jonathan P. H. Fry | Premier Investments |
| Allan Murray | Private Investor |
| David Brennan | Private Investor |
| Jim Basterfield | Private Investor |
| Sandy Buchan | Private Investor |
| Simon Bell | Private Investor |
| Alan C. Torry | Prolific Asset Management |
| Mark Hynes | Quay Associates |
| Philip Hardy | Schroders |
| David Graham | Scottish Widows |
| Clive Scott-Hopkins | Towry Law |
| Pascal Matic | Unitas |
| Martin Campbell | Virgin Direct |
| Keiron Root | What Investment |

My literary agent, Mandy Little, was the first to believe in the need for information about unit trusts and her assistant, Tahnee Wade, helped me through a maze of bureaucracy.

On a personal note, Richard and Sandra Morrison-Low often provided Scottish solace for the lonely writer and his guests. Jon Wayne Peters showed me the benefits of living life the way it should be lived. My parents continue to love and support me in my new adventures. And finally, Sophie and Tom Seale came through with ideas that you will use.

# PART

# 1

## UNIT TRUSTS: THE RIGHT IDEA FOR THE RIGHT TIME

# THE SECRETS OF UNIT TRUSTS AND PEPS

## True or false?

You can lose your entire investment in a unit trust.

True ☐   False ☐

Despite the low interest rate, my building society savings are safely growing.

True ☐   False ☐

An investment in a unit trust requires more money than I have.

True ☐   False ☐

Investing in a unit trust is very complicated.

True ☐   False ☐

Unit trusts may return more than the building society, but they are too much of a gamble.

True ☐   False ☐

Only those who are quite wealthy can invest in unit trusts.

True ☐   False ☐

All unit trusts invest strictly in shares, some of which are very risky.

True ☐   False ☐

The answers are all false. But, according to a London Stock Exchange report on investing, these beliefs are widespread[1]. This book addresses these issues. But let me say at the outset, no unit trust has ever gone to zero and you can begin a unit trust investment for as little as £50 per month.

Oh, one more thing.

**Returns after tax and charges**[2]

|  | Last year | Last five years |
| --- | --- | --- |
| Average building society account | +2.2% | 19.1% |
| Average UK equity unit trust | +9.9% | 72.9% |

At the extreme, a stockmarket investment of just £1 in the year 1700 would have grown to an astonishing £52 million by 1995. Gillian O'Connor reports in the *Financial Times* that, 'a similar investment in gilts would have increased to a comparatively modest £630,000'.[3] The margin of difference between the stock market and 'safe' investments has been constant. But investors continue to be perplexed by how to find the right investment. Let's look at how one fund manager approaches investing.

## CONSISTENTLY SUCCESSFUL

Mr William Littlewood is a little bookish: thick glasses, vast swath of blond hair, shirt-tail popping from the back of his trousers. Well-dressed, but not flashy. Behind this quiet exterior, though, lie the brains and talent of one of the most consistently successful portfolio managers in the UK. Littlewood runs Jupiter Asset Management's UK Equity Income Fund. For five straight years, his fund has ranked as the top-performing fund in its sector; his fund has gained nearly 22 per cent per year.

Let me be more explicit. Had you invested £1,000 in his fund five years ago, today you would have £2,749, a 175 per cent gain.

His efforts have not gone unnoticed. *Money Observer* magazine declared his fund the 'Best UK Equity Income Fund'; *Micropal*, the unbiased data service, awarded his performance 'Best' (for UK Equity Income Funds) over the last year and the last five years.

> Money Observer magazine provides useful personal finance information and is available at newsagents or by calling 0181-289 7960.

If this was the fund you chose for your then-£3,000 annual PEP allowance five years ago, today it would have grown tax-free to £8,784. Get out your PEP statement for the one you made five years ago to see how it compares.

He is only 30 years old and has been a fund manager for the last five years, after joining Jupiter when he was 23. Littlewood has both a fundamental knowledge of the companies he invests in and of the markets; but more than that, he has a sixth and indeed probably a seventh sense about investing.

Unlike most other fund managers, Littlewood doesn't believe in visiting companies; 'If you're on the factory floor, you get the stock view', the one that management wants you to get. 'We ask for presentations to be made in-house,' so he can make them sweat a little when they're not on familiar territory. His offices are in Knightsbridge, not the City, so he can't be swayed, he says, by skittish investing style trends in the City. 'We do our own research and rely very little on stockbrokers' recommendations for new companies in which to invest.'

He mentally divides his fund's portfolio in two: he's a loyal long-term investor for half the 200 companies in his portfolio, the others were opportunistic bargains he bought and will sell when the price is right. He says that he 'knows a little about a lot'.

Littlewood invests in companies in industries which are hard to enter; he likes companies with manageable debt loads and management who don't practise legally allowed deceits with the accounts. He says succinctly, 'Investing is an art, it's not a science.'

Details about Littlewood's Jupiter Income Fund are shown in Figure 1.1. *Micropal* has kindly allowed me to use their detailed fund reports.

# PICKING THE RIGHT UNIT TRUST

The academics say people like Littlewood are just lucky, that for every William Littlewood, there's another fund manager whose year-in, year-out returns are always below par. Maybe so, but I believe you can pick unit trusts which consistently perform well.

Dr Bill Mott, 17 years in the business, investment director at Credit Suisse: 'Investors have to work', to investigate the philosophies of the fund manager. 'If they just want to get it from their in-basket,' he says, reaching into an imaginary in-basket, 'and put it in their out-basket, [without completing any analysis] it won't work, their investments will fail.'

My aim in this book is to enable you to find the William Littlewoods of the UK unit trust market. Indeed, I found the Jupiter Income Fund exactly through a simple evaluation procedure, called Buying the Right Unit Trust (BRUT), which I'll show you in Chapter 13. This technique relies on consistent performance and is the latest used by the professionals themselves, as you'll see.

Finding the one, top best fund isn't the key to successful long-term investing. Over the years, I've developed a holistic approach to investing, which is as follows:

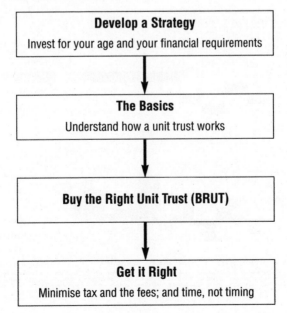

**Develop a Strategy**
Invest for your age and your financial requirements

**The Basics**
Understand how a unit trust works

**Buy the Right Unit Trust (BRUT)**

**Get it Right**
Minimise tax and the fees; and time, not timing

## Fig 1.1  Jupiter Income Fund

### Jupiter Income

Jupiter Unit Trust Mgrs, Knightsbridge House, 197 Knightsbridge, London SW7 1RB.

Information: Telephone - 0171 412 0703   Dealing - -

**Fund Objective:**
To produce a high income increasing at least in line with inflation from a managed portfolio chiefly invested in UK equities and fixed interest stocks although with some overseas exposure.

**Micropal Cumulative Performance - to 30th September 1996**

| Performance Period | 6 Months | 1 Year | 3 Years | 5 Years | 10 Years |
|---|---|---|---|---|---|
| Fund Performance | +2.3% | +17.0% | +70.9% | +174.9% | |
| Sector Average | +0.2% | +5.9% | +22.7% | +60.7% | +192.0% |
| Best Performing Fund | +5.5% | +17.0% | +70.9% | +174.9% | +308.6% |
| Worst Performing Fund | -9.5% | -8.9% | -0.8% | +10.4% | +111.5% |

Fund Performance

Sector Average Performance

(Offer-bid, net income reinvested)

| | | | | |
|---|---|---|---|---|
| Top Quartile | 14/90 | 1/88 | 1/80 | 1/78 |
| Second Quartile | | | | |
| Third Quartile | | | | |
| Bottom Quartile | | | | |

**Fund Size**

| Fund Size | £282.9m |
|---|---|
| Sector Average | £135.8m |
| Largest Fund: | £1161.0m |
| Smallest Fund: | £0.6m |
| No. of Funds: | 90 |

Fund Size

Average Fund Size in Sector

**Micropal Consistency of Performance Analysis**

— Jupiter Income
— Sector Average

% indexed accumulated return (1986 = 0%)

**Year Ending 30 September (offer-offer, net income reinvested)**

| | 1987 | 1988 | 1989 | 1990 | 1991 | 1992 | 1993 | 1994 | 1995 | 1996 |
|---|---|---|---|---|---|---|---|---|---|---|
| Performance of Fund (%) | | -15.8 | 21.9 | -21.6 | 28.1 | 5.7 | 52.2 | 11.7 | 30.8 | 24.4 |
| Performance of Sector (%) | 68.0 | -14.9 | 21.4 | -17.9 | 30.5 | -7.4 | 41.2 | 0.8 | 14.4 | 12.2 |
| Perf. of Micropal UT Total (%) | 46.8 | -18.1 | 27.6 | -20.7 | 26.8 | -3.9 | 40.8 | 4.2 | 10.0 | 12.8 |
| FTSE All Share (%) | 61.3 | -19.1 | 27.5 | -14.6 | 37.3 | -1.2 | 29.0 | 3.4 | 18.8 | 16.5 |
| UK Retail Price Index (%) | 4.2 | 5.9 | 7.6 | 10.9 | 4.1 | 3.6 | 1.8 | 2.2 | 3.9 | 1.2 |

| | 1987 | 1988 | 1989 | 1990 | 1991 | 1992 | 1993 | 1994 | 1995 | 1996 |
|---|---|---|---|---|---|---|---|---|---|---|
| Top Quartile | | | | | | 1/78 | 6/79 | 1/80 | 1/83 | 1/88 |
| Second Quartile | | | 35/72 | | | | | | | |
| Third Quartile | | | 36/69 | | 54/78 | | | | | |
| Bottom Quartile | | | | 62/74 | | | | | | |

**Micropal Rolling Period Analysis**

| | 1987 | 1988 | 1989 | 1990 | 1991 | 1992 | 1993 | 1994 | 1995 | 1996 |
|---|---|---|---|---|---|---|---|---|---|---|
| Highest 12 monthly return: 52.2% | | | | | | | | | | |
| Lowest 12 monthly return: -21.6% | | | | | | | | | | |
| Average 12 monthly return: 16.6% | | | | | | | | | | |

% return     offer-offer, net income reinvested

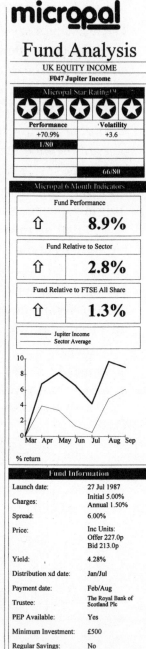

# micropal

## Fund Analysis

UK EQUITY INCOME

F047 Jupiter Income

**Micropal Star Rating™**

★★★★★

| Performance | Volatility |
|---|---|
| +70.9% | +3.6 |
| 1/80 | |
| | 66/80 |

**Micropal 6 Month Indicators**

Fund Performance

⇧ **8.9%**

Fund Relative to Sector

⇧ **2.8%**

Fund Relative to FTSE All Share

⇧ **1.3%**

— Jupiter Income
— Sector Average

% return

Mar Apr May Jun Jul Aug Sep

**Fund Information**

| | |
|---|---|
| Launch date: | 27 Jul 1987 |
| Charges: | Initial 5.00%<br>Annual 1.50% |
| Spread: | 6.00% |
| Price: | Inc Units:<br>Offer 227.0p<br>Bid 213.0p |
| Yield: | 4.28% |
| Distribution xd date: | Jan/Jul |
| Payment date: | Feb/Aug |
| Trustee: | The Royal Bank of Scotland Plc |
| PEP Available: | Yes |
| Minimum Investment: | £500 |
| Regular Savings: | No |

© Micropal Publications / Micropal Ltd 1996

*Source: Micropal*

Unit trusts are conservative investments. You establish a workable plan, and then invest. My approach doesn't require methodically watching the markets every second of the day, or even every day. Instead, like a plane flying on automatic pilot, you set the course and sit back. Of course, you need to check every so often to make sure you're still on course. Indeed, as your life changes and as you get older, you'll need to make adjustments to your investment plan.

Philip Robinson, chief operating officer of the unit trust regulatory agency, the Investment Management Regulatory Organisation (IMRO) says that 'the mechanics of investing in unit trusts are simple. Like riding a bicycle, once you learn how, you never forget.'

> For the basic facts on investing in and selling out of a unit trust, see the Appendix to this chapter.

With all the numbers and facts and figures, it does seem that investing is a precise science, with its scientific-sounding jargon, alphas, betas, gammas, standard deviations, compounded annual growth rates, and so on. Yet, the key is that markets and investments are based on human emotions and psychology: something that defies numerical classification. I'll provide clues, suggestions, and hints about the keys to look for.

In my work for this book, I have spoken with countless portfolio managers from Perpetual, Gartmore, Schroders, Legal & General, Fidelity, with independent financial advisors (IFAs), with individual investors. After a general introduction, I asked the main question: How would you pick a unit trust?

The answers I received were all sensible and reasonable. Choose a small fund, choose a large fund, choose a fund with a seasoned portfolio manager, choose a fund with a young hot-shot; choose a fund that's performed at the top for the last five years; choose a

---

**Special note to retirees:** the safety of your capital is first and foremost. You too will be given special tools to evaluate the safety of funds which promise high income in Chapters 9 and 10. Indeed, one of the best kept secrets is the cash unit trust – just as safe as a building society, but pays more interest.

fund that's a star right now, and so on. Even portfolio managers of unit trusts can't agree on the key to picking a unit trust. I'll suggest some techniques, which are fairly painless; but you must also consider other non-quantifiable variables, such as reputation or service ability.

> 'Even portfolio managers can't agree on the key to picking a unit trust.'

This book will take you through all aspects of investing in unit trusts. We'll look at unit trusts from the portfolio manager's perspective; we'll look at unit trusts from the product development point of view. We look at unit trusts from the Inland Revenue's perspective as well as from the big fund management companies. We take an in-depth look at index-tracking funds. You will hear unit trust industry executives speak about their own unit trust investments.

My aim is to make you comfortable with the terminology and the nuances. With any luck, you'll begin to get intrigued by the analysis and to find it feasible.

## MY STORY

I've been investing in unit trusts and their American and European counterparts, mutual funds, for 16 years. I began with cash funds when bank time deposit rates were too low and then moved into bond funds, and later into equity funds. I have dabbled in mortgage property funds, and now own an internationally diversified portfolio

> 'My aim is to make you comfortable with the terminology and the nuances.'

of index-tracking and stock-picking unit trusts. I also own a European bond fund and a cash fund. There have, of course, been years when my funds lost money; overall, though, I've beaten bank rates by a comfortable margin.

I'm a big believer in unit trust investing as the key for small and medium and large investors to gain professional management and to gain a sufficiently diversified portfolio. You might lose money in any one year in any one fund. But if you hold a diversified portfolio over more than five years, your chances of loss are minuscule.

I have striven to use data readily available to you, the private investor, at no or little cost. I used the brochures sent to me by unit trust fund management companies or IFAs. I read the popular personal finance magazines. I sent away for various PEP guides from IFAs that I saw mentioned in newspapers. I spoke with industry experts who emerged from my consistent unit trust picking methodology or who appeared in newspapers.

The analyses performed here are the ones recommended by the fund managers themselves for choosing a unit trust. I, like you, am a unit trust investor who needs to know how to pick the right unit trust.

## THE CASE FOR UNIT TRUSTS

A unit trust is a special type of legal entity established for the sole purpose of making investments for its investors. The legal form is that of a trust. The trust is divided into equal parts, called, not surprisingly, 'units'.

All unit trusts offer several generic benefits, otherwise unavailable to investors without huge sums of money.

Generally, the fund management company accepts money from investors such as yourself and then invests it in shares or bonds (see Figure 1.2).

> We'll go further into what constitutes a unit trust and some of the legal requirements – which are important to know – in Chapter 5.

**Fig 1.2  How a unit trust works**

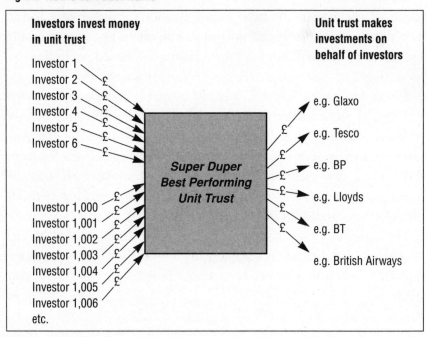

## Diversification?

All unit trusts offer investors something unavailable at such a low price – diversification. Undoubtedly, you've heard before that 'diversification' is a good thing. Very simply put, diversification is the financial equivalent of the old saying, 'Don't put all your eggs in one basket'.

*Whitaker's Almanac*, 1939, on 'Fixed and Flexible "Unit" Investment Trusts' said 'The prime objective of the [unit trust] movement is to open up to the investor of small means a wider field to enable him to spread his risks with relative safety, hitherto available only to the more influential investor.'[4] Likewise John Bogle, founder of the £125 billion ($200 billion) Vanguard Investment Group in the United States, says that, 'Diversification is at the very heart of' unit trust investing.[5]

Windsor-based Towry Law IFA Clive Scott-Hopkins, who's been investing in unit trusts for 35 years, says that in the early days, 'Unit trust investing had a cloth-cap image, that of the less affluent man's investment choice. Over the years, the unit trust has become more acceptable as a way of diversifying one's portfolio and building up a stake in overseas markets.' Scott-Hopkins adds that, 'New entrants in the last decade have livened it up and focused managers' minds, so you get better performance.'

If you own any company shares, and you're like most investors, you own shares in three companies.[3] And if you're like most people, you own a relatively high proportion of shares in one of those companies (probably the company you work for, privatisation shares, or shares from a recently converted building society) and a relatively small amount in the other two companies. The result of this share strategy is that you face the highest possible risk or volatility. Your portfolio is undiversified because it relies largely on the well-being of a few companies in a few industries.

'Volatility' is my preferred name for 'risk'. The more your portfolio bounces around, the more volatility it has, the more risk. Your undiversified portfolio bounces up and down a lot, probably more than the market in general. Suffice it to say now that volatility is how much more or less reactive your shares are as compared with the market in general.

> Volatility has an exact definition which we'll discuss in Chapter 12.

In practice, the shares in an undiversified portfolio could experience less volatility than the market as a whole; it is more likely, though, that you would find that your small, undiversified portfolio is much more volatile. As you increase the number of different companies in different industries in your portfolio, you reduce the volatility. At the extreme, you own every company's shares. This technique guarantees that your portfolio won't be any more volatile than the market.

## Cheap, too

Academic research has shown that you can achieve the benefits of diversification by accumulating shares in approximately 30 companies. By owning this number of different shares, your volatility will be very close to the volatility of the overall market. But buying shares in 30 companies would be very expensive. If you were to invest your annual PEP allowance, you would end up with £200 worth of shares in each company, of which 10 per cent would be taken in commissions alone.

Choosing which 30 stocks would certainly be a full-time job. You already have a full-time job. Equity unit trusts accomplish both tasks – choosing which stocks to buy and diversification. By pooling funds from many investors, the unit trust can afford to hire portfolio managers who select a sufficient number of shares for proper diversification. Further, the fund management company gets a better price – the volume discount – than you or I would.

> 'Academic research has shown that you can achieve the benefits of diversification by accumulating shares in approximately 30 companies.'

The same analysis holds for unit trusts which invest in bonds or money market securities instead of company shares. Minimum purchase of a market-rate instrument in the money markets is outside the reach of an average investor. In addition, these come due fairly frequently, so you'd need to continuously watch the markets. By investing in a bond or money market unit trust, you get the same benefits: better rates, professional management, and diversification.

The private holder of shares must pay capital gains tax every time he or she sells at a profit. In contrast, the unit trust fund pays no capital gains tax on profits so the fund manager can move in and out of positions without regard to tax. Thus, you, the unit trust investor, benefit indirectly from the unit trust's ability to sell unpromising shares without paying capital gains tax. As a unit trust investor, you pay capital gains tax only when your units are profitably sold.

## Getting your money when you want it

Another reason for owning units in a unit trust – as opposed to owning shares or bonds directly – is liquidity. 'Liquidity' is a fancy way of saying you can get your money when you want it. If you had purchased shares in 200 companies, it could be time-consuming and cumbersome to sell them. If you invested in a bond or made a time deposit and wanted to get your money back early, you might suffer a financial penalty.

For a unit trust, by placing a telephone request or sending in a sell order, you'll receive a cheque several days later or you can have the money directly transferred to your bank or building society account. Easy. Typically, there are no charges for selling your unit trust. Cheap. Together, 'easy and cheap' spell 'liquidity'.

## UNIT TRUSTS ARE NOT INVESTMENT TRUSTS

A unit trust and an investment trust are similar in that an investment manager chooses securities to be held collectively by holders of the trust. A unit trust's price is based solely on the underlying investments held in the portfolio. Unlike a unit trust, an investment trust trades freely on the stock exchange where its prices are determined every day by the give and take of traders.

The analysis of the underlying assets – the securities chosen by the portfolio manager – is the same for unit trusts and investment trusts. Because of the pricing, though, the investment trust adds another layer of complexity to the analysis. Investment trusts are considered cheaper than unit trusts, but suffer greater volatility: no reward without risk.

## PEPS AND UNIT TRUSTS

I've spoken with investors about their unit trust investments – some with a good deal of financial acumen – and many said, 'Right, I've got a PEP.' A PEP is not a unit trust, nor is a PEP an investment. A PEP is a legal tax dodge, a tax loophole, a set of tax rules. A PEP is a good deal. Everyone should make an investment through a PEP. A PEP is simply an incentive set up by the Treasury in 1987 to encourage investment in shares and bonds. There are other investments than unit trusts which qualify for PEP benefits. Likewise, a

> We discuss PEPs in Chapter 3, What Good is a PEP?, and throughout the book as required.

unit trust investment doesn't have to be in a PEP. A good investment is a good investment, PEP or otherwise. A bad investment won't be turned into a good one simply through the PEP tax elimination.

# OUTLINE OF THE BOOK

I've touched on the subjects to be covered in this book in depth. Let me give you the general outline, along with a brief explanation. In Chapter 2, I turn to some simple ways to choose a unit trust – and their drawbacks. After we've eliminated the simple ways, we'll set the stage with the PEP rules, and then turn to your financial situation.

## Develop your strategy

We'll put together an outline of your financial assets today and what you need for the future. Whenever I read financial planning books, I'm always tempted to skip this section. 'I want to get to the really good stuff, I don't need to be bored by what I already know.' I beg of you, plead with you, to fill out the charts in this section. They are critical to the really good stuff. To pick the right unit trust for you, you have to know what your financial brief looks like.

Many people's finances are an overly conservative, undiversified hotch-potch. Graham L. Hooper, investment director at Chase de Vere, an independent financial advisor, reports that people turn to his firm when they are about to retire. He says, 'Most people in their thirties leave their money in a building society', which is the great paradox, because they have more time to let their investments grow. If most of your financial resources find their home in a bank or building society, you're being quietly nibbled away by inflation. Unless you chart the movements of your well-being with pen and paper (or computer) you won't know. I'll plead with you more when we get to that section; at the end of that section, we will draw your financial picture and map where you want to go.

## The basics

After laying down the groundwork, we turn to the unit trust structure and the details of the costs you'll pay. This will lead to a discussion of the three categories of unit trusts, and the mélange in between. Unit trusts come in three basic flavours: cash, bonds, and equities or shares. You'll find that some form of unit trust can take care of most of your financial needs. We'll discuss how these unit trusts are made up, and how you can evaluate their performance.

## Buy the right unit trust

These following elements are critical ingredients to ensure your financial well-being – the combination of:

- best consistent performance
- least risk
- lowest costs
- lowest tax.

In Part 4, The Easy yet Sophisticated Way to Invest, we explore the work of the experts in fund selection – those whose livelihood depends on getting it right. You can invest with these experts, thereby receiving professional management.

## Get it right

The concluding section, Part 5, Getting it Right, describes ways to get ahead. Namely, why an IFA will be worth your while to use – and how much to pay, when to invest, and what to do tomorrow.

I hope to leave you with the tools to say, 'Right, I can pick the right unit trust.'

Ask an investor what he or she looks for and undoubtedly you'll hear 'Performance', almost like a mantra.

Ask an IFA why a certain unit trust was recommended. 'It's the best-performing.' If you flip through the pages of *Financial Advisor* or *Investment Advisor*, two trade newspapers for the IFA, guess what unit trust adverts focus primarily on?

## PERFORMANCE!

Since performance is so important, we move on to it in Chapter 2.

### REFERENCES

[1] 'Report of the Committee on Private Share Ownership' by the London Stock Exchange, (London: Gee Publishing Limited, July 1996), pp. 64–71.

[2] 'Trust Update', *Money Management*, December 1996, p. 102.

[3] 'The £1 stake that grew to £51.5m' by Gillian O'Connor in the *Financial Times* – 'Weekend Money – Section 2', 25–26 January 1997, p. 9.

[4] 'Fixed and Flexible Unit Investment Trusts', *Whitaker's Almanack*, 1939, p. 1068.

[5] *Bogle on Mutual Funds* by John C. Bogle (Burr Ridge, Illinois: Richard D. Irwin Publishing Inc., 1994), p. 52.

# APPENDIX:

# THE MECHANICS OF INVESTING IN A UNIT TRUST

## Buying a unit trust

The actual mechanics of making a unit trust investment scares away non-investors. If you've never done it, you may fear that you'll be asked technical questions that you can't answer.

The reality is that it is no different from opening a current account or savings account at your bank or building society. After you've done it once, you'll recognise its simplicity. You provide such basic information as name, address, phone number, and the amount you intent to invest. You will be asked in which unit trust fund you wish to invest and whether you wish to receive the dividends when they are paid or if you would instead prefer for dividends to be reinvested.

The fund management companies want you to invest. If you ring them up with questions, it's their job to provide you with answers you understand. If you don't understand, ring back and ask again. If still you don't understand, ring another firm and ask them. You're not stupid and it's their job to explain the procedure in clear terms. If nonsensical jargon is used, ask what the term means in plain English. After all, you're the customer.

Below are the actual steps you'll follow in making a unit trust investment, either direct by telephone or by post or via an IFA.

### Direct

Two ways to invest directly.

*By telephone:*

1 Ring up fund management company.
2 Open account, specifying particular unit trust and amount to be invested.
3 Fund management company will ask how you wish to receive dividends:
   - reinvested in more units in fund;
   - cheque sent to you when dividends distributed.

4 Unit fund management company sends you contract note with price and units acquired.
5 You send fund management company cheque for investment amount.
6 You receive confirmation of investment or certificate of investment.

*By post:*

Alternatively, you can fill in the form provided with unit trust brochure, answering the dividend distribution question and send in form along with cheque for the desired investment amount. The fund management company then sends you confirmation and possibly a certificate, depending on fund management company policy.

**Through an IFA**

1 Agree with IFA on unit trust in which to invest.
2 IFA provides fund management company's form for you to fill in and sign.
3 Make cheque out to fund sponsor or IFA.
4 You have 14 days to rescind investment, though you are liable for decrease in value of investment during that period. (Rescinding investment is not possible with direct investment above).
5 Fund management company sends you confirmation and possibly certificate of holdings, if that is fund management company policy.

# Selling a unit trust

Direct
1 Call fund management company and say you want to sell units – all or a portion.
2 Fund management company requests you send in signed certificate, if you have one, or a letter indicating instructions.
3 Fund management company sells units.
4 You receive contract note confirming sale.
5 Fund management company has five days to send you cheque.

**Through an IFA**

1 Ring IFA to indicate your desire to sell.

2 IFA handles all interaction with fund management company.

3 Fund sponsor sends you cheque.

# SUMMARY

- Unit trusts allow investors to pool together their resources.

- A unit trust invests in a large number of securities, which provides investors with lower risk than owning a few shares.

- Like any large volume purchase, investors get a better deal than if they were to act individually.

- You can sell your investment and get the proceeds sent to your bank with just a phone call.

Key to long-term investment success is:

- know your personal requirements

- understanding the basics

- use BRUT (Buying the Right Unit Trust) technique to choose consistent high performers with lowest risk

- getting the finer points right makes it successful.

# Chapter 2

# SIMPLE RULES FOR PICKING A UNIT TRUST

## Staying on top of the situation

Like you, the individual investor, a fund of funds selects the best-run unit trusts. You can invest in these funds of funds, thereby letting the experts decide which is best.

Then how do you explain the following performance?

The Old Mutual Fund Managers offers the International Growth Fund of Funds, whose charter is 'to maximise capital growth'. In 1996, the world's principal stockmarkets were up a combined 14 per cent. Old Mutual's International Growth Fund acually lost its investors 1.3 per cent. If you bought the fund that year and paid 6.5 per cent in up-front charges, you'd be down 7.8 per cent.

Oh, there were the glory days. Four years earlier, the fund was ranked at the top, earning 3.3 per cent when the Footsie index was down 1.2 per cent; in 1994, the fund earned 12 per cent while the Footsie index was up only 3.4 per cent. Then, apparently, the manager hit a bad patch, because in 1995 and 1996, the fund was ranked at the bottom (45th out of 58 and 71st out of 71).

You need to stay on top of the situation.

As a unit trust investor, you are charged with the difficult task: to choose a unit trust that will yield you the best possible results consistent with your objectives. According to Emma Weiss of The Association of Unit Trusts and Investment Funds (AUTIF – the official voice of the unit trust industry), there are 1,571 available for investment today: nearly 1,600 provided by 169 fund management companies. Each claims to do a good job at providing financial success and security.

Open today's *Financial Times*, turn to the second section, look at the 'Managed Funds' page. You'll see all the funds available. Choosing one can be a nightmare. How do you know it's the right one? How do you know it's 'safe'? How can you tell whether it will perform well in good markets as well as bad?

You have to work to uncover the true details.

In my discussions with unit trust investors, IFAs, and the fund managers themselves, it appeared most investors use one of the following rules, or a combination, to make the all-important decision, of which fund to invest in – each of the following simple ways of choosing a unit trust is valid, though each has some glaring deficiencies as well:

- Choose the best-performing.
- Choose the largest.
- Trust the performance advertisements.
- Choose the trust with the lowest fees.
- Invest through a PEP.
- Trust your financial advisors.
- Choose a familiar fund management company.
- Trust consistent performance.

We will examine each technique in due course. The great secret of this book is to trust consistent performance. But we need to work through all the details and nuances of the unit trust business to make this conclusion meaningful.

## CHOOSE THE BEST-PERFORMING

Investors desire the best performance, the highest return. Grant Phillips, former head of Barclays Unicorn unit trusts, says, in his private investments, he looks first towards performance. Every single person I've spoken with, young, old, knowledgeable, novice, professionals, hobbyists, all of them bar none, said 'Performance', like a mantra.

Unfortunately, all you have to go on is the past; and the recent past poorly predicts the future, as the example shows.

### The higher they climb . . .

You pick up *Money Management* magazine to choose that best-performing unit trust over the last year. You look in the summary column: Top Five Unit Trust Performers in each sector. Your eye falls on Kleinwort Benson's European Special Situations. You learn that the fund earned investors 16 per cent, £160 on a £1,000 investment after fees. You think to yourself, 'Europe is a good place to be, why not?'

*Money Management* magazine provides good fund data and is available at newsagents or by calling 01444 44520.

A year later, you turn back to *Money Management* to see how your investment has fared. You're aghast to find that your top-performing fund has now dropped to the bottom quartile, 119th out of 123 funds. The fund's absolute performance was +7.3 per cent: less than half the sector average of 16.5 per cent. While this is an extreme example, it's not unique.

It's very difficult to do extremely well consistently. Figure 2.1 proves the point as well. I chose from the same issue the top performers in the largest sectors held by UK investors. I picked up the same magazine, exactly one year later to see how they had fared. Between the first year and the following year, sector names changed and Perpetual's fund changed sectors. I simply used the top performers in the initial year and used the sector they appeared in the following year. The last column shows how well the fund performed compared to the average fund in the sector. For example, the first entry, Lazard UK Capital Growth, was at the top of its sector in the first year. In the following year, it grew 2 per cent less than the average fund in its sector – not so bad, you say; but it only ranked 74th. In other words, Lazard's top performer did worse than average the following year.

**Fig 2.1 Top-performing funds, by sector one year later[1]**

| 1995 category | Fund | 1995 rank | 1996 rank |
|---|---|---|---|
| UK growth | Lazard UK Capital | 1st | 74th |
| UK general | Lazard UK Income & Growth | 1st | 62nd |
| UK equity income | Perpetual Income | 1st | 88th |
| UK smaller companies | Waverly Penny Share | 1st | 36th |
| International | Prolific Technology | 1st | 1st |
| Europe | Kleinwort Benson Euro. Spec. | 1st | 119th |
| Average of six categories | | 1st | 57th |

Unfortunately, the pattern seen in Figure 2.1 shows up consistently. For these funds considered in the year following their exemplary performance, the growth was 7 per cent on average, better than the sector. And this figure is buoyed considerably by one fund, Prolific Technology Fund, which exceeded the average of its sector by 60 per cent.

> Here's a hint: no reward without risk.

Prolific Technology was first in both years. In fact, Prolific Technology has consistently shown up as number one. In Chapter 13, we'll talk with Alan Torry, the fund manager, to learn how he has managed to produce these results consistently.

---

**A Note on the Performance Figure Dates**

The writer of a financial book always suffers from timing. A long lead time exists between when I have written these words and the book is edited, typeset, published, delivered to booksellers, and finally ends up in your hands. Invariably, performance of the funds highlighted in this book will change: some will go down, some will increase, some of the funds will be eliminated, and so on. However, I use these figures to highlight a point of unit trust investment, which should remain. To not confuse matters, I have deliberately left some dates out of the text.

---

## CHOOSE THE LARGEST

At the beginning of 1996, the following was the largest UK unit trust:

*Fund:* M&G Recovery
*Size:* £1,396,000,000

Many, many people have chosen to invest considerable sums in this fund. It must have something going for it. Let's look at the record. Its five-year compounded growth amounted to 14.3 per cent per annum. Not too bad. £1,000 invested five years ago would have yielded an additional £954, almost double.

But ... in the following nine months, its one-year performance had dropped from 11.2 per cent to 3.3 per cent (figures are reported after deducting fund's initial charge). In one-year rankings, it had dropped from 93rd to the tenth-worst out of 152 funds. Its size, apparently, had become overwhelming.

I performed a similar analysis, looking at the largest funds in each sector and seeing how they compared one year later (see Figure 2.2). Again, we find that size is no guarantee. Size reflects the growth in the value of the fund through increases in share price *and* increased investment in the fund. Increased investment in the fund shows the sales acumen of the marketing department at convincing investors of the likelihood of strong performance of that fund.

> 'Just picking a large fund is no guarantee of performance.'

In each instance, while the fund grew, the performance relative to other funds in the same sector was worse. To be fair, the returns of these funds increased in the second year, reflecting the general increase in share prices overall. Had it been a bad year – and these happen – the returns could have been negative, but the ranking is telling.

Just picking a large fund is no guarantee of performance.

Fig 2.2 Size and performance ranking of largest funds in sector (initial charges taken into account)[2]

| Sector | Largest available fund | Size £ million | Performance rank | One year later | |
|---|---|---|---|---|---|
| | | | | Size £ millions | Performance rank |
| UK general | Allied Dunbar Accum. | £1,154 | 23 | £1,294 | 86 |
| UK growth | M&G Recovery Accum. | £1,350 | 92 | £1,522 | 110 |
| UK smaller companies | Baillie Gifford Small Companies | £333 | 24 | £469 | 57 |
| Intl. growth | Perpetual PEP Growth | £648 | 49 | £982 | 65 |
| UK equity income | M&G Dividend | £1,039 | 9 | £1,174 | 74 |
| Europe | Fidelity European | £546 | 10 | £805 | 65 |
| **Six-fund average** | | £845 | 35 | £1,041 | 76 |

Note: Size in £millions; rank 1 is top performer, 23rd is 23rd best, and so on. List includes only those funds available to private investors and therefore excludes large institution-only funds.

## TRUST THE PERFORMANCE ADVERTISEMENTS

Dr Bill Mott, investment manager with Credit Suisse, says it best: 'You see the advertisements, they all say 1-1-1-1-1-1', he trails off.

Dr Bill Baker, private investor, says, 'Everyone seems to be number one at everything.'

The managing director of one fund sponsor, which shall remain unnamed, said, 'You skew the graphs, you can make the numbers look like

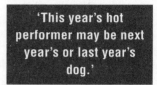

'This year's hot performer may be next year's or last year's dog.'

what you want them to.' Even I have done this data mining. Whenever I wanted to prove a point for this book, I looked through the data and found the numbers that proved my point, which, in fairness to me, was not very difficult to do.

There are just many, many ways to measure performance. This year's hot performer may be next year's or last year's dog. You, the investor, need to ensure that you compare like with like: same sector, same calendar period.

## CHOOSE THE TRUST WITH THE LOWEST FEES

Mr Grant Phillips is the engaging, energetic man who used to run Barclays' unit trust division. His success is demonstrated by the fact that Barclays is the only high street bank among the ten largest fund management companies.

I asked if he personally invested in unit trusts. He did. And then I asked him, how did he choose them? He said he looked at 'performance'; he was 'cost-conscious', and that he could 'afford to be a long-term investor'.

His comments are astute, given his position. Like most people I spoke with, he invested in his own product, and understood unit trusts from the investor side. He said he 'actually had a capital loss at the end of 1994. But I still own these trusts, and they have performed well since then.'

The initial charge you pay has little to do with the long-term performance of the fund. I'll say it again, because it runs in the face of common accepted wisdom and general sense. How much you pay upfront will have little, if anything, to do with your long-run performance. The key word here is 'long-run': or as Mr Phillips says, it is important to be a long-term investor.

As an investor, I had long held the view that the fees paid upfront were to be avoided like the plague. I believed more importantly that the level of fees upfront played no role in predicting the future performance of the fund; after all, this was just a sales fee paid to the sales person; it had nothing to do with the fee earned by the portfolio manager, the person really running the fund. I tried to find data to support this view (see Figure 2.3); surprisingly, I found almost the opposite – the higher the initial fee, the higher the performance!

**Fig 2.3  Relationship between fees and performance of UK equity-related unit trusts**

| Initial fee | Five-year average return before initial fee | Average initial fee | Five-year average return after initial fee |
|---|---|---|---|
| >6.1% | 16.9% | 6.5% | 15.2% |
| between 5.9% – 6.1% | 15.4% | 6.0% | 13.9% |
| <5.9% | 15.8% | 4.9% | 14.4% |

*Source:* HSW Ltd. StatsWise 29 December 1995 for data, includes all UK equity-related unit trusts, excludes cash and gilt and fixed-interest trusts; author calculations.

HOWEVER ... and it's a big however, if you intend not to stay long in an investment, then the level of fees plays a role. It's just common sense. Obviously, if you pay, say 5 per cent, and you sell the following year, the fund has to grow 5 per cent just to pay back your initial charges; conversely, if you stay in the fund for five years, the fund must grow only slightly less than 1 per cent a year to pay back your charges. One per cent a year isn't much of a hurdle; whereas 5 per cent can be.

Does this mean that I'm just a mouthpiece for the industry, saying don't worry about the fees? Far from it. I believe that the marketing people, not a stupid lot, observed which of their funds were doing well, and said, 'Hang on, we should charge more for these high performers.' There is a public perception that a Mercedes or a Bentley or a Rolls, is a great-performing car; hence, the manufacturers charge a premium over and above other cars. And that's what we see with unit trusts: right now, there is a price war going on, and initial fees have dropped throughout the industry. Probably, the relationship is not as clear-cut as above. I used statistical data from HSW Ltd. for this analysis; the reality is that the initial fees are changing frequently.

But, there are lot of funds with poor performance combined with high fees. The fees should be just one of the several ingredients in your considerations.

> '. . . develop a group of consistently high-performing, low-volatility funds, and then make the expenses of the fund the deciding factor.'

There's a way to beat these fees which offers the best of both possible worlds: you get the expensive, high-performance funds, but at a discount price; but I'll save that for Chapter 7.

However, the above analysis is valid only if, like Phillips, you're a long-term investor. If you sold out a year after you initially purchased the trust, the relationship changes dramatically.

My suggestion: develop a group of consistently high-performing, low-volatility funds, and then make the expenses and initial charges of the fund the deciding factor.

## INVEST THROUGH A PEP

You buy a unit trust through your bank, which has advertised that 'It's PEP time – have you got yours?' Many people first begin to become aware of unit trust investing through PEPs (Personal Equity Plans). Seventy per cent of new unit trust investments is in PEPs.

Investing on the last day of the tax year into a PEP is better than no PEP at all. But it is far better to choose an investment first, and then add the PEP wrapper second.

> Chapter 3 looks in brief at PEP-able unit trusts.

## TRUST YOUR FINANCIAL ADVISOR

Many people look to a financial advisor to recommend investments. The Financial Services Act of 1986 requires IFAs (independent financial advisors) to be – well – independent. The other kind of advisors are 'tied agents'. 'Tied agents' are those who work solely for one firm; accordingly, the products they advise you to invest in are only those offered by the firm they are working for. You need to understand from the outset whether your agent is independent or whether he or she works for only one firm.

Though well-intentioned, and though IFAs should be guided by your best interests, not surprisingly, their own best interests may also guide them. I've had several advisors confirm that, given a choice between two very similar unit trusts, they'll push the one with the higher commission. This is not necessarily evil; nor will you lose money. They are paid a commission by the unit trust houses for steering your investments in a certain direction. Use your IFA as a guide; he or she is certainly well-informed. But armed with the information in this book, you can further analyse his or her suggestions in a thoughtful manner.

## CHOOSE A FAMILIAR INVESTMENT HOUSE

Richard Royds, managing director of the unit trust division for Mercury Asset Management, one of the largest fund management companies said, 'Our marketing studies show that brand name is one of the most important means by which people choose unit trusts.' While you want to ensure that your unit trust is 'safe', there are many brand-name houses. But, brand-name houses can have dogs just as well as some unknown management company. And no matter how good the manager, they are all affected by the general direction of that particular market. All the big fund management companies have good and bad funds and indeed, there are simply bad years in particular markets; and even good funds lose money on occasion as shown in Figure 2.4.

**Fig 2.4 Ten largest fund management companies, by total size of unit trusts: Best and worst one-year fund returns[3]**

| Fund sponsor | Size £ millions | Best | One-year return | Worst | One-year return |
|---|---|---|---|---|---|
| M&G | 6,841 | American & General Accum. | 24% | Japan & General Accum. | −17% |
| Schroders | 6,049 | US Small Cos. | 34% | Japan Small Companies | −16% |
| Gartmore | 4,226 | American Emerging | 36% | Emerging Markets | −18% |
| Mercury | 3,798 | American | 20% | Gold and General | −12% |
| Barclay Unicorn | 3,517 | Financial | 26% | Japan Special Situations | −16% |
| Allied Dunbar | 3,055 | American Special Situations | 31% | Japan | −9% |
| Perpetual | 3,107 | American Small Companies | 35% | Latin American Growth | −30% |
| Standard Life | 2,952 | UK Equity Growth | 23% | European Accumulation | 7% |
| Save & Prosper | 2,901 | American Income & Growth | 28% | Latin America | −20% |
| Fidelity | 2,859 | American Special Situations | 42% | Japan Smaller Companies | −15% |

# TRUST CONSISTENT PERFORMANCE

I spent the better part of an afternoon with two senior, respected Gartmore Fund managers, Duncan Trinder and Bryan O'Neill. Duncan manages Gartmore's British Growth Fund, while Bryan manages Gartmore's European Fund. Both these managers have paid their dues and know all the techniques in the industry. Both men said the key measure should be consistency of performance. But this highlights some serious questions. What is performance and what is consistency? We discuss performance, volatility, and consistency in Chapters 11, 12, and 13.

All the above measures are useful in putting together a unit trust portfolio. But the bottom line is consistency of performance. You want a unit trust which will perform admirably in all kinds of markets, up markets and down markets. This book will show you the ingredients of consistent performance. The fund may not be last quarter's or even last year's best performing fund. But I hope to persuade you that top performance in any one year alone is not the key to long-term, successful unit trust investing: the key is to invest in the right funds for your situation and to your comfort. We move on to evaluate your situation today after briefly looking at what constitutes a PEP-able investment in Chapter 3.

## REFERENCES

[1] 'Statistics, Top Five Unit Trust Performers in Each Sector', *Money Management*, July 1995, p. 79 and 'Statistics', *Money Management*, July 1996, pp. 67–85.

[2] 'Statistics, Five largest unit trusts in each sector', *Money Management*, July 1995, p. 79 and 'Statistics', *Money Management*, July 1996, pp. 67–85. *Note:* Excludes Schroders UK Small Cos. Institutional, largest small company fund, because fund is available only to institutions.

[3] 'Management Groups in Order of Size', *Unit Trusts Yearbook 1995*, p. 72 for fund management company order and size; HSW Ltd., StatsWise, 29.12.95 for one-year return statistics.

# SUMMARY

- Last year's performance is no guide to the future.

- Even investing in the largest funds does not guarantee success.

- Don't make your decision based solely on the higher return promised in the advertisement.

- Just to take advantage of PEP tax benefits is no reason alone to invest in a unit trust.

- A fund management company or bank or building society that's a household name doesn't guarantee consistent performance.

- Select funds with track records of consistent, long-term performance.

# WHAT GOOD IS A PEP?

Do you have a PEP? You should. Given the fierce price competition, today's Personal Equity Plans (PEPs), which now can also invest in less volatile, lower-return corporate bonds, are one of the cheapest saving and investment forms around.

As I made clear in Chapter 1, a PEP is only a set of tax laws; it's not an investment. No investment is ever justified on the basis of its PEP-ability alone. There are so many PEP possibilities available today, the odds are you can find a good unit trust that is PEP-able. You don't have to invest in a unit trust to receive PEP benefits, you can invest in investment trusts or individual shares.

The PEP opportunity began in 1987. If you had invested the maximum amount each year since the beginning, your total PEP contribution could be £79,200 and this is excluding any tax-shielded gains you would have received. Keiron Root, editor of *What Investment?* concludes that, 'The PEP represents a practical method for most investors to put a substantial part, if not the whole, of their investment portfolios outside the tax net.'[1]

## KEY FACTS ABOUT PEPs

Here are the key facts about PEPs:

### Investment

Each person may invest up to £6,000 in a General PEP and an additional £3,000 in a single-company PEP. Of the £6,000 General PEP allowance, £1,500 may be invested in 'non-qualifying' assets, while the remaining £4,500 is restricted to 'qualifying' investments (see Figure 3.1).

'Each person may invest up to £6,000 in a General PEP and an additional £3,000 in a single-company PEP.'

Qualifying investments in a General PEP include: The following securities either held individually or in collective funds (unit trusts, investment trusts, or open-ended investment companies [a new form of unit trust]):

**Fig 3.1 PEP allowances**

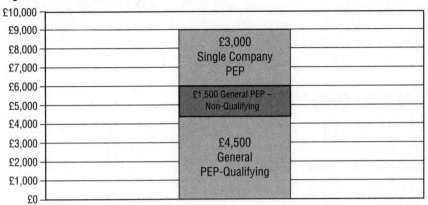

- Ordinary shares of companies registered in the UK or in other European Union (EU) countries.
- Corporate bonds and convertibles (fixed-interest securities which may be converted to equities at some future date) of UK or European companies. The companies must not be authorised credit institutions (no banks). Corporate bonds must have a minimum lifespan of five years at time of purchase (see Chapter 10 to learn why).
- Preference shares (shares that pay dividends at a fixed rate) of UK and other EU companies.
- All investments must be in quoted companies.

Non-qualifying investments for the £1,500 maximum can be invested in non-qualifying collective funds, which hold at least half of their assets in ordinary shares listed on international exchanges recognised by Inland Revenue.

From Debbie Harrison's *The Good PEP Guide*[2].

# Keeping cash in a PEP

Can't do it. After 42 days, cash in a PEP is subject to tax.

# Benefit

All dividends and capital gains in the PEP are free from tax.

> **Hint:** Because £6,300 of capital gains are already free from tax, you should consider income-oriented investments over capital growth-oriented ones for your PEP allowance.

## Investment managers

You are allowed to have only one PEP plan per year, and that PEP can be managed by only one sponsor, e.g., one fund management company. However, firms such as the Skandia Company allows you to get around this rule. You invest in their PEP, from which you can invest in a variety of unit trusts run by different fund management companies (provided you meet the rules outlined above).

'You are allowed to have only one PEP plan per year, and that PEP can be managed by only one sponsor, e.g., one fund management company.'

Because of the benefits of not having to put all your eggs in one basket, other firms may begin offering the Skandia-type smörgåsbord menu for investing in unit trusts. Further, the advantage offered by such a programme is to minimise the charges associated with transferring your PEP from one fund management company to another.

## Charges

Many fund management companies no longer charge an additional fee associated with establishing a PEP. However, you will face the normal charges associated with any unit trust investment. In fact, some fund management companies charge a lower fee just to get you in the door. Because so many unit trust companies are eager for your PEP business, it pays to shop around to find one that doesn't levy an additional PEP fee.

We go into considerable detail about the charges associated with a unit trust in coming chapters.

## Restrictions

Once you take the money out of a prior year's PEP, you lose that portion of that year's PEP allowance. In other words, you cannot reinvest that money for that year's PEP allowance. Studies show that many people do withdraw their investments after a few years for various reasons.

## PEPs vs pensions

'PEPs give you free access to capital, if you suddenly need to lay your hands on money fast', says *Investors Chronicle*. While contributions to pensions can be deducted immediately from tax, which is a significant advantage, they 'block access to capital in an emergency'.[3] Another benefit of PEPs over pensions is that you can pass the entire PEP capital on to future generations, while pensions typically pass only a portion of your contribution on to your heirs. However, the PEP inheritance is no longer in a PEP and is then subject to tax.

## PEPs as mortgages

At the same time as you borrow the funds to buy a house or flat, you establish a PEP. You only pay interest to the bank for your mortgage loan. Your PEP contributions are established with the intent of paying off the mortgage at the end of the loan. The key question is whether the PEP investment will grow sufficiently to pay off the loan amount when the loan becomes due.

## THE BEST TIME TO INVEST

You save up your money and then, on 5 April, just before the gates slam shut, you invest your money. In any given tax year, you can invest at any time. Most people invest right before the tax deadline, 5 April. From a tax perspective, this is the worst time to invest because you have missed the tax-shielding PEP advantage for the prior 12 months.

Alternatively, you could set up a savings plan where, say, £500 each month is invested directly from the funds in your bank account. By the end of the tax year you will find you have calmly filled your annual PEP allowance.

Two advantages emerge if you invest monthly, as opposed to once at year-end. First, you gain the profit in the market that you would miss by investing only at year-end. The stockmarket has appreciated 7.8 per cent annually for the last 70 years. By keeping your money in a current account, you lose the gain that year.

> '... if you invest monthly ... you gain the profit in the market that you would miss by investing only at year-end.'

The second great advantage of investing monthly is that you're not making a particular bet on the market on 4 April. That is, you're averaging out the price at which you invest over the course of a year.

## GUARANTEED PEPS

If it sounds too good to be true, it probably is. In the last year, we've seen the emergence of a new product whose name should be 'Have Your Cake and Eat It Too'. They promise stockmarket level returns, while at the same time guaranteeing no risk to your capital. These products typically offer a below-market rate of return coupled with a 'participation' in any rise in a stockmarket index. There's a lock-in period before which, if you withdraw your money, you do not get the guaranteed benefits.

This type of offer, while appealing at first glance, is usually less valuable over the long haul than straight unit trust investments. For example, one guaranteed-type PEP offered 18 per cent. Closer examination showed this to be not annually but over five years, which works out to 3.4 per cent per year: significantly worse than you might expect to achieve in a bank with a five-year term deposit.

A far better approach is to invest some of your money in a low-risk bond fund or even a building society account which assures you a certain return, and then invest the balance in an equity unit trust. This offers you certainty coupled with the potential for high returns. This is exactly what the guaranteed PEP does, only you're paying for the privilege of having a bank do it for you.

# WHO DOESN'T NEED A PEP?[4]

The benefits of this tax-advantaged investment are in the short-term fairly minimal. If you invest £6,000 and the market moves up 7.8 per cent, your capital gain is £468. If that was your only capital gain, your profit would be exempt from capital gains anyway.

If the dividends you received were 5 per cent, your income would be £300. If you're a basic rate taxpayer, the tax would be £60. If you only made one investment and you only had one year to live, the fees associated with the PEP investment could be upwards of 6 per cent to 7 per cent (£360 to £420) in the first year, which would far out-weigh the £60 reduction in tax.

However, presumably you're investing for the long-term. If your £6,000 appreciates along with the general market, in 20 years your £6,000 would grow to £27,000. Tax-free.

**Get a PEP.**

## REFERENCES

[1] 'A World of Tax-Free Savings' by Keiron Root in 'How to Use Your PEP', A *What Investment & Personal Finance* supplement, in association with Skandia Multipep, p. 3.

[2] *Good PEPs Guide* by Debbie Harrison, Pitman Publishing, 1996, pp. 18–19.

[3] 'Planning Investment for a Lifetime,' by Dido Sandler, *Investors Chronicle*, 6 December 1996, p. 40.

[4] Even non-taxpayers can benefit from a PEP by not having to reclaim the basic rate tax on interest paid to Inland Revenue.

# SUMMARY

- Income and capital gains from investments under the PEP umbrella are free from tax forever.

- Each person may invest up to £6,000 in a General PEP, consisting of unit trusts, investment trusts, or shares each year.

- Of the annual General PEP allowance, £4,500 must be in UK or European Union securities.

- The remaining £1,500 may be invested in non-UK, non-European securities.

- PEP-able unit trusts include equity and gilt and fixed interest funds.

- You cannot keep cash or short-term deposits in a PEP for more than 42 days without attracting tax.

- Take the money out of your PEP from an earlier year, and you cannot reinvest in that year's PEP.

- The best time to invest is at the beginning, not the end, of the tax year.

# YOUR FINANCIAL PICTURE TODAY

## Tidying up

Mr Fritz Amselmann, 35, looks poised to move to the executive suites in the not-so-distant future. He manages an important, highly profitable division of an international bank. The profits of his business have been growing at 50 per cent a year for five years, and his boss has not forgotten Amselmann at bonus time.

But, to look at his personal investment portfolio, you would have thought that Amselmann was a nervous pensioner ... £250,000 sitting in six-month time deposits. He's just been too busy making money for his company to worry about his own money.

He had also invested in a PEP ten years ago which had 'appalling' results in the first year, after which he stopped looking at it. Since that time, the investment has recovered and grown 149 per cent or 11 per cent per year – which recommends the strategy of patience and watching your investment over the years.

Finally, he decided to tidy up his financial affairs, and called an IFA recommended by a friend. The IFA completed a fact find, and suggested a diversified portfolio of national savings and UK, European, and international equity-based unit trusts.

Since then, Amselmann has tidied up his financial affairs. He has diversified investments in various volatility categories reflecting that he has at least 20 more working years ahead. In addition, Amselmann would like to buy some property in the next few years. The IFA also proposed some investments in medium-term gilt and fixed-interest funds to provide some certainty, combined with better returns than the six-month deposits.

---

The key point, almost above choosing a particular unit trust, is to pick the right unit trust category for your particular investment need. Unfortunately, this can be a daunting subject. Life can be simple, and so should this.

I categorise investments by the length of time likely to ensure a positive return: this is the Timing Outlook for Investments.

> 'The key point ... is to pick the right unit trust category for your particular investment need.'

First, we'll calculate where you are today: your Actual Financial Asset Timing. You will decide how your investments, deposits, and current accounts funds *should* be divided up among short-term, medium-term, and long-term: your Desired Financial Asset Timing.

We'll then compare your *Actual* Financial Asset Timing with your *Desired* Financial Asset Timing. That is, we look at whether your current distribution of investments matches up with your desired timing needs.

The Timing Outlook for each investment is probably far more important in investment

> 'The Timing Outlook for each investment is probably far more important in investment selection than whether you're an "aggressive" investor or a "conservative" investor.'

selection than whether you're an 'aggressive' investor or a 'conservative' investor. I know this seems like heresy, but bear with me as I try to persuade you that being 'aggressive' or 'conservative' won't help you to achieve your goals.

I believe the all-important characteristic is the time available for investment: short-, medium-, and long-term, and returns and volatility are by-products of the Timing Outlook for Investments.

## CONSIDER THE EXPERTS

The wise investor, who is therefore safety-conscious, allocates investments across the Timing Outlook for Investments. Consider an investment manager for an assurance company. He or she is out of work if the money is not available when the beneficiary comes knocking on the door. You would think that an assurance company, above all else, would invest cautiously. Yet, you find the investments of assurance companies in property, in stock markets, in leveraged buy-outs, in Eastern Europe and other far reaches of the investment globe, and in gilts; basically, you'll find them across the Timing Outlook for

> The Timing Outlook for Investments categorises investments by the length of time likely to ensure a positive return.

Investments. Have these investment managers gone mad? Far from it – these investment managers know they won't need all the funds immediately tomorrow. Some funds they'll need tomorrow; some funds they'll need in three to five years; and the balance of funds will be needed from five years to a lifetime.

Consider these other examples of expert investors choosing so-called risky investments.

**Richard Royds**, managing director of the unit trust division for Mercury Asset Management, one of the UK's largest asset management firms, has two children, aged seven and three. Royds invested in Mercury's Emerging Market Fund on their behalf because they won't need the money for a minimum of ten years. Royds could have taken the attitude, 'This is my children's university money, I don't want to risk losing it, so I'll keep it in a low-yielding, "safe" deposit account.' Instead, he chose to invest in an area with high-growth potential because he knows these funds won't be needed for quite some time.

**Mary Blair** is one of the heavyweights in the unit trust business. She began by working for a predecessor organisation to Invesco, back in the mid-1970s, turned to the then-start-up Fidelity in 1979, where she worked as head of marketing, product development, and communications, before leaving to have her third child. She put in 20 years for these two companies.

But the call of the unit trust business rang again; today, she's director of product development at Threadneedle Asset Management (which owns Allied Dunbar and Eagle Star). Her name appears often in the papers, as she comments on the state of the unit trust business.

She says if she didn't have to work, she'd pick stocks for fun and profit. But she doesn't have the time, so she relies on unit trusts. Where does she invest safely for her children, to ensure funds for their university education?

'Ever since my first child was born, I have invested in Fidelity Special Situations. We started at £30 per month, then later increased it to £50 per month and now it has close to £10,000 in it.' Fidelity's Special Situations Fund is among the most volatile funds as compared with other UK equity growth funds. In other words, it's risky; it has also been extremely successful: generating an average 16 per cent per year over the last ten years.

For example, in 1987, 'Fidelity Special Sits' (as it is called) shot up

114 per cent, only to fall 22 per cent the following year. That see-saw performance was repeated in 1989 when it grew 38 per cent, only to be followed by a loss of 24 per cent the next year. Since 1993, it has never had a loss-making year, though the wide swings have continued.

The *Micropal* report on Fidelity Special Situations in Figure 4.1 shows what a long-term fund – high return, high volatility – looks like.

**Clive Boothman**, managing director for Schroders' Unit Trusts, the largest unit trust house, keeps some investments in emerging markets. He says, 'I regard these as long-term investments, to be left alone.'

In my research, I found numerous similar examples of unit trust experts investing funds for their children or for their retirement in highly volatile investments, not building society savings accounts. They weren't gambling recklessly; just the opposite. They were making an extremely informed judgement about when they needed the funds and what the most likely investment vehicle would be to take them there.

## WHERE YOU ARE TODAY

The first step is determining your Actual Financial Asset Timing, implicit in your existing portfolio. Please, please complete the exercises.

Stephen C. Abbott, unit trust marketing director at Legal & General, describes a simple programme of building a portfolio of unit trusts. Abbott says the logic for determining generally what you need is 'not all that different from buying a car'. You say to yourself, in selecting a car,

> Don't worry about getting your financial figures correct to the nearest penny; the aim is to give you a general direction.

'I need to transport myself, my wife, and my two kids and sometimes a dog.' So you exclude two-seater sport cars, and basically consider only cars with four doors and back space for man's best friend.

## Fig 4.1  Fidelity Special Situations

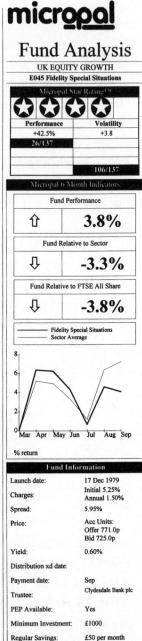

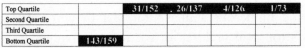

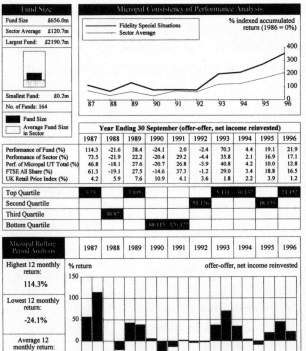

### Fidelity Special Situations

Fidelity Investment Services, Oakhill House, 130 Tonbridge Road, Tonbridge, Kent TN11 9DZ.

Information: Telephone - 01732 361 144   Dealing - 0800 414 161

**Fund Objective:**
Capital growth by investing primarily in the shares of companies in the UK considered to bespecial situations"".".

#### Micropal Cumulative Performance - to 30th September 1996

| Performance Period | 6 Months | 1 Year | 3 Years | 5 Years | 10 Years |
|---|---|---|---|---|---|
| Fund Performance | -2.4% | +14.6% | +42.5% | +136.7% | +325.7% |
| Sector Average | +1.3% | +10.7% | +32.2% | +71.7% | +177.0% |
| Best Performing Fund | +17.0% | +36.7% | +71.0% | +143.8% | +325.7% |
| Worst Performing Fund | -6.4% | -1.7% | +6.8% | +2.4% | +59.6% |

(Offer-bid, net income reinvested)

| | | | | | |
|---|---|---|---|---|---|
| Top Quartile | | 31/152 | 26/137 | 4/126 | 1/73 |
| Second Quartile | | | | | |
| Third Quartile | | | | | |
| Bottom Quartile | 143/159 | | | | |

#### Fund Size

| | |
|---|---|
| Fund Size | £656.0m |
| Sector Average | £120.7m |
| Largest Fund: | £2190.7m |
| Smallest Fund: | £0.2m |
| No. of Funds: | 164 |

Micropal Consistency of Performance Analysis

Fidelity Special Situations
Sector Average

% indexed accumulated return (1986 = 0%)

87 88 89 90 91 92 93 94 95 96

#### Year Ending 30 September (offer-offer, net income reinvested)

| | 1987 | 1988 | 1989 | 1990 | 1991 | 1992 | 1993 | 1994 | 1995 | 1996 |
|---|---|---|---|---|---|---|---|---|---|---|
| Performance of Fund (%) | 114.3 | -21.6 | 38.4 | -24.1 | 2.0 | -2.4 | 70.3 | 4.4 | 19.1 | 21.9 |
| Performance of Sector (%) | 73.5 | -21.9 | 22.2 | -20.4 | 29.2 | -4.4 | 35.8 | 2.1 | 16.9 | 17.1 |
| Perf. of Micropal UT Total (%) | 46.8 | -18.1 | 27.6 | -20.7 | 26.8 | -3.9 | 40.8 | 4.2 | 10.0 | 12.8 |
| FTSE All Share (%) | 61.3 | -19.1 | 27.5 | -14.6 | 37.3 | -1.2 | 29.0 | 3.4 | 18.8 | 16.5 |
| UK Retail Price Index (%) | 4.2 | 5.9 | 7.6 | 10.9 | 4.1 | 3.6 | 1.8 | 2.2 | 3.9 | 1.2 |

| | 1987 | 1988 | 1989 | 1990 | 1991 | 1992 | 1993 | 1994 | 1995 | 1996 |
|---|---|---|---|---|---|---|---|---|---|---|
| Top Quartile | 3/73 | | 3/105 | | | | 5/131 | 30/137 | | 21/152 |
| Second Quartile | | | | | | 51/126 | | | 18/159 | |
| Third Quartile | | 48/87 | | | | | | | | |
| Bottom Quartile | | | | 88/115 | 170/122 | | | | | |

#### Micropal Rolling Period Analysis

| | 1987 | 1988 | 1989 | 1990 | 1991 | 1992 | 1993 | 1994 | 1995 | 1996 |
|---|---|---|---|---|---|---|---|---|---|---|
| Highest 12 monthly return: 114.3% | | | | | | | | | | |
| Lowest 12 monthly return: -24.1% | | | | | | | | | | |
| Average 12 monthly return: 20.8% | | | | | | | | | | |

% return   offer-offer, net income reinvested

---

### micropal

## Fund Analysis

**UK EQUITY GROWTH**

**E045 Fidelity Special Situations**

#### Micropal Star Rating™

| Performance | Volatility |
|---|---|
| +42.5% | +3.8 |
| 26/137 | |
| | 106/137 |

#### Micropal 6 Month Indicators

Fund Performance

⇧  **3.8%**

Fund Relative to Sector

⇩  **-3.3%**

Fund Relative to FTSE All Share

⇩  **-3.8%**

Fidelity Special Situations
Sector Average

Mar  Apr  May  Jun  Jul  Aug  Sep

% return

#### Fund Information

| | |
|---|---|
| Launch date: | 17 Dec 1979 |
| Charges: | Initial 5.25% Annual 1.50% |
| Spread: | 5.95% |
| Price: | Acc Units: Offer 771.0p Bid 725.0p |
| Yield: | 0.60% |
| Distribution xd date: | |
| Payment date: | Sep |
| Trustee: | Clydesdale Bank plc |
| PEP Available: | Yes |
| Minimum Investment: | £1000 |
| Regular Savings: | £50 per month |

---

**To subscribe: Micropal Publications / Micropal Ltd  Tel: 0181 741 4100  Fax: 0181 741 0939**    © Micropal Publications / Micropal Ltd 1996

*Source: Micropal.*

Then you look at your budget. You have, say, £15,000 to spend. This limits your choices again. You visit the Ford, the Vauxhall, the Honda, and the Peugeot dealerships. You get an idea of what you like. Your list gets shorter. You talk to your insurance agent to find out how much insurance will cost for the various cars. You buy a consumer magazine detailing estimated upkeep costs. Your list is now down to two or three cars.

You take each out for a test drive. Your wife takes them out for a test drive. Then, with brochures in hand and calculations in head, you sit down to make the hard-headed decision to buy a car. The mental steps involved in building a unit trust portfolio turn out to be very similar.

Abbott gives the following examples:

- 'You may have £20,000 in a building society with a very low return. You want a better return.' So you start looking around.

- Or, you want to buy a house or flat: 'How much will I need, and how much do I need to save and what kind of return will I require to have sufficient funds in one, three or five years' time?'

- Or you say: 'I'm going to retire in ten years, I want to build capital for ten years, then I want the investment to start paying income to live from.'

- You could be self-employed and require very little loss in your capital.

- Alternatively, you could be young and ably employed, earning a salary with good prospects for continued employment, and needing the money only for the future, at least five years hence.

Abbott says, 'When you finish the exercise, it'll give you a good feeling, like the way you feel once you've tidied the garage.' You may have been saying to yourself, 'I should sit down and write out where I am.' This will give you the chance to take a quick look at your overall financial picture.

Proceed to fill in the form shown in Figure 4.2. This need not be a cumbersome exercise. Don't get out all your documents and files. Do it in your head or check a few key statements. Fill it in now.

**Fig 4.2  What is your net worth?**

| | |
|---|---|
| Current account | |
| Deposits (less than one year) | |
| *less any debt due within one year* | ( ) |
| **Total short-term** | |
| Notice savings accounts (more than one year to mature) | |
| Gilts and corp. bonds, | |
| Corp. bond PEPs – unit trusts or individual bonds | |
| *less any instalment or other debt over one year* | ( ) |
| **Total medium-term** | |
| Shares and single-company PEPs | |
| Unit trusts and unit trust PEPs | |
| Equity in property* (total value less loan owed) (Not your flat or house) | |
| Other** (Not including your house and your car) | |
| Total long-term | |
| **TOTAL NET WORTH** | |
| Subtract equity in property and *other (except pension assets)* | |
| **NET FINANCIAL ASSETS** | |

*I never include the car or house in the net worth calculation. If you sell your car, you'll probably buy another one. If you sell your house, where will you live? You can't turn these assets into cash to invest, because you need the benefits these assets throw off, namely transportation and shelter. If you did turn them into cash, you'd have to use that cash to get the benefits some other way, e.g., taking taxis or staying in hotels. In other words, you cannot sell these assets to invest in unit trusts.

**Pension funds and assurances* can be included in the Other category if you know the surrender value; likewise, you can include them in the Unit Trusts category. The value of pensions and life assurances is sometimes unclear, so you may not know this figure.

Thus, using the subtotals from Figure 4.2, you know your Actual Timing Class of Investments (see Figure 4.3).

**Fig 4.3  Your actual financial asset timing**

|  | (from Figure 4.2) | Actual % |
|---|---|---|
| Short-term | £ | % |
| Medium-term | £ | % |
| Long-term* | £ | % |
| **Total** | £ | 100% |

\* Subtract equity in property and other, except pension assets, from long-term.

This is where you are today. Congratulations. We're not finished, though. Your garage is only half-tidied.

# YOUR DESIRED FINANCIAL ASSET TIMING

Abbott paints a picture of three types of cash needs, the figures for which we'll calculate together shortly.

## Daily needs and dire emergency funds

These are the funds you need to pay your daily bills, to get by during the month. Add to this any amount you feel you need for emergencies. This amount should be small.

## Medium-term needs

Planned and unplanned expenditures. You know you'll need to buy a car in five years and you know generally what it will cost. You know you need to spend some money on painting your house or some other kind of upkeep. If you want to buy a house, how much will you need, again in rough terms. This category could also include your children's school fees or university costs in a few years.

## Long-term future needs

Depending on your age and stage in your financial life, these funds represent your nest-egg. This could be the funds you have earmarked for retirement, to pay off your mortgage in 25 years, or for your children's future university education.

To determine where you want to be, take the net financial assets from Figure 4.2 and fill that in in the top row (see Figure 4.4). Second, calculate your short-term requirements and fill that number in. Third, calculate your medium-term requirements; fill that in. The difference between your net total financial assets and the sum of your short- and medium-term needs is your desired long-term assets.

**Fig 4.4  Desired financial asset timing**

| | | |
|---|---|---|
| Total assets (from Figure 4.2) | £ | 100% |
| less *estimated* short-term day-to-day requirements | £ | % |
| less *estimated* medium-term funds requirements | £ | % |
| = desired long-term assets | £ | % |

## DO YOUR ASSETS FILL YOUR DESIRES?

The next step in the process requires choosing the right assets to match against these needs. As I wrote that last sentence, I thought to myself, that sounds like a financial planner talking to a group of financial planners: further explanation is necessary.

Consider the two examples shown in the boxes: 'Going to France' and 'Working in your garden'.

---

**Going to France**

If you need to get from London to Paris right now, you'll take a plane from Heathrow or the Eurostar.

If you're taking your family to the Continent and plan to spend the summer on the Côte d'Azur, you'll probably drive to take a summer's worth of clothes, games, books, and other summer goods.

If you're moving to France, you'd hire a removal firm with a large lorry.

---

> **Working in your garden**
>
> If you have a few weeds, you could get them out by hand or with a small trowel.
>
> If your garden was dry, you would use a hose.
>
> If your garden was as big as the lawns on a huge estate, you would install sprinklers and hire gardeners.

For each general topic, you had unique requirements, and you used a different vehicle to achieve those needs. And that's exactly the point with your financial needs and unit trusts. Identify the need and then find the right tool, the right vehicle, to get there.

> In Chapter 8, we look further at what the classes of investment actually are.

All financial investments provide a return to satisfy a need in the future. The key words here are 'return' and 'future'. Below, we list the attributes that are important to you.

## Short-term

Tomorrow, you may need money. Thus, the current account, which generally pays no interest would satisfy that requirement. There are a myriad of immediate-access-type investment/ savings accounts paying low interest. The building societies and banks provide this service. These types of investments, immediate-access deposit accounts, short-term notice accounts, and cash unit trusts all serve this same need: current monthly needs plus a rainy-day source where you can get at your money right away. Its main characteristic is stability.

> Fund management companies offer cash funds. As a rule, they pay about three-quarters to one per cent more than a typical high-street building society. More about that in Chapter 9, when we turn to the various types of unit trusts.

## Medium-term

The second category of investment are corporate bonds and gilts with a time to maturity of over three years. (Anything under three years won't fluctuate that much and is more suitable to the short-term category.) Corporate bonds and gilts and time deposits can be used to plan for longer-type needs: the university fees in five years, the first house in three years, new car, the home refurbishment, and so on.

Because you don't need the money right away, you can afford to bear more volatility – the chance that the price will go down in the near term, because within five years, the combination of interest received and the bond's price will most likely be greater than when you invested the money.

## Long-term

The investment for the long-term are shares in companies. Of the three categories, equity values bounce around the most. If you need the money with certainty in three years, you cannot be certain the value will not have decreased. Over five years, there's an 80 per cent chance you'll have gained; and over ten years, you're virtually assured of a real profit.

**Fig 4.5  Timing class of investments**

| Timing class | Investment | Return | Volatility |
|---|---|---|---|
| Short-term | Cash | Lowest | Least |
| Medium-term | Bonds | Medium | Medium |
| Long-term | Equity | Highest | Highest |

In 1995, Barclays de Zoete Wedd Securities performed an exhaustive study of returns from financial instruments, as they have for the past 41 years. The study authoritatively answers the question, how well would investors have done in short-term deposits, longer-term bonds, and equities. This shows you the trade-off between equities, which have the longest investment time horizon, bonds, with a medium term horizon, and cash (shown as Treasury bills), with the shortest investment time horizon (see Figure 4.6).

**Fig 4.6 Summary statistics 1919–95 (per cent per annum)**

|  | *Real* | *Inflated at 3.9%* |
|---|---|---|
| Non-interest-bearing cash deposits | –3.9% | 0% |
| Gilts | 1.94% | 5.84% |
| Treasury bills | 1.45% | 5.35% |
| *Average gilts and Treasury bills* | *1.70%* | *5.60%* |
| Equities | 7.81% | 11.71% |

*Source:* Summary Statistics, *The BZW Equity-Gilt Study*, Barclays de Zoete Wedd Securities Limited, 41st edition, January 1996, p. 4.

In his book, *Stocks for the Long Run*, Professor Jeremy J. Siegel states that 'over the long run the returns on shares are so stable that shares are actually safer than either government bonds or Treasury Bills. The constancy of the long-term, after-inflation returns on stocks is truly astounding, while the returns on fixed-interest assets posed higher risks for the long-term investor.'[1]

Thus, the message emerges. The more you move into equities, the greater the return you might have. The more you stay in bonds or your current account, the greater the return you give up: this is the cost of missing the opportunity.

The greatest opportunity cost is paid by those with funds in a current account, because of inflation. Inflation is a secret tax created by the government which eats away at the value of our savings, our cash, and our investments. Presently, it's fairly 'low' – around 3 per cent per year. At this 'low' inflation, the value of investments gets eaten up at the rate of 26 per cent every ten years. In ten years, your rainy-day money, kept in a current account, would be worth a quarter less than it is today.

> 'The more you move into equities, the greater the return you might have. The more you stay in bonds or your current account, the greater the return you give up ...'

The average rate of inflation since 1945 has been 6.2 per cent. Since 1990, it has been only 3.9 per cent. Whatever it is currently, it has been proven historically that it won't be zero. Only in the 1920s were there years of deflation. Inflation needs to be considered in any review of financial investments: building society, government deposit offerings, and unit trusts.

If inflation resumes to its annual historical rate of 6.2 per cent, the value of any funds kept in a current account for a decade would be worth 47 per cent less than today. Sobering thought.

Now, the moment of truth: Repeated in Figure 4.7 with some sub-totals are the charts you filled in earlier. Compare them with the percentage of your actual investments:

**Fig 4.7  Your desired vs actual financial asset timing**

| | Desired | Actual | Difference between desired and actual | Your net financial wealth (same in each cell) | Suggested change in investment |
|---|---|---|---|---|---|
| Short-term | % | % | % | × £ | |
| Medium-term | % | % | % | × £ | |
| Long-term | % | % | % | × £ | |
| Total | 100% | 100% | % | | |

For example:

| | Desired | Actual | Difference between desired and actual | Your net financial wealth (same in each cell) | Suggested change in investment |
|---|---|---|---|---|---|
| Short-term | 10% | 50% | −40% | × £100,000 | −£40,000 |
| Medium-term | 40% | 30% | 10% | × £100,000 | +£10,000 |
| Long-term | 50% | 20% | 30% | × £100,000 | +£30,000 |
| Total | 100% | 100% | | | |

Is your desired allocation in sync with your financial needs?

These exercises will alert you to the effects of inflation and to demonstrate how you might want to tilt your investments towards a longer time horizon.

The reality is simple: the more you keep in 'safe' investments, the less you earn. How much less? I've created two portfolios – one is overly cautious, while the other has more in longer-term equities (see Figure 4.8). The overly cautious investor keeps 80 per cent of his or her money in the building society while the wise investor keeps 60 per cent of his or her money in equity unit trusts. The wise investor's portfolio earns 4.8 per cent, nearly four times as much, in real terms

**Fig 4.8  A tale of two portfolios**

| Asset | Real historical return | Per cent of assets Overly cautious | Wiser |
|---|---|---|---|
| Current account* | –3.90% | 10% | 10% |
| Savings account | 1.45% | 80% | 10% |
| Bonds | 1.94% | 5% | 20% |
| Equities | 7.81% | 5% | 60% |
| | | 100% | 100% |
| **Real return** | | **1.3%** | **4.8%** |
| **+Inflation of 3.9%** | | **3.9%** | **3.9%** |
| **Reported return** | | **5.2%** | **8.7%** |

*Note: Because the current account pays no interest, amounts kept in a current account lose value due to inflation.

as the overly cautious investor, 1.3 per cent or, including inflation, 8.7 per cent versus 5.2 per cent.

We go back to the real world to look at the mechanics by which a unit trust is established, the different types of unit trusts, and how they can fill short-, medium-, and long-term requirements.

REFERENCE

[1] *Stocks for the Long Run* by Jeremy J. Siegel (Burr Ridge, Illinois: Richard D. Irwin Publishing Inc., 1994) p. iv.

# SUMMARY

- Take into account your own financial situation and determine when and for what purpose you'll require the funds.

- The Timing Outlook for Investment is the time you should wait for the return to materialise.

- The longer the time for investment, the higher the likely gain.

- Rather than worry about aggressive or conservative investments, divide your financial resources into categories and invest accordingly:
  - immediate
  - medium
  - long.

- Choose investments based on the time category.

- Some managing directors of the largest fund management companies invest their own money in emerging market sectors because they offer great, long-term growth potential.

# PART

# TYING YOUR DETAILS TO UNIT TRUST DETAILS

# INSIDE A UNIT TRUST

In autumn 1996, Portfolio Funds, a small-but-successful unit trust group, actively marketed a new unit trust, dedicated to investing in Asia. Raising £14.3 million, the fund, reported *The Daily Telegraph*,[1] hopes to smooth 'out [the] bumpy road to Oriental reward' for investors intending to invest in Asian securities. What made the fund unique was that it didn't invest in individual securities, but instead invested in other unit trusts. This is called a Fund of Funds, because it is a *fund* compromised *of* other unit trust *funds*. It was not unique, in that, like all unit trusts, it pooled investors' funds together to make investments on behalf of the investors. These funds purport to offer higher returns coupled with lower volatility than could otherwise be achieved by investing in one unit trust.

In this chapter, we explore some of the mechanics of assembling a unit trust, using the new Asia Fund and an established fund, Mercury Asset Management's Mercury Portfolio Fund, as examples.

My game plan over the next few chapters is:

- to develop an understanding of the inner workings of a unit trust;
- to explain how unit trust prices arise out of the inner workings.

You'll be able to take this information about the inner workings coupled with unit trust pricing to make sure you're getting the best possible deal and setting yourself up properly for a lifetime of performance.

The use of these living, breathing examples allows us to explore the subject more realistically, rather than legally. Following from a brief, brief look at the creation of a unit trust, we'll move on to slightly more lively topics, such as the underlying value of unit trusts and where dividends come from.

## THE RIGHT IDEA AT THE RIGHT TIME

Mary Blair, currently product development director with Threadneedle Asset Management (owner of Allied Dunbar and Eagle

Star), as she was at Fidelity, explained that her firms introduced a new product when the fund manager came to them with a new idea for a fund. Generally, fund management companies see what's hotting up in the market, and decide to offer new funds.

At the time of writing, several new funds are aimed at the Asian market and the European markets. In the last few years, new funds dedicated to the then-newly expanded Eastern European market have arisen. Ever since Richard Branson's Virgin Direct introduced the Virgin Growth PEP, which is a simple index-tracking fund, there has also been an explosion in index-tracking funds. The biggest news in new funds, however, has to be the vast number of gilt and fixed-interest funds introduced to meet the demand for the new corporate bond PEP. The UK unit trust investor can choose from approximately 1,600 unit trusts. In other words, a shortage of available products will never be your problem as a unit trust investor.

## WHAT A UNIT TRUST IS: AN OVERVIEW

To read sales brochures, you'd think that unit trusts can do everything; take care of the kids, pick up the groceries, and clean the car. A lot more mundane, the unit trust just offers the promise of life-long security.

A unit trust is born when the legal document, called the trust deed, becomes effective. Debbie Harrison in the *Unit Trust Yearbook 1996* explains that 'The concept of trust law ... was first used in the Middle Ages' to protect Holy Crusaders' property during the Crusades 'and since then has evolved in a complex and piecemeal fashion. The trustees' job is to act in the best interests of the beneficiaries (in this case the unit holders).'[2]

A unit trust is a legal vehicle, a legal fiction, which is established by a trust deed whose sole purpose is to invest on behalf of its unit holders. Like any trust, there's really no one owner. Instead, this legal vehicle acts on behalf of its beneficiaries and investors.

A unit trust begins with the idea: what the unit trust will invest in. Typically, a fund management company will organise the venture, which consists of creating a trust deed, choosing an investment manager, trustee and various other parties to manage its operations.

But hang on, you say, isn't the fund management company the same as the fund? Isn't Mercury Asset Management's UK Equity Fund and Mercury Asset Management the same thing? Isn't Gartmore's British Growth Fund Gartmore? No. And this distinction is what affords protection to investors. The company that manages the fund does not own the fund.

> 'A unit trust begins with the idea: what the unit trust will invest in.'

Rather, the fund is created through a trust indenture which states that it will employ the services of Morgan Grenfell, Mercury, or Schroders to manage the portfolio of securities on behalf of unit holders. Indeed, the person or team actually choosing the portfolio may not even be associated with the fund manager.

For example, Tony Woods, Virgin Direct's marketing director, notes that Virgin Direct's Growth PEP is managed by Norwich Union; however, the administration, the telephone client service people, and the general direction of the trust is managed by Virgin Direct.

The trust deed lays out the roles of the various participants in operating the fund: who shall perform administration, who shall be the trustee, and who shall be the investment manager. This may seem illogical or confusing. The fund is set up by the fund management company, e.g., Perpetual or Mercury. But the fund itself hires companies to perform services for it, such as administration, investment management, and trusteeship. Unlike a normal company with a board of directors, the trustee's role is to oversee the fund's activities independently. But it is the fund – and ultimately you, the investor – who pays for these services.

The situation is shown in diagrammatic form in Figure 5.1.

In reality, the investment manager, the fund administrator, and sometimes the registrar is the same firm. The trustee and the accounting firm are never the fund management company.

For example, the new Asia Fund is managed by Portfolio Fund Management Limited, whose offices are at 64 London Wall. However, the trustee for the fund is the Midland Bank. The registrar

**Fig 5.1 The fund management company co-ordinates the unit trust**

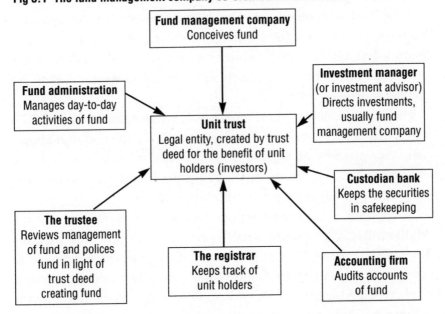

is Premier Administration Limited of Essex, while the auditors are Price Waterhouse. The investment advisor is Portfolio Funds, the fund management company. The scheme particulars tell us that 'The investments of each of the funds are managed by the Manager [Portfolio Fund Management Limited]. No investment advisors have been appointed.'[3] We will understand the roles of the investment advisor as the book unfolds; however, now we focus briefly on the trustee.

## THE TRUSTEES OF THE TRUST

The trustees play an incredibly important role, albeit behind the scenes. Conceivably, the trustees for the fund could sack the fund management company and choose another one. This is unlikely; in a sense, it'd be like a son claiming he doesn't like his parents and would rather have his next door neighbour's parents; though an orphan as a ward of the court could petition to have his foster parents changed.

Trustees are companies like Royal Bank of Scotland, Lloyds Bank, and the Bank of Scotland.[4] The trustees are responsible 'for separating the assets from the fund management company'. This is key. The *Yearbook* states that 'if the fund goes bust, the investors' money is safe'.[5] The trustees are completely independent of the fund management company.

The central function of the trustee is to oversee the fund's activities with regards to its trust-deed-mandated policies about cash management, investments of the fund, and pricing. The trustee does not choose the actual investments; it just ensures that the fund is invested according to what is set out in the trust deed.

As mentioned, the trustee for the Portfolio Funds' Asia Fund is the Midland Bank. The scheme particulars for this new fund describe Midland Bank as 'a Public Limited Company incorporated in England and Wales on 15 August 1836'. The scheme details go on to explain that Midland Bank's 'principal business activity is to provide a comprehensive range of domestic and international banking and financial services. As a Trustee, the company [Midland] is regulated by IMRO in the conduct of investment business and is authorised to carry on investment business in the United Kingdom by virtue of that membership.'[6]

This certainly adds an air of reputability: 'incorporated in … 1836' – that's over 150 years ago. However, remember, the trustee's assets are on the line only if there is a breach of trust, not if the investments were poorly chosen. The only guarantee offered by the trustee is that the fund will be managed by the means set out in the trust deed.

The trust deed establishing the unit trust lays out several key requirements:

- **Aims:** specifying the goals of the fund;
- **Charges and fees:** the maximum level of charges and fees that the fund can pay to the management house running the fund;
- **Expenses:** those fund-related expenses allowed to be charged to the fund;

- **Dividends and yields;**
- **Pricing:** detailing the formula for pricing the units.

We turn to each of these requirements.

## Fund aims

The trust deed sets out what the fund's aims are, what the fund can do to reach these aims, and, very importantly, how much the fund can pay to its managers.

The aim of the Asia Fund is:

> to provide capital growth by investing in any Asian market, other than Japan, through authorised unit trust schemes or recognised schemes. Investment will not be confined to any particular economic sectors.
>
> from Scheme Particulars, Portfolio Funds.

The trust deed for the Asia Fund specifies that 'all the property [money] of each Fund must be invested in authorised unit trust schemes which are not themselves funds of funds or equivalent parts of umbrella funds, except that cash or near cash may be held for liquidity purposes or the efficient management of the Fund or any other purpose ancillary to its objectives'.[7] The Limitations of Type of Investments states that the fund may enter into transactions in derivatives, such as options and futures for the purpose of reduction of relevant risks or the reduction in costs. This last comment about derivatives is fairly commonplace these days.

This is a little dry. You have to dig further to find out why you should invest in this fund. I rang up Portfolio Funds and asked them to send me all information, all articles, everything, about the new Asia Fund. I received a packet of articles as well as the Scheme Particulars. From the articles, I discovered that Richard Timberlake, head of Portfolio Fund Management, visited the Far East on a fact-finding mission. Mr Timberlake said he 'was impressed after inter-viewing 44 managers from 15 leading investment houses in Hong Kong and Singapore. I like Asia because it is the only region that still gives me a buzz at the ripe old age of 52.'[8]

He continued, saying that 'Asia has had its problems recently and the stock markets have suffered a low-down. But it is still the fastest growing part of the world. The genuine equity investor with a five to ten-year view cannot go wrong investing 20 per cent of a portfolio in Asia.''

That certainly sounds inviting. But the same article – included in the pack of information I was sent – stated that Mercury unit trust managing director Richard Royds, whom we met earlier when we learnt that he invested money for his children in emerging markets unit trusts, opposed Timberlake's view, saying, 'The Asian stock markets have become increasingly vulnerable to change in sentiment on American interest rates. Market volatility is exacerbated by local politics, while trade problems between US and China continue to be a concern. On top of that is the increased political turbulence in Hong Kong.'

> 'Whenever you're considering investing in a fund, you should ring up the fund management company and request that all information be sent to you.'

So, it's not as clear-cut as Mr Timberlake would have us believe.

The Mercury Portfolio, which falls under Mr Royds' directorship, has been around for over ten years. Its aim is:

to provide capital growth and a yield, after charges, equivalent to approximately two-thirds of the yield on the FTSE Actuaries All-Share Index. It may invest in any and all geographical areas or economic sectors.

Dry again. We also learn that The Mercury Portfolio mirrors the investment strategy adopted for individual UK-based private clients of Mercury Asset Management plc. In other words, you get your money managed in the same fashion as the rich folks.

Whenever you're considering investing in a fund, you should ring up the fund management company and request that all information be sent to you. Everything. Scheme particulars, comparisons of performance, all the fund brochures. You receive a huge packet in the mail. It doesn't cost anything; and your job is to understand as best you can how the fund is managed and how well it has done. All the information cited above came to me via the post.

# Charges and fees

One of the first things to look at in picking a unit trust is the initial charge which you must pay to invest in the fund. This is an ingredient in the eventual success of your performance. As pointed out earlier, the longer you hold the investment, the less important the initial charge. However, this is money straight off the top of your investment.

> In Chapter 7, I'll describe a technique for reducing the initial charge which is safe, foolproof, and can be used, regardless of what investment you eventually make.

For the Asia Fund, we find that the initial charge amounts to 5 per cent of the value of the underlying assets. For investments of £10,000 or more, a discount scheme comes into action (see Figure 5.2).

**Fig 5.2  Portfolio's Asia Fund: discount scheme**

| Amount invested | Discount |
|---|---|
| £3,000 to £9,999 | nil |
| £10,000 to £24,999 | 1% |
| £25,000 to £99,999 | 2% |
| £100,000 and over | 3% |

For Mercury's Mercury Portfolio Fund, the preliminary charge, as they call it, is normally 5 per cent of the underlying assets. There is no mention of any discount scheme. But see Chapter 7 for how to get a discount on unit trust investments.

The initial charge can vary from 0 per cent to upwards of 7 per cent. The market dictates the charges, though the trust deed spells out the maximum allowable charge. Presently, there is a pricing war in the unit trust marketplace. This is good. Initial charges are dropping. Some firms, however, in place of an initial charge have instituted a sliding scale of exit charges. If you sell your investment, typically, within five years, you pay a fee based on the value of your investment when you sell.

For example, Legal & General unit trusts today charge no initial fee, but have instituted the scale of withdrawal fees shown in Figure 5.3.

**Fig 5.3 Legal & General unit trusts: withdrawal fees**

| Year | Year 1 | Year 2 | Year 3 | Year 4 | Year 5 | After year 5 |
|------|--------|--------|--------|--------|--------|--------------|
| Exit fee | 5% | 4% | 3% | 2% | 1% | 0% |

There is nothing wrong with this fee scheme; it is specifically to encourage long-term holdings. If you hold the investment for over five years, you pay no initial or exit charges. If you hold for less than five years, what you pay is based on the value of your investments when you sell. If you sell, say, in the third year, and pay a 3 per cent exit fee it is a better deal than paying the 5 per cent initial charge at the beginning.

The important point, however, is to check whether a fund which charges 0 per cent upfront institutes exit charges.

## Fund income and expenses

The unit trust is very much like a separate, unique company. It has assets like any company. The assets aren't factories, though; the assets are securities. And just like a factory which produces widgets to generate revenues called 'widget sales', the unit trust's assets, its shares, generate revenues called dividends and interest income. And just like a company which sells its factory because it is obsolete and no longer capable of generating sufficient revenue, the unit trust sells shares in companies which are no longer promising. The company may also hold cash balances which generate interest income. This unit trust, like any company, has expenses.

Harry Nash, one very knowledgeable individual in charge of unit trust accounting for Mercury Asset Management, who will take us on our tour of unit trust accounting, explained the issue of expenses to me. 'The expenses are strictly regulated in that they must be disclosed in the scheme particulars,' he said handing me a copy of the Scheme Particulars for Mercury's unit trusts. 'You must specify them.'

He added, 'There's no regulation saying you can't charge 10 per cent per year, but no-one would buy your units.'

When you look at the accounts of the unit trust, you'll see only those categories specified in the scheme particulars. For Mercury's funds, the following are allowable charges:[10]

### Annual charge

'Payable to the Managers [Mercury Fund Managers Ltd, in this particular instance] and charged to the relevant fund. Currently 1½ per cent of the average of bid and offer values of the fund', and then the particulars go on to list some exceptions where the charge is less.

This is the amount paid to portfolio managers. It is typically stated as a percentage of the volume of funds under management. Unfortunately, there is usually no correlation with performance and payment to the fund manager. Thus, if the fund is successful in raising more money because the performance is strong, then the amount paid out to the manager would increase. Likewise, if the performance is weak, investors depart, then the size of the fund shrinks, and with it the annual charge would be reduced. I would like to see more performance charges where the managers benefit from good performance and suffer for bad performance.

The Asia Fund addresses this issue in that the fees payable to the manager decrease as the fund size grows. In the Scheme Particulars, we find the schedule shown in Figure 5.4.

**Fig 5.4  Portfolio's Asia Fund: schedule of annual charges**

| Funds invested | Annual charges |
|----------------|----------------|
| First £100 million | 1.50% |
| Next £150 million | 1.25% |
| Above £250 million | 1.00% |

While it is a step in the right direction, to raise more than £100 million is quite an achievement, as only one in five funds is valued at over £100 million.

### Trustee's charges

These consist of fees for safe custody, insurance, acquisition, holding the collection of dividends or interest, any deposit or loan charges and so on. You get the picture. The fees for Mercury's trustee are shown in Figure 5.5.

**Fig 5.5 Mercury Fund: trustee's charges**

| Up to £200,000 | 0.0225% |
|---|---|
| On the next £300,000 | 0.020% |
| On the remainder | 0.0175% |

### Other expenses

The list is long. It includes brokers' commissions, interest on borrowings, taxation and duties, annual general meeting costs, audit costs, registrar costs and so on.

# UNDERSTANDING A WINNER: UNIT TRUST ACCOUNTING

The expenses are only one side of the equation. The other side is the revenues or gross income of the fund. Mercury's Nash talked me through the accounting for unit trusts. His jovial spirit and keen understanding of the topic made it interesting. He also made me understand its relevance. Even if you hate accounting, please forge on. I promise not too much accounting, but it is essential to see where performance comes from – which you are interested in – that you have a minor understanding of unit trust accounting. Let's call it 'understanding a winner' instead of 'accounting'.

And, as I imply by my chart (shown in Figure 5.6), the path to investment success and failure is charted via understanding a winner (accounting).

## Dividends

The typical fund holds investments which pay dividends from equities or interest payments from bonds to the fund. Not all funds receive dividends, notably those funds which invest in Asian shares which generally don't pay dividends. The dividends and interest represent revenues for the fund. I go back to the analogy of a factory. The 'machines' of the 'factory' are stocks and bonds. Those

**Fig 5.6 Understanding a winner (accounting)**

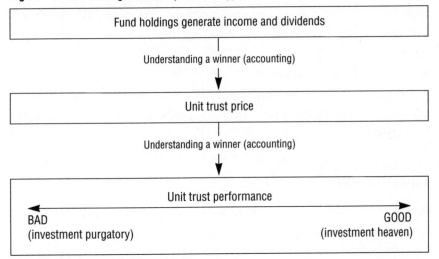

'machines' generate revenues called dividends or interest. It is from the dividends and interest paid to the fund that dividends from the fund are paid to you. However, the fund first deducts the charges and expenses outlined above from the fund to determine the amount available for payments as dividends.

We use again Mercury Portfolio as an example of a typical income statement for a unit trust (see Figure 5.7).

**Fig. 5.7 Mercury Portfolio Income Account (15 March 1995 to 16 March 1996)[11]**

| | Amount £ millions |
|---|---|
| *Gross income* | |
| Dividends received from security holdings | £7.02 |
| Interest paid from cash or bond holdings | £2.10 |
| *Other income* | *£0.32* |
| Total Income | £9.44 |
| | |
| *Expenses* | |
| Managers' service charge | (£3.08) |
| Registrars' fee | (£0.03) |
| Custodian fee | (£0.06) |
| Trustee fee | (£0.05) |
| *Securities and Investment Board and audit fees* | *(£0.01)* |
| Total expenses | (£3.23) |
| | |
| *Taxation* | *(£1.27)* |
| Income available for distribution | £4.94 |

Several comments: as you can see by far and away, the largest expense is the fund management company's fee. Secondly, dividends generate most of the revenues; however, the interest earned on cash balances is not insignificant. We'll see where this comes from when we turn to the holdings of the fund.

This last line is important. It's the amount of net income from the unit trust available for distribution to unit holders as dividends of the unit trust.

## Equalisation

Before the dividends can be distributed, the administrators must take into account another confusing item, called 'equalisation'. Equalisation prevents you from gaining advantage by investing the day before dividends are paid or likewise, losing out because you sold out before the dividend was paid. Equalisation basically spreads out the dividends paid by the fund over the entire period, and then pro-rates the amount you receive to make sure the dividends are fairly distributed.

Mercury's Nash says that 'typically, dividends are paid from the fund two times per year and all net income must be paid out of the fund by law'.

## The issue of dividends

The units entitle the holders – you, the investor – to share ownership of the property of the fund – the underlying investments, and any income arising from ownership of those units. This means when the underlying investments pay dividends to the unit trust, holders of those units are entitled to their share of the dividends, after expenses of the fund are paid. Thus the level of expenses directly affects the amount you will receive in dividends (see Figure 5.8).

The annual management charge can be deducted from the capital of the fund, its investments, and not from income (as in Figure 5.8) at the fund management company's discretion. This frees up more income to be paid out in dividends. But it's robbing Peter to pay Paul.

**Fig 5.8 Mercury Portfolio: abbreviated income statement**

|  | Amount<br>£ millions |
|---|---|
| Gross Income<br>Dividends, interest and other income | £9.44 |
| Managers' charges and other expenses | −£3.23 |
| *Taxation* | −£1.27 |
| Income available for distribution | =£4.94 |
| *Equalisation* | +£0.12 |
| Total to be distributed: | =£5.06 |
| Interim dividend | £1.86 |
| Final dividend | £3.21 |

Any advantage to income has to come from somewhere, and it comes out of capital. We'll look at this issue and the resulting yield calculation when we turn to gilt and fixed-interest funds.

### How to get dividends

Generally, fund managers set up two classes of funds: one called 'income units' and the other, 'accumulation units'.

Every time the unit trust declares a dividend, the income holders receive the cash. For the accumulation holders, the managers simply add the value of the dividend to the price of the unit trust. Accordingly, the price of the accumulation units will never be the same as for the income units after the first dividend distribution.

However, the price difference between the two kinds of units would never be affected by market conditions reflecting investors' preferences between income or accumulation units. The price reflects the composition of the underlying assets, and not market conditions for the unit trusts.

This is probably confusing. Let me clarify. The unit trust's value is based on the value of the underlying assets of the trust. Each day, the fund management company adds up the value of all the securities or unit trusts in the fund, divides by the number of units, and this is the value of the fund. It's a bit more complicated, but that will be explained shortly.

> 'The unit trust's value is based on the value of the underlying assets of the trust.'

Some unit trusts do not create two classes, income and accumulation. These funds will, at your discretion, pay out income or simply reinvest it to give you more units.

Thus, the unit trust has three different methods of distributing the dividend income:

- **paying out cash;**
- **giving out more units;**
- **increasing the price of the units.**

In all instances, tax is withheld at the basic rate. Hence, no tax savings are possible, regardless of your choice of distribution. We turn now to the investments which generate those dividends.

## The fund's investments

The unit trust is formed by the initial investment of capital by investors. This capital is then invested in stocks and bonds, consistent with the fund's aims, by the investment manager on behalf of the unit trust holders.

Mercury's Nash says, 'The capital of the unit trust is comprised of the investments plus net assets, which equal the total value.'

As we saw, the Mercury Portfolio had the world as its oyster and was conceived to invest all over the world in all investments. We'll see this below. On 15 March 1996, the Mercury Portfolio was valued at £229.0 million, comprising investments equalling £218.4 million and, cash and other net current assets of £10.5 million. Nash handed me the annual statement (see Figure 5.9).

**Fig 5.9  Mercury Portfolio Fund: location and type of investments**

| Location/type | Equity | Bonds | Total |
|---|---|---|---|
| United Kingdom | 60% | 10% | 70% |
| Overseas | 22% | 8% | 30% |
| Total | 82% | 18% | 100% |

As Figure 5.9 shows the investments of the fund in general are consistent with the aims to invest in a wide range of stocks and bonds from around the world.

Further examination shows the following details. There were four pages of tiny printed securities. Rather than repeat them all, just a few are included in Figure 5.10 to give you a flavour.

**Fig 5.10  The Mercury Portfolio: Composition 15 March 1996[12]**

| Location/ type | Category | Security | Holding | Market value £ millions | Per cent of total holdings |
|---|---|---|---|---|---|
| UK equity | Bldg matrls | Wolseley | 800,000 | £3.7 | 1.59% |
| UK equity | Electronics | Gen. Elec. | 900,000 | £3.3 | 1.43% |
| UK equity | Electronics | Racal Elec. | 650,000 | £3.3 | 0.89% |
| : | : | : | : | : | : |
| : | : | : | : | : | : |
| : | : | : | : | : | : |
| Overseas bonds | Denmark | 10/12/99 6% bonds | DKr 9 million | £1.0 | 0.45% |
| Overseas bonds | USA | 15/2/1999 5.25% Notes | US $1 million | £4.2 | 1.83% |
| : | : | : | : | : | : |
| : | : | : | : | : | : |
| : | : | : | : | : | : |
| Other equities | Mercury European | Privatisation trust | 250,000 | £0.2 | 0.1% |
| Subtotal investment | International | | | £218.4 | 95.4% |
| Net current assets | Liquidity* | | | £10.5 | 4.6% |
| Total | | | | £229.0 | 100.0% |

\* Net current assets are cash and bank balances; monies owed to and from investors; income due. This represents the liquidity: the money available to the fund management company for investment and to investors for redemptions.

Note the last item, net current assets. This reflects primarily cash in the bank, money owed from investors and money owed to investors and other funds owed to or by the unit trust within the next year. It's important because it reflects funds not invested in securities in the fund.

All portfolio managers keep some money in the bank in case you redeem your units and the fund must pay out cash. If the fund management company didn't keep some funds in the bank, he or she would have to sell some holdings to pay you, and the timing might be inopportune.

# HOLD ON TO THAT LIQUIDITY: THE TWO SCHOOLS

But the other reason the fund manager might keep cash holdings is that he or she believes the market may be going down and the fund manager is not prepared to invest at the current time. An expression I always hear when talking about the cash balances is 'keeping your powder dry'. That is, the fund manager may want to be ready to blast away, that is, to invest fully, as soon as he or she believes the market presents some opportunities.

There are two schools of thought regarding the cash balance held in the fund. The first view is that you are paying the manager to keep fully invested in the market. That is, if you yourself can make the decision to reduce your holdings depending on your view of the market, why should you have the fund manager making either the same or the opposite decision? Some funds remain fully investing, assuming the investor can make that decision.

Along the same lines, if the manager is holding cash in the bank, earning a paltry interest, why should you invest your money, paying upwards of 5 or 6 per cent in initial fees, only to have the investment manager take a portion of your funds and invest them the same way?

The other school of thought is that you hire the portfolio manager to keep his or her ear closely tuned to the state of the market. If the manager believes that the whole market is in for a downward spiral, and that no opportunities present themselves, then the manager should begin to build up the fund's cash holdings so that the fund won't suffer as the market moves downward.

There is no right or wrong answer here. Indeed you do hire the fund manager to keep his or her ear to the ground, to sense big and small shifts in the market. Building cash reserves can be a sensible strategy.

Occasionally, you'll see studies in the investment magazines of the change in the cash balance position of some of the leading funds. This aims to assess professional investors' sentiments. When the cash balances rise, this suggests a bearish or negative sentiment. Fund managers, in aggregate, believe that there are not as many opportunities and are building cash reserves instead of investing.

Conversely, when the cash balances fall, the opposite view holds: that investment managers in sum are bullish, more positive, than previously.

However, cash balances change all the time for many reasons. For example, the manager may have recently received a big in-flow, and may be taking his time to invest the money. Alternatively, he could have sold some shares and is waiting for prices to improve slightly. I wouldn't pay much attention to this indicator, because there are countless individual fund accounting reasons why the liquidity balance may grow unrelated to the fund manager's actual view. We'll look at a far more effective indicator which will inform you about whether investors are moving in or out of the fund, and can save you or make you some money.

## HOW EXPENSIVE IS YOUR FUND?

I turned back to the annual report to determine what percentage of total fund size was received in income and what was paid out to the manager and others (see Figure 5.11).

**Fig 5.11   Mercury Portfolio income and as percentage of total net assets**

|  | Income | As % of assets |
|---|---|---|
| Dividends received from security holdings | £7.02 | 3.38% |
| Interest paid from cash or bond holdings | £2.10 | 1.02% |
| Other income | £0.32 | 0.15% |
| Total Income | £9.44 | 4.55% |
| EXPENSES |  |  |
| Managers' service charge | (£3.08) | (1.48%) |
| Registrars' fee | (£0.03) | (0.01%) |
| Custodian fee | (£0.06) | (0.03%) |
| Trustee fee | (£0.05) | (0.03%) |
| Securities and Investment Board and audit fees | (£0.01) | (0.01%) |
| Total expenses | (£3.23) | (1.56%) |
| Taxation | (£1.27) | (0.61%) |
| Income available for distribution | £4.94 | 2.38% |

Far and away, the biggest expense is the annual management charge, which amounted to 1.48 per cent, slightly less than the 1.5 per cent which the fund states will be charged by the investment manager. The fund administrators calculate the amount each and every day during the period. However, the investments are shown as they stood on the last day of the period. Hence, if the investments are growing, either through additional investments or if the value of the underlying investments increased, we would expect the figure to be slightly less than what is set out in the charges. Rest assured, though, that the fund administrator is taking out the full charge. The amount the fund management company, Jupiter, Gartmore, Prolific and M&G, can charge is set out in the trust deed and generally ranges from 0.50 per cent per year to 1.5 per cent to 2.0 per cent. For the Portfolio Asia Fund, the annual management charge is 1.5 per cent per year, though the trust deed allows Portfolio Management to charge up to 2.00 per cent per year.

This can affect your performance. Here's where you can begin to see the effect. You can see for Mercury's fund that 3 per cent of the fund value was received in income while 1 per cent was earned in interest. If the fund had no expenses, the dividend paid would have equalled 4 per cent of fund value. Yet, there are expenses to which attention must be paid.

## VALUING UNITS

The final step of the equation is the value per unit of the fund. This is a comparatively simple step. You take the value of investments, cash, and other net current assets, and divide by the number of units outstanding. Let's go back to the new Asia Fund, which only recently began trading and is easier to understand and then we'll turn to Mercury's value.

As we discussed, the unit trust begins its life when the trust deed is made effective. The blood flows into the new unit trust with the investment of the first pound sterling. The new Asia Fund had £14.3 million invested when it began trading on 4 November 1996. The units were priced at 50p per unit; hence, there were 28,600,000 units created.

A lower-priced unit is seen as more attractive and more appealing to a wider group of investors and reduces the problem of dividing units into fractions. Portfolio Funds chose to price the units at 50p. Portfolio could have set the price at 100p, in which case 14,300,000 units would have been created. Or they could have set the price at 200p per unit, in which case 7,150,000 units would have been created.

The actual price per unit in fact is irrelevant. For unit trusts, you will invest a certain sum, say £1,000 or £10,000 or £100,000, regardless of the number of units it buys. If you own 100 units or 1,000,000 units, it doesn't matter; what matters is the value of the units.

As we saw (Figure 5.10), the Mercury Fund had £229.0 million in investments and cash; at the annual accounting date, there were 253 million units; and the value per unit was 90.35p.

We move forward from this exposition of the underlying value of the fund to the next step in our journey, pricing and where the price comes from.

## REFERENCES

[1] 'Smoothing out bumpy road to Oriental Reward', by Tristan Stein, *The Daily Telegraph*, 12 October 1996.

[2] 'What is a unit trust and how does it work?' by Debbie Harrison, in the *Unit Trust Yearbook*, 1996, p. 16.

[3] *Scheme Particulars*, Portfolio Funds, revised October 1996, p. 2.

[4] From AUTIF from *Guide to Investment Trusts & Unit Trusts*, p. 48.

[5] *Unit Trust Yearbook*, 1996, p. 16.

[6] *Scheme Particulars*, Portfolio Funds, revised October 1996, pp. 1–2.

[7] *Scheme Particulars*, Portfolio Funds, revised October 1996, p. 7.

[8] 'Star funds could rise in the East', by Claire Burston, *Financial Mail on Sunday*, 13 October 1996, p. 17.

[9] Ibid., p. 17.

[10] Charges section in 'Scheme Particulars', Mercury Fund Managers, 12 March 1996, pp. 15–19.

[11] *Annual Report*, The Mercury Portfolio, 16 March 1995 to 15 March 1996, Mercury Asset Management, p. 12, p. 15.

[12] 'Portfolio Statement', *Annual Report*, The Mercury Portfolio, 16 March 1995 to 15 March 1996, Mercury Asset Management, pp. 7–11, p. 12.

# SUMMARY

- Many new unit trusts have recently been established which can be used in a PEP – including bond funds and index-tracking funds.

- The fund management company acts as the coach co-ordinating the different departments or companies necessary to secure the performance and integrity of the unit trust and PEP.

- The trust deed of the unit trust establishes:
  – objectives of the fund
  – charges and fees
  – dividend policies
  – pricing practices.

- You can tell how expensive your fund is, compared with other funds, by looking at the expenses as a percentage of total assets.

- The value of the units is the total investments, cash, and other assets divided by the number of outstanding units.

# FINDING
# THE RIGHT
# PRICE

'If you understand pricing', marketing head for Scottish Widows, David S. Graham, told me, 'you can get an edge – nobody understands it.' Presumably, he understood it, as he spent the next three-quarters of an hour trying to explain a nuance to me. Graham let on that 'it's easy once you understand it', and that 'you can learn a lot from pricing in the *Financial Times*'.

The pricing of unit trusts, the formula for which is prescribed both by the trust deed and securities law, is incredibly complex and, at the same time, simple. I was thoroughly confused by the subject of pricing. The more I looked into the matter, the less I knew. Bob Hale, the technical representative from AUTIF, who understands it better than anybody, says, 'I wish [the mechanics of pricing] weren't so complicated'. I spent time with experts from the Investment Management Regulatory Organisation (IMRO), with AUTIF, with Scottish Widow's Graham, and several other knowledgeable industry types. Then I met Mercury's Harry Nash, the man who guided us through the unit trust accounting. Finally, I understood it; I realised it was quite simple. I will talk you through the concept, which is no different from any other commercial transaction.

> 'The pricing of unit trusts . . . is incredibly complex and, at the same time, simple'.

Like many things in the business world, those who understand the rules profit more than those that don't. After you get through this chapter, you'll understand the concepts. You'll get an 'edge'. The chapter concludes by discussing when is a better time to sell and how to get a better price.

A new pricing scheme looms on the horizon, which should greatly simplify matters. It comes from a European Union imperative to sell unit trusts across Europe. The legal form of unit trusts can be changed from a trust-based fund to what's called an Open-Ended Investment Company, or OEIC – pronounced 'OICH' or the plural, 'OIX'. The change that you'll notice is that only one price will be quoted for investing in the new form of fund. At the time of writing, the industry is still wrangling over the rules, and the speed at which unit trusts will convert is unclear. What follows below is a summary of the existing structure with a brief discussion of the effect on the price of the new rules.

# A LITTLE HISTORY

First, a little history. The unit trust was introduced to this country in the 1930s. M&G's current direct marketing director, Roger A. Jennings, explained that George Booth of Municipal and General Securities (now better known as M&G) had been to America and saw the popularity of mutual funds in the States. He exported the idea to the United Kingdom, though he added a few wrinkles which make unit trust pricing different from in the States. The initial issue of the UK's first unit trust, called the First British Fixed Trust, was made on 23 April 1931, at a price of 31s 9d per unit.

Booth's biography said that, 'This first trust was a fixed trust, so called because it had an absolutely fixed "hamper" or portfolio laid down in the trust deed.'[1] This proved unworkable because some shares grew in value while others diminished; thus, later purchasers ended up with shares disproportionate to what was stated in the trust deed. This was remedied by allowing the investment manager to invest in any shares on a 'permitted list of securities'.

Jennings, who has been in this business for 30 years, said, 'Investment trusts are allowed to gear up', which means they can borrow funds and then invest those funds on top of the funds provided by investors. George Booth had been 'staggered' by the losses in investment trusts on Wall Street and wanted to create a 'type of trust distinct from what the Americans had had'.

Municipal and General's Booth applied for a stock exchange quotation to allow investors to go to an exchange to buy or sell units. He believed the best way to introduce collective investments was to make them look and feel like stocks or investment trusts, with which the public was familiar. Hence, when you buy a stock, an investment trust, or a unit trust, you pay what's called the 'offer' price; likewise, when you sell a stock, an investment trust, or a unit trust, you are paid what's called the 'bid' price.

However, a small world of difference exists between the price of stocks or investment trusts and unit trust prices. The bid and offer prices on unit trusts are not really created in the market, as described below. The terminology confuses.

First of all, a unit trust – as opposed to an investment trust – is called an 'open-ended' fund. By comparison, an investment trust is a 'closed-end' fund. This is the main legal distinction between the two types of investment. The open-ended unit trust creates and cancels units in the trust depending on the demand of the investing public. The trustee issues certificates of unit holdings and destroys them as investors sell back their investment. With an investment trust, a pre-specified number of shares is created at inception, the number remains fixed for the life of the investment trust, and these investment trust shares trade freely in the market.

The investment trust's value is determined by the constant tug and pull of the marketplace. Just like any company whose shares trade on an exchange, the value of the investment trust reflect market conditions, confidence, and fear.

In the case of a unit trust, there is no market for its units. The fund management company agrees to buy or to sell the units at the price reflecting the value of the underlying assets. The price is set at a pre-determined time once a day.

When you buy or sell unit trusts, the fund management company will buy or sell units from you at either the most recent price (called historic pricing) or the price at the next price setting (called forward pricing).

## TO BID OR TO OFFER

To purchase a security in the marketplace, investors need to go to the company which specialises in buying and selling these securities. If, for instance, you wanted to buy shares in BT, your stockbroker must go to the stockbroker who specialises in buying and selling BT shares. The stockbroker in this particular instance is called a market-maker, because this firm is said to 'make a market' in the particular security.

The market-maker charges a higher price to sell you the security than he would to buy the security back from you. The difference between what he'll sell it to you for and what he buys it back is his profit for making a market in the stock.

Think of a food retailer. Tins of food were purchased from a wholesaler. The grocery store marks up the price of the tins to cover costs, storage, the labour, and to make a little profit. Hence, you pay more to buy this can than the grocer did.

The same system holds with securities. However, unlike the grocer who only purchases tins of soup *to sell* to you, the market-making security company is willing both *to sell* you securities and *to buy* them back from you. Just the same in the market, however, the price he buys the securities from you is lower than the price that he'll sell it to you. This is his mark-up for keeping the securities on the shelves, for all those screens, the computer systems, and the labour.

Thus, when the unit trust fund management company goes into the marketplace to buy securities for your fund, the fund management company pays more to buy the shares than to sell the shares. However, the fund management company gets a better deal than you would, because the fund makes transactions in the hundreds of thousands or even millions of pounds, while yours most likely would be a lot smaller.

> '. . . the market-maker buys shares at the bid price, and sells at the offer price. The difference is known as the 'bid/offer spread'.

Again, the price at which the market-maker sells securities is known as the 'offer' price, the price which the market-maker is *offering* shares for sale. The offer price is what the fund management company must pay to buy shares for the fund. On the other hand, when the market-maker buys shares from sellers, the market-maker pays the 'bid' price. The difference between the price at which the market-maker sells shares or buys shares is known as the 'bid/offer spread'.

Let me repeat: the market-maker buys shares at the bid prices, and sells at the offer price. The difference is known as the 'bid/offer spread'.

| Offer price | Price at which the market-maker *sells* shares |
| less bid price | Price at which the market-maker *buys* shares |
| Bid/offer spread | Difference between selling price and buying price |

Please be patient. You'll see the forest for the trees in a minute.

# PRICING THE UNITS

With unit trusts, it's the same story. When you buy a unit trust you'll pay more for it than if you were to turn around and sell it back immediately. That's the central concept. The difference between the price you pay and the price you would receive immediately thereafter is called the unit trust spread or just the 'spread'. The spread is fixed at the time of pricing of the units, which occurs once a day.

The pricing of the units occurs once a day because it's fairly complex to work out every second of the day. Prices must be verified before setting. Sometimes the data services get the price of the underlying securities wrong, especially for less frequently traded securities, or sometimes there are decimal point errors with foreign currencies. The fund management company must authenticate the price, therefore, before establishing a price at which units in the fund can be bought or sold.

If you hear of a spread of 5.71 per cent, this means the difference between the price at which you buy and that at which you sell is 5.71 per cent. Put differently, your investment must grow by slightly more than 6.05 per cent before you're in profitable territory (see **Calculating the spread percentage**). The Trust Deed specifies the maximum allowable spread. This, not surprisingly, is the maximum difference between the buying price and the selling price, in percentage terms, for the units.

The market has a way of reducing the spread; accordingly, most likely, the actual spread is less than the maximum allowable spread.

I rang up the client service line at Mercury to find out the spread on the Income Portfolio when I wrote this. The helpful fellow explained that the price I could buy units today was 122.7p and the price at which I could immediately sell my units was 115.7p. Hence, the spread was 7p.

---

**Calculating the spread percentage:**

To calculate how much the bid price must grow to equal the offer price you paid, subtract the bid price from the offer and then divide by the <u>bid price</u> . (For some strange reason, the official calculation is to take the spread and then divide by the <u>selling price</u>. This latter calculation results in a smaller spread than in the former case. Unfortunately, the latter calculation doesn't tell you what you need to know: how much the bid price must increase for you to get back what you invested.)

| | |
|---|---|
| Investing price | 122.7p |
| Selling price | 115.7p |
| Spread | 7.0p |

Spread as % of investing price $^{7.0}/_{122.7}$ or 5.71%

Spread as % of selling price $^{7.0}/_{115.7}$ or 6.05%

---

If you invested £100 in the Mercury Portfolio, you would need the selling price to advance by 6.05 per cent to start back where you began.

**Example**

| Investment | | Investing price | | Number of units purchased |
|---|---|---|---|---|
| £100 | ÷ | 122.7p | = | 81.49 |

Sell immediately:   81.49 units  ×  bid at 115.7p = £94.30

Selling after bid price rises 6.05% to 122.7p

Sell     81.49 units  ×  bid at 122.7p = £100.00

Since 1960, there have been 19 years when the UK stock market rose at least 6 per cent. But if you left your investment in the market for five years during that same time, the market would have risen enough to cover the costs 80 per cent of the time. That's just a not-so-subtle argument for investing and staying put.

The prices reported above are not random, nor were they determined by traders buying and selling units. They are built up from the underlying investments and the value of the fund's cash holdings and expenses. The investing price, the amount which you must pay, is equal to an estimate of what the fund management company would have to pay to buy the shares in the marketplace, uninvested cash, and the net income of the portfolio up to that point. This is where the discussion of investments, liquidity, and the income statement, which we called 'understanding a winner' and what the rest of the world calls 'accounting', becomes important.

Again, we turn to the Mercury Portfolio to help flesh out the dry discussion of pricing (see Figure 6.1). I have revalued the numbers as a percentage of the bid price of £100. This will simplify the analysis because all values can be seen as a percentage of the bid price.

The first step is to look at the investments. This lists the value of investments in the fund in terms of what it would cost the fund management company to buy these investments all over again at today's prices and what it would receive if it was to sell at today's prices. The first column shows the bid prices for the underlying investments and the second column shows the offer prices of the underlying investments.

We saw this list earlier when we analysed the list of investments of this particular unit trust. We go a little deeper now.

The second section includes results internal to the fund itself. If the fund management company had to return to the marketplace and re-purchase all these investments, it would face dealing charges. Thus, in calculating the value of the fund today, it is required to add in an amount it would pay to repurchase the investments, £0.39.

On the other hand, if the fund management company was required to sell the investments, it would again face dealing charges, which would reduce the value of the investments. Hence, this time, we must deduct it from the value it would receive if it were to sell the securities.

Next, we add in uninvested cash. These are funds received from new and existing investors and from the sale of investments.

**Fig 6.1  Mercury Portfolio: Bid and offer prices of underlying investments: (revalued so that bid price equals £100)**

| Source of value | Bid value | Offer value |
|---|---|---|
| **Investments** | | |
| UK equities | £62.39 | £62.85 |
| European equities | £6.49 | £6.50 |
| North American equities | £3.89 | £3.91 |
| Japanese equities | £4.06 | £4.06 |
| Pacific equities | £4.14 | £4.19 |
| Other equities | £1.89 | £1.91 |
| UK fixed-interest | £7.05 | £7.06 |
| Overseas fixed-interest | £5.79 | £5.79 |
| *Mercury funds* | *£1.45* | *£1.48* |
| Total | £97.15 | £97.75 |
| **Other Assets** | | |
| Dealing exp. and stamp tax | £–0.11 | £0.39 |
| Uninvested cash | £2.09 | £2.09 |
| *YTD fund net income* | *£0.87* | *£0.87* |
| Total other assets | £2.85 | £3.35 |
| **Total** | **£100.00** | **£101.10** |

Finally, we come to the net fund income. You'll recall from Chapter 5 that YTD net income reflects the results of the unit trust: the dividends and interest received less the charges, such as the manager's fee, trustee's fee, and so on. We add this in because it is part of the property of the unit trust, and as a holder of this particular trust, you are entitled to the income generated by the trust's activities.

Thus, with these building blocks, we finally see how the buying and selling prices are arrived at. The investment totals are added together with the internal fund results, and the final values are calculated. To the buying amount, we add the manager's initial charge, and end up with the buying and selling price for the fund (see Figure 6.2).

**Fig 6.2 Buying and selling prices: (revalued so that bid price equals £100)**

| | Bid value | Offer value |
|---|---|---|
| Investment totals | £97.15 | £97.75 |
| Internal fund results | £2.85 | £3.35 |
| Total portfolio value | £100.00 | £101.10 |
| Managers' initial charge @ 5% of offer price | | £5.06 |
| **Price to invest** | **£100.00** | **£106.16** |

Even though I use the words 'bid/offer', as highlighted above, a true bid/offer price is only quoted by a market-maker. The fund management company isn't really making a market in the unit trusts because it can create as many new units as are necessary, or destroy them as necessary. Accordingly, if the supply of new units is infinite, the price paid and received for a unit trust isn't the result of investors bidding up the price or driving down the price for the units, instead it's calculated very methodically, as described above.

The new legal form of fund, called the Open Ending Investment Company (OEIC), requires a single purchase and selling price. For these new funds, you receive the same price for buying as for selling the fund. The fund managers simply take the average of the bid and offer prices of the underlying investments. However, they are still allowed to add on the initial charge.

Now, let's add some terminology. The underlying securities are purchased at the offer price from market-makers. The fund management company creates the portfolio by buying at the offer price. Thus, in the unit trust world, the creation price is what it costs to create the fund by purchasing securities at the offer price.

If the fund managers decided to wind down the whole affair, to cancel the unit trust, they would go into the marketplace to sell the underlying securities at the bid price. This is also known as the 'cancellation price'.

## CREATING AND CANCELLING

The price you'll pay or receive for your unit trusts lies somewhere between the price that it costs to create the units plus the initial charge, and the price to sell off all the investments and cancel the units.

This maximum difference between the creation price and the cancellation price is called the 'maximum allowable spread'. However, market forces usually make this spread – the difference between what you pay to buy units and what you receive when you sell your units – called the 'Quoted Spread', less than the maximum allowable spread.

You can calculate this spread. Buy the *Financial Times*. Find the 'Managed Funds' pages in the second section. There you'll find the initial charge, the bid price, the offer price, the yield, and the change from the previous day. See the box on page 93 for the two ways of calculating the spread.

Figure 6.3 shows some examples of quoted spreads on large unit trusts.

**Fig 6.3 Examples of quoted spreads**

| Fund | Spread |
|---|---|
| Hill Samuel Capital | 6.64% |
| Barclays Unicorn General | 6.64% |
| Perpetual High Income | 6.51% |
| Perpetual UK Growth | 6.50% |
| Schroders UK Enterprise | 6.25% |
| Schroders UK Equity | 6.25% |
| STD Life UK Equity General | 5.89% |
| M&G Dividend | 5.51% |
| M&G Recovery | 5.46% |
| Scot. Amicable Equity | 5.43% |
| M&G Managed Income | 4.79% |

Source: *Micropal Expert*, data for October 1996.

You'll note that the spread can vary between different funds. The spread arises from different bid/offer values of the underlying securities, the manager's initial charge, and the internal fund results.

## THE INSIDE SCOOP ON PRICING

Put yourself in the fund management company's shoes. If you buy units in the fund, the manager has to go out and buy additional shares – paying the offer price – in the marketplace. But let's say that right before you called, another holder of units wanted to sell exactly the same number of units as you wanted to buy. The fund management company wouldn't have to buy more securities at the offer price, but would simply give you the units belonging to the person who wanted to sell. Under some circumstances, however, the fund management company would be liable to pay stamp tax.

The fund itself wouldn't incur any charges, except for the clerical ones relating to the changes of names on the register and on the certificate. If it only happened once, then the fund management company wouldn't gain or lose from the transaction. But if the fund charged buyers the higher offer or creation price, and sold at the lower bid or cancellation price over and over and over again, the fund management company would stand to gain.

If the fund is expanding, that is, the fund management company has to increase the number of outstanding units and enter the marketplace to buy more securities, the fund is said to be on an 'offer basis'.

If, on the other hand, the fund is contracting, there are more sellers than buyers, the fund management company does not need to buy more underlying securities, and the fund is said to be on a 'bid basis'.

It's possible that the fund management company will buy back units from an investor and not be able to sell them to someone else immediately. It has a choice: it can instruct the trustee to destroy or cancel the units. Alternatively, it can put them in the 'box', that is, it can hold them until someone comes in to buy units. The risk is that by the time someone calls to invest, the price may have gone down, and the fund management company may be forced to sell the units for less than it bought them. Alternatively, the price may rise, allowing it to sell the units back for more than it paid for them.

If, on calculating the difference between the creation price and the cancellation price, the fund management company discovers it is greater than the market-driven spread, it has to decide how much to charge to buy and sell units.

The fund management company can choose to price the units for purchasing and selling so long as:

- the price for *you* to sell (the bid price) is at least as great as the cancellation price;
- the price for *you* to buy (the offer price) is no more than the creation price plus the published initial charge;
- the spread between the two prices does not exceed its agreed-upon spread.

**Fig 6.4 Creation and cancellation**

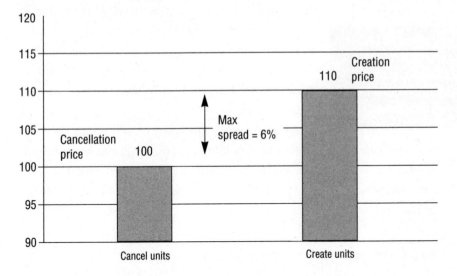

If the fund is on an offer basis, the fund management company sets the offer price such that it equals the creation price, which is the highest amount it can charge. However, once setting the offer price to equal the creation price, it has to set the bid price within the spread range. Thus, if the difference between the creation and cancellation prices was greater than the pre-specified spread, the fund management company is forced to set the bid price, that it pays to you when you sell units, at a higher price than the cancellation price.

Alternatively, if the fund is on a 'bid basis', then the spread moves down such that the lowest price the fund management company can buy back units is at the cancellation price. In this case, because of the spread constraint, the fund management company is forced to sell you units at less than the creation price.

Figure 6.5 gives a summary.

**Fig 6.5 Bid basis and offer basis**

| Basis | Bid price | Offer price | Best |
|-------|-----------|-------------|------|
| Bid basis | Lowest selling price | Medium buying price | **Buy** |
| Offer basis | Medium selling price | Highest buying price | **Sell** |

The implications are clear: you want to buy when the fund is on a bid basis, and sell when the fund is on an offer basis. Unfortunately,

> '. . . you want to buy when the fund is on a bid basis, and sell when the fund is on an offer basis.'

a fund will be on a bid basis when the fund management company is buying more units then selling; i.e., a time when investors are cashing in their investments and probably when the market is moving down.

Alternatively, you want to sell when the fund is on an offer basis, because this is when you'll get the better price. However, by the same token, when the fund is expanding, the market is probably doing well; hence, you'll be selling when prices are going up.

**Fig 6.6  Same unit trust, same spread: different prices**

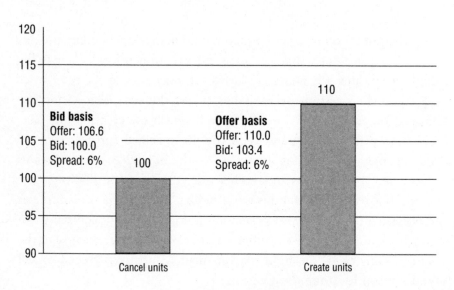

Now, you know more about pricing of units and how it relates to the internal mechanics of a unit trust. David S. Graham, the Scottish Widows marketing director we met at the beginning of the chapter, says it best: if you understand pricing, you'll get the edge. In addition, armed with this information, you'll be able to evaluate which funds are 'cheap' and which ones 'expensive' and when it's a good time to buy.

Next we move on to a related topic: how the expenses affect your performance, and again, how can you get the edge by determining which funds are more likely to perform well.

REFERENCES
[1] *A Man of Push and Go* by Rupert-Hart Davis, 1965, p. 178.

# SUMMARY

- Two prices are presented for unit trusts:
  - the offer price is what you pay to invest
  - the bid price is what you receive when you sell.

- The initial charge, included in the offer price, pays the fund management company and the IFA.

- The 'bid/offer spread' or just the 'spread' is the difference between the bid price and the offfer price.

- The spread is quoted in pence or as a percentage of the offer price.

- Spreads vary across types of investments and among fund management companies.

- Getting a better deal:
  - buy when the fund is on a bid basis – when the fund is contracting
  - sell when the fund is on an offer basis – when the fund is expanding.

# THE CHARGE
# TO PAY

'The prospective [unit trust] holder is not always able to calculate easily for himself whether the managers are making a low or an unduly high charge for their services as midwives or managers of the Trust'[1] decried the authors of *Unit Trusts and How They Work* which was published in 1937.

Some things never change.

It is as sure as the sun will rise tomorrow that you'll pay to invest in a unit trust. According to *Money Management*, 'Many managers maintain that performance is the be-all and end-all, with charges a very minor consideration.'[2] I always hold my wallet tightly when someone tells me not to worry about charges.

The good news is that competitive forces in the last few years have caused 'quite a sea change in pricing though, spurred in large extent by fierce competition in the PEP market'.[3] Philip Warland, Director General of the Association of Unit Trusts and Investment Funds, says that price competition has never been like it is today.

Jeremy Soutter, product director at Henderson Touche Remnant, divides unit trust investors into two camps: those that care about fees and those that don't. When you see what fees can do to your results, you'll care about fees.

Continuing on from the discussion in Chapter 6 about pricing, this chapter will highlight the explicit and hidden charges you'll pay. I'll introduce 'the flat earth', a concept to isolate clearly the charges from performance. And then I will show you a remarkably simple means of comparing expenses from fund to fund. Finally, we conclude with a legal, above-board mechanism for cutting your charges in half. Specifically, I can save you as much as £120 from your PEP charges. 'Doesn't sound like much', you say. How about £1,200 over ten years? Read on.

> 'It is as sure as the sun will rise tomorrow that you'll pay to invest in a unit trust.'

Fund managers and financial advisors deserve to get paid for their efforts. They should be paid for performance and consistency, which in a roundabout way, they are. Consistent performance attracts investment and, therefore, they earn more in fees. For example, William Littlewood's Jupiter Income Fund has grown from £2 million to £283 million during its reign as consistently high-performing king. Compensation to fund managers and financial advisors should be more closely linked to performance. With the advent of new regulations, it is possible we'll see more performance-related fees.

## THE FIRST STEP

Four sources of fees pay the fund management company and associated professionals. Even though you don't get a separate bill, don't think you're not paying it.

The four sources of charges are:

- Initial charge (included in spread): *you pay directly*;
- 'Other bit' initial charges (included in spread): *you pay directly*;
- Exit fees (separate): *you pay directly*;
- Annual management charges and 'other bit' fund expenses (in bid price): *you pay indirectly*.

### Initial charge

The initial charge is very straightforward and you'll see it mentioned explicitly when you make an investment. It can range from 0 per cent of the offer price (called a 'no-load' fund), to 6 per cent and upwards. This money comes off the top. You invest £1,000 into a 6 per cent initial-fee fund, and you'll only have £940 working for you. The benefit for paying the lowest fee, all other things being equal, is obvious. The initial charge covers the commission paid to IFAs.

The typical commission paid to an IFA is 3 per cent. Thus, with an initial charge of 6 per cent, this leaves the fund house with 3 per cent to play with.

The price, besides telling you how much it costs, tells you how much the fund is worth. There is some evidence that the better-performing funds charge at the high end of the scale, and in such instances, you are paying for performance. However, it is not a universal truism. You can also pay 6 per cent for a dog. That's why it's important to consider the performance-consistency trade-off when choosing a fund to invest in.

# 'Other bit' initial fees

The second category of fees is 'other bit' initial fees. This is the unit trust industry's dirty little secret.

In Chapter 6, we went into quite some detail about the bid/offer spread. The bid/offer spread is the difference between what you pay for the fund and what you'll sell it for. Most of the spread is the initial fee. But, there's also the other little bit which is the difference between the spread and the initial fee.

## Legally permissible

*Bid/offer spread = initial fee + 'other bit'*
6.5%               5.25    + 1.25%

Once I bought into a unit trust where the brochure indicated a 5.25 per cent initial fee. Fair enough. I received the confirmation, and the price seemed higher than I was originally quoted. I rang up the fund management company and discovered that the actual difference between what I bought the fund for (the offer price) and what I could have immediately turned around and sold it for was 6.5 per cent.

I sent a letter to the fund management company requesting an explanation. I received a nice letter back saying that it was stated in the brochure. I sent back another letter saying, 'No it wasn't'.

I received back another nice letter saying that these extra charges were legally permissible, and provided the industry averages for the 'other bit' initial fees. I reread the summary sheet about the fund and saw, in small print, what possibly could be charged. A per cent here, a per cent there, pretty soon it adds up.

Besides the manager's initial charge, stamp tax or sales taxes, and investing charges on the securities in the portfolio make up the 'other bit' initial fee. Though these charges are easily explainable, there is quite a wide range among 'other bit' fees.

I obtained a list of spreads, initial charges and one-year performance for the most popular sectors. I've included those funds with the largest bid/offer spread. You'll notice that the one-year results for some of the funds are dramatically below the average for the group, while others hover right around the average.

You must take care to look at the bid/offer spreads sector by sector. In the bond markets where buying and selling prices between the underlying securities are small, you would expect to find smaller bid/offer spreads. Conversely, in the Far East and in the emerging markets, bid/offer spreads are larger due to the relative expense of trading securities in these markets. Spreads for Far East funds typically exceed 6 per cent and can reach up to 8 per cent.

Don't be misled by the mechanical aspects of spread calculation described in Chapter 6, the spread can also indicate the scope for the profit to the house. As Scottish Widows' Graham said, 'The higher the spread, the higher the profit.' This should be obvious from the chart in Figure 7.1. We're looking at funds all in the same sector; presumably they face the same costs of raw materials (i.e., the securities they purchase), labour, trustee's fees, rent. The only explanation for the variation in spreads is the variation in profits.

## Exit fees

The advent of exit fees is relatively new on the scene. They generally are charged if your investment in the fund doesn't last for five years. Typically, there is a sliding scale, 5 per cent, 4 per cent, 3 per cent, 2 per cent, 1 per cent, depending on your year of exit. They promote long-term investment, which is a good thing. They allow the fund manager to claim 0 per cent initial fee; in the *Financial Times*, funds with an exit fee are denoted by an 'E' – it's important to know which ones. Exit fees are not included in performance reports, as the fee is charged at the end, and not at the beginning.

## Annual management charges and 'other bit' fund expenses

As we saw in Chapter 6, the annual management charge and other fund expenses, such as trustee's fees are taken off the income of the fund and reduce the income payable as dividends. Timberlake and

## Fig 7.1 Ten largest bid/offer spreads in most popular sectors[4]

| Fund | Initial charge | + 'Other bit' | = Spread | 12-month performance after charges |
|---|---|---|---|---|
| **Growth & income** | | | | |
| Barclays Unicorn 500 | 5.3% | 3.3% | 8.6% | 3.3% |
| Halifax Accumulation | 7.5% | 0.2% | 7.7% | New fund |
| MAMPI Income | 6.0% | 0.9% | 6.9% | 10.0% |
| London & Manch. General | 6.0% | 0.8% | 6.8% | 8.9% |
| Barclays Unicorn General | 5.3% | 1.4% | 6.6% | 9.0% |
| Gartmore UK Equity Income | 5.3% | 1.4% | 6.6% | 6.8% |
| Edinburgh UK Income & Growth | 5.0% | 1.6% | 6.6% | 6.1% |
| Barclays Unicorn Trustee | 5.3% | 1.3% | 6.5% | 8.3% |
| Cazenove UK Equity | 5.0% | 1.5% | 6.5% | 13.2% |
| Dolphin UK & General | 5.5% | 1.0% | 6.5% | 3.4% |
| **Average in sector** | | | | **8.3%** |
| **Equity income** | | | | |
| London & Manch. Income | 6.0% | 0.8% | 6.8% | 4.9% |
| Exeter High Income | 6.0% | 0.7% | 6.7% | −4.3% |
| Clerical Med. Equity High Income | 5.3% | 1.4% | 6.6% | 0.5% |
| Baring Equity Income | 5.0% | 1.5% | 6.5% | 8.7% |
| Sun Alliance Equity Income | 6.0% | 0.5% | 6.5% | 9.3% |
| Barclays Unicorn Extra Income | 5.3% | 1.3% | 6.5% | 5.6% |
| GT Income | 5.0% | 1.5% | 6.5% | 15.4% |
| Refuge Equity Income | 6.0% | 0.5% | 6.5% | 8.7% |
| Abbey High Income Equity | 6.0% | 0.5% | 6.5% | 3.6% |
| Abtrust Extra Income | 3.5% | 3.0% | 6.5% | −6.7% |
| **Average in sector** | | | | **5.9%** |
| **Equity growth** | | | | |
| Cavendish Opportunities | 3.5% | 3.6% | 7.1% | 9.6% |
| Mercury Asset Income Portfolio | 6.0% | 0.8% | 6.8% | 8.3% |
| Morgan Grenfell UK Growth | 5.3% | 1.5% | 6.8% | 10.0% |
| Baring UK Growth | 5.0% | 1.8% | 6.8% | 16.5% |
| Exeter Capital Growth | 6.0% | 0.8% | 6.8% | −1.7% |
| Barclays Unicorn Spec. Sits. | 5.3% | 1.5% | 6.7% | 15.8% |
| Sovereign Ethical | 5.3% | 1.5% | 6.7% | 16.7% |
| Old Mutual CAM British Growth | 5.3% | 1.4% | 6.6% | 1.9% |
| Barclays Unicorn Capital | 5.0% | 1.6% | 6.6% | 8.1% |
| Tilney UK Equity | 5.0% | 1.6% | 6.6% | New fund |
| **Average in sector** | | | | **10.7%** |

*Source: Micropal Expert, 30 September 1996.*

company estimates that these expenses add around 0.30 per cent to the average fund's annual management fee of 1.30 per cent.

*Investors Chronicle* says that '"Other Expenses" can add a hefty whack to a fund's annual management fee . . . In extreme cases, these "other expenses" . . . can more than double the total costs taken out of the fund.'[5]

Viewed this way, your dividend cheque or reinvestment is directly reduced by the management fee and 'other bit' expenses.

## THE 'FLAT EARTH'

A new regime of disclosing fees will enter the promotional literature shortly. This aims to make more clear the effect of charges on your performance. There was heated debate about exactly how all funds would demonstrate the effect of fees. Because of the diversity of fund types and the diversity of fees, the effect of fees on performance is to be shown in a standardised way.

An easy way to consider the effect of fees on performance is called 'nil growth', or what I call the 'flat earth'. Assume that there is no growth and no loss on your fund. Assume that no taxes are paid, as if the investment is held in a PEP. Thus, we can isolate the effect of fees. We will consider two holding periods, one year and five years. After one year, for example, you change investments because of poor performance, or because you need the money for personal affairs. Alternatively, you hold your investment for five years, the industry-recommended holding period, and then decide to invest differently.

One comment you'll often hear is, 'If the fund isn't performing well, switch to another fund.' I asked some of those in the industry, 'How long do you wait before selling?' The answers varied from six months to four years, seemingly, to my surprise, dictated by the age of the respondent, with the younger ones showing more impatience than the older ones.

The problem is that the front-end costs tend to be so high – 5 or 6 per cent – you need to think very carefully about switching out of a dog fund. If you buy a fund and then switch in the same year, your charges could exceed 10 per cent plus whatever loss you incurred on the first fund. Clearly, you need to think long and hard before changing funds.

You should also consider the one- and five-year fees both in terms of cash fees and also on a present value basis. 'Present value' is a mathematical technique which recognises that a pound received today is better than a pound received tomorrow.

Consider a typical fund, which charges 6 per cent upfront, and 1.60 per cent per year in management fees and other fees.

On the 'flat earth' basis (see Figure 7.2), there is no increase in asset value, but instead, a decrease, as the annual management charge continues to eat away at your investment.

**Fig 7.2 The flat earth**

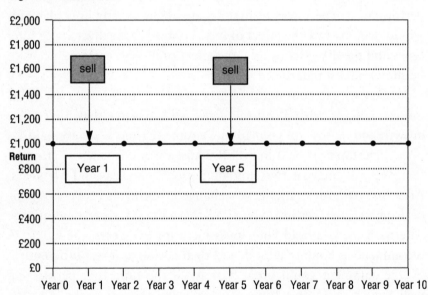

On a £1,000 investment, the typical fund costs £60 right away, and then 1.60 per cent on your investment. Because your investment starts at £940, the 1.60 per cent is slightly less than £16 per year. The amount decreases each year because your investment is eaten away by the administrative costs. After the end of one year, your investment is worth £75 less than when you began. After five years, total costs amount to £132.83, or £117.30 on a present value basis (see Figures 7.3 and 7.4).

Thus, returns from the fund must be strong to counteract the charges. As you can see, the typical fund's charges amount to 7.5 per cent of the amount you'll pay in the first year. Given that the stock market index over the last 75 years has earned on average 7.8 per cent per year, you shouldn't plan on selling during the first year.

**Fig 7.3 Typical fund, flat earth**

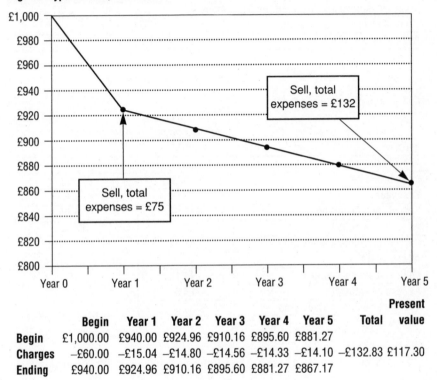

| | Begin | Year 1 | Year 2 | Year 3 | Year 4 | Year 5 | Total | Present value |
|---|---|---|---|---|---|---|---|---|
| **Begin** | £1,000.00 | £940.00 | £924.96 | £910.16 | £895.60 | £881.27 | | |
| **Charges** | −£60.00 | −£15.04 | −£14.80 | −£14.56 | −£14.33 | −£14.10 | −£132.83 | £117.30 |
| **Ending** | £940.00 | £924.96 | £910.16 | £895.60 | £881.27 | £867.17 | | |

Restated, after five years, almost 12 per cent of your investment is not working for you.

Consider now if you will, a fund with 0.5 per cent bid/offer spread and 0.50 per cent in annual charges and the same 0.30 per cent 'extra bit'. We'll call this the 'Cheap Fund' (see Figures 7.5 and 7.6). The benefits are obvious.

**Fig 7.4  Results of Typical Fund**

|  | Actual amount | Present value at 5% |
|---|---|---|
| Initial fee | 6.00% |  |
| Annual expenses | 1.60% |  |
| Initial investment | £1,000 | £1,000 |
| **First year** |  |  |
| Expenses: spread and annual | –£75 | –£71 |
| Value of investment afterwards | £925 |  |
| As % of investment | –7.5% | –7.1% |
| **After 5 years** |  |  |
| Expenses: spread and five years annual charges | –£133 | –£117.30 |
| Value of investment afterwards | £867 |  |
| As % of investment | –13.3% | –11.7% |

**Fig 7.5  Results of Cheap Fund**

|  | Actual amount | Present value at 5% |
|---|---|---|
| Initial fee | 0.50% |  |
| Annual expenses | 0.80% |  |
| Initial investment | £1,000 | £1,000 |
| **First year** |  |  |
| Spread and annual charges | –£12.96 | –£11.98 |
| As % of investment | –1.3% | –1.2% |
| Value of investment afterwards | £987.04 |  |
| **After 5 years** |  |  |
| Initial and annual charges | –£44.17 | £37.09 |
| As % of investment | –4.4% | –3.7% |
| Value of investment afterwards | £955.83 |  |

The first catch is that no evidence exists that by paying more money, you end up with a better fund. The second catch is that these charges are always masked by performance. Remember, these charges are eating into your return.

We can see the trade-off between high and low annual fees and high, low, and no fees in the table in Figure 7.7, which lists the present value for the various scenarios we've outlined so far.

The cost difference between the Cheap Fund and Typical Fund is £85 or 8.5 per cent of your investment money. Put another way, the Typical Fund manager must make at least 8.5 per cent over five

**Fig 7.6  Total fees: Cheap Fund vs Typical Fund**

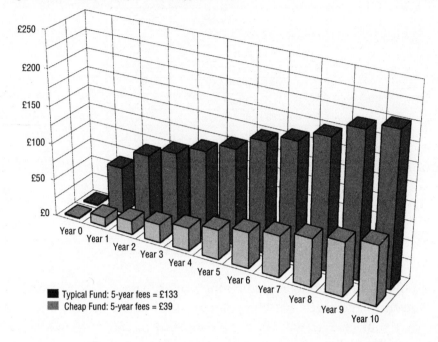

Typical Fund: 5-year fees = £133
Cheap Fund: 5-year fees = £39

**Fig 7.7  Total charges after five years: various scenarios (present value)**

|  | High annual fee | Low annual fee |
|---|---|---|
| High initial fee (6.0%) | (£117) | (£88) |
| % | (11.7%) | (8.8%) |
| Low initial fee (3.0%) | (£91) | (£60) |
| % | (9.1%) | (6.0%) |
| No initial fee (0%) | £64 | (£32) |
| % | (6.4%) | (3.2%) |

years, as opposed to the Cheap Fund manager who only needs to make 3.2 per cent.

Yes, performance counts above costs, and there are managers who continually do better than the averages. Yet, consider 1992, when the FTSE All-Share index decreased in value, or 1994, when it went up by only 3 per cent.

The final wrinkle is to add in exit fees (see Figure 7.8). Typically, these funds charge 0 per cent upfront, a management fee, and then a sliding scale depending on when you exit. Whether it's better or not

**Fig 7.8  Typical exit fees**

|  | Per cent |
|---|---|
| Amount paid initially | 0% |
| Exit fee in first year | 5% |
| Exit fee paid in second year | 4% |
| Exit fee paid in third year | 3% |
| Exit fee paid in fourth year | 2% |
| Exit fee paid in fifth year | 1% |
| Exit fee paid thereafter | 0% |

to choose a fund with these fees depends upon when you sell. Clearly, it's to your advantage to hold on for five years.

# AN EASY WAY

Rather than go through these complex machinations, you can simply add the percentages that you will pay as a rough approximation of what your charges will be. For example, if the fund charges 6 per cent upfront and an annual management charge of 1.80 per cent, calculate the following:

$$6\% + (1.8\% \times 5 \text{ years}) = 15.0\%$$

Total five years' fees, calculated as above (see Figure 7.4) amount to 13.3 per cent of your investment. While this method doesn't take into account the time value of money, for our purposes it will be close enough.

Similarly, for the Cheap Fund, the calculation is:

$$0.5\% + (0.8\% \times 5 \text{ years}) = 4.5\%$$

Whereas the correct value is 4.4 per cent.

# GETTING THE EARTH SPINNING AGAIN

We've seen what high fund charges can do to your performance. Most industry experts I spoke with, when they were wearing their investor hats, said, 'Make sure not to pay too much in fees.' A unit trust investor who's a stockbroker said, 'I always look for the cheapest alternative.' I'm not interested in fund managers. I go for whatever is cheapest: the markets and I never pay the full rate.

You don't have to pay those high charges, even if the fund you desire has those high charges. The answer? The execution-only broker.

The *Independent on Sunday* described it:

> Execution-only: it sounds like the promise of a hangman with a conscience – hanging without drawing and quartering. In fact, it is a curious piece of jargon in the financial services industry used to describe a particular way of buying and selling.[6]

In the stockbroking world, traditionally, a stockbroker would earn a commission for selling you a security. The unit trust business, originally established to look like the stockbroking world, also established the commission or initial fee. The purpose was to pay salesmen to entice investors into the unit trust. Independent Financial Advisors (IFAs) today serve as salesmen for the unit trust industry. Consequently, they earn commissions as compensation for advising you to invest in a particular unit trust.

As the world of investors grew more sophisticated, some people began to make their own investment decisions and didn't need to hire an advisor. The unit trust industry agreed to sell direct to customers over the telephone. However, they didn't want to alienate this huge force of IFAs by allowing customers to get the advice from the advisor, and then go direct to the fund management company and not pay a commission. Hence, whether you called the fund management company directly or went through an advisor, you'd still pay the same commission. Well, it used to be that way.

> 'Most industry experts I spoke with, when they were wearing their investor hats, said, "Make sure not to pay too much in fees".'

Then along came a few enterprising IFAs who said, instead of doing a complete fact-find for a customer and advising him, I can just buy the unit trust he desires. The unit trust initial charge typically is 5 per cent to 6 per cent. Of this amount, 3 per cent goes to the IFA who brought the business. The enterprising IFAs will rebate 2 per cent of the commission and keep 1 per cent for themselves.

On a £6,000 PEP, this can amount to £120. Multiply this by ten years or 20 years, however many years you have left in your investing life, and you're looking at saving £1,200 to £2,400. All for the cost of making a phone call. In fact, many IFAs will buy unit trusts for you on an execution-only basis. Even further, if you call a fund management company, they might even negotiate the discount for you, right over the phone. The point is: if you research, evaluate, and decide yourself, why pay the commission?

Some IFAs offer services half-way between full service and execution-only. Typically, they provide a detailed fund ranking by investment value. Some of the better reports include: Chase de Vere's *PEPGUIDE*, BESt Investment's *Portfolio Advice*, Whitechurch's *Pedigree Investment Ratings Service*, Unitas's *Newsletter*, and the Allenbridge Group's *PEP Talk*.

'The point is: if you research, evaluate, and decide yourself, why pay the commission?'

If you use information from one of these firm's reports, the fair approach is to invest through the firm. They conduct the research with the expectation that users will invest through the firm. To use a firm's research, and then invest through another firm on an execution-only basis is not fair.

#### Fig 7.9 IFAs providing discounts and advice as required

| Firm | Phone number |
| --- | --- |
| Allenbridge Group | 0800 33 99 99 |
| BESt Investment | 0990 11 22 55 |
| Chase de Vere | 0800 526 091 |
| Chelsea Financial Services | 01902 711764 |
| Garrison Investment | 0114 250 0720 |
| PEP Direct | 0800 413186 |
| The PEP Shop | 0115 982 5105 |
| Premier Investment Management | 01483 306090 |
| Whitechurch Investment Securities | 0800 374413 |
| Unitas | 01724 849481 |

Source: 'Bargain Basement Deals on PEP', *Investors Chronicle*, 22 March 1996, p. 37; author additions.

Alternatively, if you require advice or request an opinion, then you should pay for the service. But we're getting ahead of ourselves. We'll discuss the role an IFA can play for you later, in Chapter 17.

## REFERENCES

[1] *Unit Trusts and How They Work* by C. L. Rosenheim and C. O. Merriman, (London: Sir Isaac Pitman & Sons, Ltd., 1937), p. viii.

[2] 'Why Pay More?' by Pauline Skypala, *Money Management*, May 1995, p. 51.

[3] Ibid., p. 46.

[4] *Micropal* and *Money Management*, Nov. 1996.

[5] 'Beware Hidden Charges,' *Investors Chronicle*, 1 November 1996, p. 33.

[6] 'Middle Man Fades Away' by Anthony Bailey, *Independent on Sunday*, 10 March 1996, p. 17.

# SUMMARY

- The upfront spread consists of the initial fee and the 'other bit'.

- Investigate whether your fund charges exit fees.

- You pay indirectly annual management and other allowable charges.

- Beware of the charges: they vary considerably across unit trusts.

- An easy way to consider all charges together is to assume you will own the fund for five years and add together percentage charges:

  **Example**

  | | | | |
  |---|---|---|---|
  | Spread | | | 6.0% |
  | Annual management charge: | | Year 1 | 1.5% |
  | " | " | Year 2 | 1.5% |
  | " | " | Year 3 | 1.5% |
  | " | " | Year 4 | 1.5% |
  | " | " | Year 5 | 1.5% |
  | " | " | Total | 13.5% |

- Use an execution-only IFA and save two to three per cent off the initial charge – if you pick your own unit trust.

# PART

3

# TYPES OF
# UNIT TRUST

# NARROWING DOWN YOUR CHOICES

Imagine you are a private client of an investment management company. You're ushered into a wood-panelled room where classic original art adorns the walls. You're offered a seat in an old leather-bound chair around a deep-rich mahogany round table, with a window view of the Thames and London Bridge. Men and women in chalk-striped suits speak confidently, persuasively, and they're friendly. You've arrived, and you demand the excellence of the best service, the best advisors, the best research staff, the best administration, the best of everything.

The lead advisor, speaking in hushed tones, talks about the strong performance of the person who will be investing your portfolio. You'll see bar graphs to the heavens, all pointing to the high success you can expect as a private client. You'll also receive a cup of tea and some biscuits. You agree to this highly personalised service which a person of your means deserves. You arrange to transfer the funds.

Behind the scenes, something altogether different is taking place. It's as if you've walked into the kitchen of an expensive restaurant, or the engine room of a big locomotive. Behind the scenes, you discover, your funds are being shovelled into a big pot with the rest of the funds under management. You've succumbed to the marketing of investments.

In the back room your money gets added to the funds from other investors. The portfolio manager, say, for European equities, may manage a European equities unit trust, the pension fund monies invested in European equities, the life assurance funds invested in European equities, and the private client money earmarked for European equities. It's not a fiddle; in fact, the manager of European equities may be top flight; but he or she's only one person with only so many investment ideas.

Indeed, you, the private client, want only the best investments; so does the unit trust investor; so do the life assurance and pension fund investor. Even though your private client portfolio may be marketed as a bespoke service, the truth is the private client's European equity portfolio will look a lot like the European equity portfolio for the others.

In reality, the unit trust, which collects funds from many smaller investors, may hold more funds than the total of private clients, therefore generate more revenues for the fund management company and, as a consequence, may be a lot more interesting to management.

'. . . you, the high-street unit trust investor, may get exactly the same service as the private client . . .'

In other words, you, the high-street unit trust investor, may get exactly the same service as the private client – without the tea and biscuits.

Respected *Investors Chronicle* and *Financial Times* writer Bernard Gray complains that '. . . finding a winning unit trust from the 1,300-odd [1,600 today] around seems almost impossible. In many ways, picking unit trusts is harder than picking shares; with shares you only have to select the right company, with unit trusts you have to find the right investment and the right fund manager!'[1]

I don't agree at all. Picking the right unit trust is a matter of narrowing down the choices, indeed. But we will outline a procedure, the same one that is used by independent financial advisors (IFAs), professional unit trust selectors, and other personal financial experts, to provide you with the right unit choice, without having to calculate the price of oil in the Middle East or interest rates in ten years' time.

'. . . we will describe the three classes of investment in general terms, and then list the unit trust sectors contained within these broad classes.'

We've already begun the narrowing-down process by allocating your financial assets among three classes: short-term, medium-term, and long-term. Not surprisingly, there are three classes of investments ready to fill your needs which correspond exactly with these three classes.

In this short chapter, we will describe the three classes of investment in general terms, and then list the unit trust sectors contained within these broad classes.

# THE CLASSES OF INVESTMENT

In Chapter 4, we looked at the Timing Class of Investment from the point of view of the benefit to you, the investor; now we look at these same financial instruments from the company's perspective.

## Cash

If you lend money to a corporation overnight, you are virtually certain you'll get this money back the next day. There is little risk that the money will not be returned to you and you know with 100 per cent certainty what interest rate you'll receive.

Step back a little bit, and lend the money to the corporation for a month. Well, a lot can happen in a month. The company's solid credit rating can dissipate, the Chancellor can raise the discount rates, leading to a general increase in interest rates. Thus, if you lend your money to a corporation for a month, it's a little riskier. For this extra risk, you demand to earn a slightly higher rate of interest.

For reasons I've never really liked, short-term lending is called 'cash', with the implication that it is like cash under your mattress. The truth is that 'cash' is lent out for very short periods of time and will earn interest. 'Cash' is usually lent for six months or less (sometimes just overnight).

## Bonds

Now, if you were to lend your money to a corporation for 20 years, you would demand a much higher interest rate. The buggy-whip corporation, looking so good now, could lose out to an invention called the motor car. Inflation could be quite strong in ten years, rendering the value of your loan to the corporation worth only half as much. A lot can happen in 20 years: hence, the interest rates on money lent for 20 years is normally significantly higher than for such short terms as a month.

# Equity

The final extension of this example: if rather than lending the company money, you invested in its shares. You have made a payment to a company that will not be returned. The only way you get your money back is by selling the investment to another party. And to continue the thread of our analysis, the value of such an investment can change significantly until the end of time.

Now, those smart fellows and ladies in the City have figured out all sorts of permutations and combinations of these three categories, but these are the main definitions.

**Fig 8.1 Timing class of investments[2]**

| Timing class | Investment | Return | | Volatility |
|---|---|---|---|---|
| Short-term | Cash | Lowest* | 4.7% | Least |
| Medium-term | Bonds | Medium** | 7.3% | Medium |
| Long-term | Equity | Highest† | 12.8% | Highest |

\* Cash fund sector average.
\*\* UK gilt and fixed-interest sector average.
† FT S&P World Index.

**Fig 8.2 The return classes**

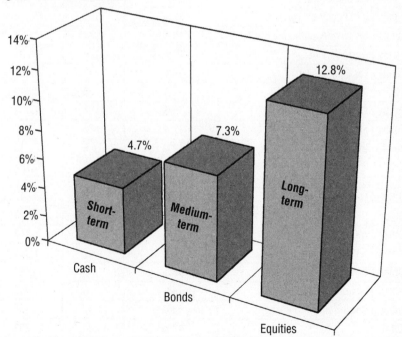

The returns on these three investment types over the last five years are shown in Figures 8.1 and 8.2. I prefer to use the five-year figures because they are more identifiable with today's situation. These figures are higher than the 77-year average results we looked at in Chapter 4 (Figure 4.6), reflecting the buoyancy in today's market versus the long-term trend.

**Fig 8.3  Unit trust sectors: returns and size**

|  | Unit Trust Sectors (Association of Unit Trusts and Investment Funds) | Five year average annual return | Number of funds | Total funds: £ millions |
|---|---|---|---|---|
| Cash | Cash funds | 5% | 28 | 324 |
|  |  |  |  |  |
| Bonds | UK gilt and fixed interest | 7% | 104 | 1,772 |
| Bonds | Intl fixed interest | 7% | 43 | 738 |
| **Total** |  | **7%** | **147** | **2,510** |
|  |  |  |  |  |
| Equity | UK growth and income | 10% | 152 | 16,600 |
| Equity | UK equity growth | 11% | 164 | 11,896 |
| Equity | UK equity income | 10% | 90 | 8,999 |
| Equity | Europe equity | 14% | 128 | 8,163 |
| Equity | Intl. equity growth | 12% | 163 | 7,304 |
| Equity | UK smaller companies | 13% | 77 | 5,337 |
| Equity | North America | 18% | 128 | 4,793 |
| Equity | Far East ex. Japan | 20% | 77 | 4,403 |
| Equity | Japan | 3% | 96 | 4,349 |
| Equity | Far East and Japan | 13% | 38 | 1,520 |
| Equity | Emerging markets | 12% | 35 | 918 |
| Equity | Intl. equity income | 12% | 9 | 445 |
| **Total** |  | **12%** | **1,157** | **74,727** |
|  |  |  |  |  |
| Other | Fund of funds | 11% | 79 | 3,847 |
| Other | UK equity and bond income | 8% | 43 | 2,293 |
| Other | UK equity and bond | 11% | 25 | 1,948 |
| Other | Intl. equity and bond | 10% | 42 | 1,721 |
| Other | Investment trust units | 13% | 14 | 793 |
| Other | Financial and property | 14% | 9 | 445 |
| Other | Commodity and energy | 18% | 12 | 204 |
| **Total** |  | **12%** | **224** | **11,251** |

# WHERE THE MONEY IS

The Association of Unit Trusts and Investment Funds (AUTIF) sets the standard for unit trusts by dividing them into various sectors. Thus, the unit trust's investment policies are reviewed to find the particular unit trust sector which is most appropriate for it. The sectors change from time to time. Sometimes, a fund will be reclassified from one sector to another, due to changes in investment policies or investment results. However, this provides clues as to the next step in allocating your financial assets.

Figure 8.3 gives a list of unit trusts with returns. I've grouped them into our three main categories and added a fourth category for those sectors which cross over the main three investment categories. I've also included the five-year average annual return for each of these sectors and categories.

> 'The Association of Unit Trusts and Investment Funds sets the standard for unit trusts by dividing them into various sectors.'

In each of the coming chapters, we'll describe what each of these sectors aims to achieve, we'll look at the records, and describe your considerations for each investment.

## REFERENCES

[1] *Beginners' Guide to Investment* by Bernard Gray, (London: Century Books), 2 edn. 1993, p. 165.
[2] 'Statistics', *Money Management*, November 1996.

# SUMMARY

- Unit trust investors get the same level of professional investment advice as the well-to-do because their funds are pooled together.

- The three broad classes of investment, corresponding to the timing needs of investors, are:

| Investor timing | Product | Unit trust |
|---|---|---|
| Immediate | Cash | Cash funds |
| Medium | Bonds or loan stock | Gilt and fixed interest |
| Long-term | Equities or shares | funds |
| | | Equity funds |

# CASH FUNDS

'Why do you save?,' 30-year M&G veteran Roger Jennings seriously asked me.

I said nothing.

'People save because they've been told, "You gotta save".' Jennings went on. 'This woolly idea isn't quite on. You've got to be focused.'

'Unless you've got a firm rationale of why you're saving, it's possible you won't get it right.'

'Why do you save?,' he asked me, again.

I stumbled, and said something about being a long-term investor who writes.

'Why do you save?,' he asked me again.

I said, not too specifically, 'For the future.'

Jennings' point is clear and takes us back to the financial planning exercise we completed a few chapters ago. You have to make up your mind about your plans and requirements: e.g., school fees, mortgage repayment, home purchase, pension planning, vacation plans, a new car. You're more certain of being successful. Without a plan, it's as if you were to take a trip in your car to go to a destination you have never visited before, without a road map. You might get to your destination, but by luck. Most likely, you'll end up somewhere on a motorway, not really getting to your destination at all.

The rest of this book will consider each category separately. In this chapter, we look at the home for your short-term emergency-type money. Our first unit trust variety is cash funds. They are the unit trust industry's best kept secret. Cash funds can house your emergency money, to which you have immediate access, and still earn a higher interest rate than from your high street bank or building society.

> 'Without a plan, it's as if you were to take a trip in your car to go to a destination you have never visited before, without a road map'.

First, we'll take a look at inflation. Then we'll look at where building society deposit rates come from. Then, we'll turn to cash funds as

**Fig 9.1 Timing class of investments**

| Timing class | Investment | Return | | Volatility |
|---|---|---|---|---|
| **Short-term** | **Cash** | **Lowest** | **4.7%** | **Lowest** |
| Medium-term | Bonds | Medium | 7.3% | Medium |
| Long-term | Equity | Highest | 12.8% | Highest |

an alternative to the building society. Your emergency funds are not the same as your day-to-day money, which should be kept where you can access it constantly, according to the ebbs and flows of your monthly requirements.

# INFLATION

In the ten years since 1985, prices have increased 55.7 per cent. Conversely, that same pound in your current account is only worth £0.64 today (see Figure 9.2). Figure 9.3 gives some average annual rates of inflation. Unfortunately, every single person makes an 'investment' in this loss-making proposition.

**Fig 9.2  Value of £1 in 1995 compared to its value in 1985**

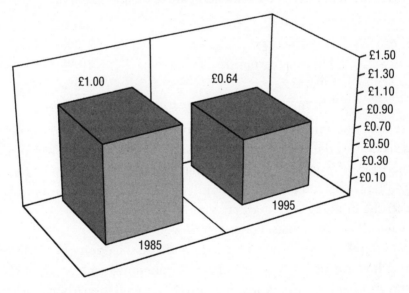

**Fig 9.3  Average annual rates of inflation since 1919**

| Period | Years | Avg annual Inflation |
|--------|-------|----------------------|
| 1919–95 | 75 | 3.72% |
| 1945–95 | 50 | 6.23% |
| 1970–95 | 25 | 8.59% |

There are many ways to outrun inflation; the point here is that you just have to do something; otherwise, you're doing worse than standing still – you're running backwards.

# BUILDING SOCIETY DEPOSIT RATES

Many people believe that a unit trust isn't for them, 'too risky' they say. The building society's 'safe' savings account is for them. They'll be sure that their funds are there, when the rainy day comes.

Unfortunately, this belief substantially penalises those that hold it. As I write this, typical savings account interest rates at the high street building society are about 3 per cent. Inflation is running at around 3 per cent. But the 3 per cent rate paid on savings is gross, before tax. After tax, for a higher rate payer, the earnings are about 1.8 per cent. This leaves a loss of 1.2 per cent after tax and inflation are taken into account.

| | |
|---|---|
| Gross savings rate: | 3.0% |
| High-rate tax: | –1.2% |
| After-tax earnings: | 1.8% |
| Inflation: | 3.0% |
| After-tax, after-inflation earnings: | –1.2% |

At best, the inflation figures are estimates and give only a general direction of the rate of price increases. This means the effect of the increases of prices on your particular lifestyle – the prices of things you buy – could be more or could be less. The conclusion is apparent: the building society offers you at best inflation-protection, but that's all. Your savings, your capital, won't grow.

Philip Warland, Director General of the Association of Unit Trusts and Investment Funds, notes that, 'People don't understand if they stay in a bank for five years, they're at risk to inflation.' Now, clearly, Mr Warland has a vested interest in unit trusts; nevertheless, his comment is borne out by the facts shown in Figure 9.4.

These figures are illustrated in the chart shown in Figure 9.5, (sometimes a chart is worth a thousand words and figures!).

As you can see from Figures 9.4 and 9.5, the actual growth of your savings after inflation is non-existent with a building society account.

**Fig 9.4  The real story: building society returns after tax and after inflation**

|  | 1986 | 1987 | 1988 | 1989 | 1990 | 1991 | 1992 | 1993 | 1994 | 1995 |
|---|---|---|---|---|---|---|---|---|---|---|
| Halifax Solid Gold 90 Day deposit over £500 | 14.9% | 12.9% | 10.7% | 12.5% | 12.7% | 8.9% | 6.4% | 3.6% | 3.2% | 3.3% |
| Higher rate tax @ 40% | −6.0% | −5.2% | −4.3% | −5.0% | −5.1% | −3.5% | −2.6% | −1.5% | −1.3% | −1.3% |
| Retail Price Index – Capital return | −5.3% | −5.9% | −8.8% | −9.8% | −11.2% | −4.8% | −3.2% | −1.4% | −2.7% | −3.1% |
| Actual return | 3.6% | 1.9% | −2.4% | −2.3% | −3.6% | 0.6% | 0.6% | 0.7% | −0.8% | −1.1% |

*Source:* HSW Ltd., StatsWise, 29 December 1995.

Use it for the convenience, use it for the memory, but don't use it to increase for capital growth, or even for safety. As I mentioned above, the inflation rate is only an estimate based on a specified price change on a standard set of goods. The increases in prices you face will depend on what

> 'you should view a building society account as a means of capital preservation, and little else'.

you buy. In other words, you should view a building society account as a means of capital preservation only, and little else.

**Fig 9.5  Building society rates vs Tax and and inflation-adjusted return**

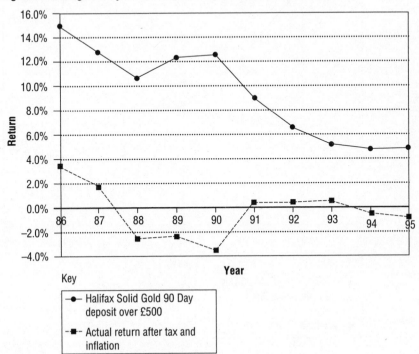

Key

—●— Halifax Solid Gold 90 Day deposit over £500

–■– Actual return after tax and inflation

*Source:* HSW Ltd., StatsWise, 29 December 1995.

You're still not convinced. 'Yes, McWilliams, what you're saying makes sense – but unit trusts are too risky.' This is like saying, 'cars are too risky, I'm going to walk.'

# CASH FUND RATES

All unit trusts, like cars, are not created the same. Some unit trusts, cash funds, offer an interest rate slightly higher than building society rates, and move along with building society rates (see Figure 9.6).

You'll notice instantly that the cash fund like the building society never lost money. No capital has been lost on the cash fund – it is safe, predictable, and profitable. You won't be racing up swells in the

**Fig 9.6  Cash unit trust vs building society**

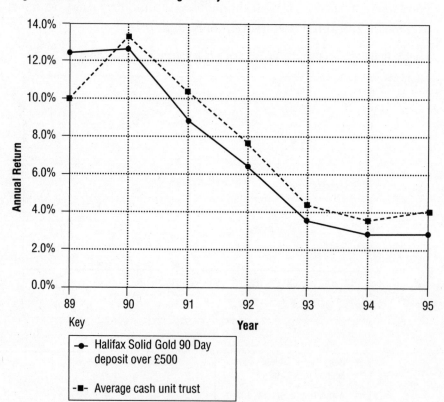

*Source:* HSW Ltd., StatsWise, 29 December 1995.

FTSE Small Cap Index, nor will you be falling down the precipices. In only one of the seven years highlighted in Figure 9.6 was the building society rate superior to that of the cash fund. These numbers are from year-end, not annual averages. Most likely, the building society was trying to attract funds and was offering an unusually high rate to do so. But the main point is, you can almost always do better with a cash unit trust than you would with a building society account.

> 'The margin of difference between the building society and the cash fund has been diminishing in the last few years'.

The margin of difference between the building society and the cash fund has been diminishing in the last few years. This has been due entirely to the competitive pressure of the cash funds. As investors became wiser, they realised they could always do better with the cash unit trust. The building societies have had to increase their rates to compete for funds. This has benefited you, the investor.

## THE ADVANTAGE OF CASH FUNDS OVER BUILDING SOCIETY DEPOSITS

'OK,' you say, 'you've convinced me, cash funds will pay a per cent or two more. Why should I go through the hassle of opening up such an account for such a small amount of money?' The answer is that over a year, a per cent or two more is indeed a small amount. But over 20 years, it amounts to quite a difference. And presumably, you will have this money in such an account for 20 years.

Richard Royds, managing director of Mercury's unit trust division, says, 'Cash will always comprise a large proportion of an investor's assets. For this reason, you need to go for the best rates.' And the performance test shown in Figure 9.7 assumes you'll have the money in the account for 20 years. However, you will have access to these funds for every day of those 20 years – it's not as if you're locking up these funds.

To demonstrate the advantage, I assumed a £10,000 deposit is made at the building society or in a cash fund. I used *Micropal* statistics, comparing the return over the last three years for the ten largest cash funds and the average UK building society rate for £2,500 or more for instant or postal access. These are net figures, after tax has been paid at the basic rate. The results are shown in Figure 9.7.

Figure 9.7 depicts two phenomena: first, the advantage of cash funds over building society funds, and second, the magic of compounding. The magic of compounding isn't really magic, though the results are stupendous. The idea is that year after year, your funds add a little bit of interest to the amount you originally invested. Year in, year out. You'll note with the cash fund, your funds have more than doubled. With the building society account, your funds have grown by less, but still more than 72 per cent.

**Fig 9.7 Comparing average cash fund results to average building society results over 20 years (results after tax)**

| | Average cash fund | Average building society | Advantage |
|---|---|---|---|
| Last 3 years average/year | 3.87% | 2.76% | 1.10% |
| | Average cash fund £10,000 | Average building society £10,000 | Advantage |
| Year 1 | £10,387 | £10,276 | £111 |
| Year 2 | £10,788 | £10,560 | £228 |
| Year 3 | £11,205 | £10,852 | £353 |
| Year 4 | £11,638 | £11,152 | £486 |
| Year 5 | £12,088 | £11,460 | £628 |
| Year 6 | £12,555 | £11,777 | £778 |
| Year 7 | £13,041 | £12,102 | £939 |
| Year 8 | £13,545 | £12,436 | £1,109 |
| Year 9 | £14,068 | £12,780 | £1,288 |
| Year 10 | £14,612 | £13,133 | £1,479 |
| Year 11 | £15,177 | £13,496 | £1,681 |
| Year 12 | £15,763 | £13,869 | £1,894 |
| Year 13 | £16,373 | £14,252 | £2,121 |
| Year 14 | £17,005 | £14,646 | £2,359 |
| Year 15 | £17,663 | £15,050 | £2,613 |
| Year 16 | £18,346 | £15,466 | £2,880 |
| Year 17 | £19,055 | £15,894 | £3,161 |
| Year 18 | £19,791 | £16,333 | £3,458 |
| Year 19 | £20,556 | £16,784 | £3,772 |
| Year 20 | £21,351 | £17,248 | £4,103 |

*Source: Micropal Expert*, 30 September 1996.

The important feature is that after 20 years, a 1.1 per cent difference, the small amount referred to above, results in an advantage to the cash fund holder of more than £4,000. To be precise, you'd do £4,103 better than the building society account – £4,103 is 41 per cent of your original investment.

Again, this investment does not require you to lock up your funds for 20 years; it just shows the difference that'll take place over 20 years.

## BEHIND THE WIZARD'S CURTAIN: HOW INTEREST RATES ARE SET

Every so often, the interest rates paid by the banks and building societies for various kinds of deposits change. If you were to ask your bank manager why this is, the answer is always 'market forces'. And then you quietly walk away, overpowered by the market forces.

I had never understood the link between the interest my bank paid me for my deposit and the omnipotent market forces. And then I started to work for a bank, and understood that market forces were a little bit like the Wizard of Oz. The Wizard of Oz, you'll recall, was able to make all sorts of miracles and disasters occur, but at the end, was just a little old, wizened man behind a curtain.

And so it is with banks and the interest rates they pay. Every day or week or month, a committee of wise men and women sit down at each bank to determine the interest rates to be paid to depositors. And how do they do this? Usually, their economists predict the future direction of rates. Their accountants argue for the lowest conceivable rates to save the bank money, while the marketing people argue for the best rate of interest to bring in more customers. And then, using this scientific evidence, this committee, the asset and liability committee, make a decision. How do they do it? They look at what everyone else is paying.

The big American bank I used to work for never wanted to be in a position of paying the highest interest rate; they wanted to be competitive, but they viewed their market position was to pay around the average.

The interest rate paid to you as a depositor is a cost borne by the banks. They borrow money from many sources: the bank goes to the securities markets to borrow money for a day, for a week, for a month, for a year, for 20 years. They also borrow money from you whenever you deposit money. They pay you interest, where you earn higher amounts, depending how long you are willing to lock away your funds. Generally, the longer you lend the bank money – the term of your deposit – the higher rate of interest you earn.

If you were to lend the bank money for a month, and if a corporation or a pension fund were to lend the bank money for a month, it's likely the corporation or pension fund would be paid a higher rate of interest. Because the local depositor market isn't very efficient, it is cheaper for the bank to borrow £1,000,000 from one corporation than to build branches, hire staff, and accept £1,000 from 1,000 separate depositors.

An efficient market means that the big institutions who lend money to companies like your bank are very well aware of what other similar banks are paying in interest rates all over the world. They know if your bank isn't willing to pay enough in interest, there are other similar banks that will. Small savers may look in the newspaper to try to determine which bank or building society pays the best interest rate, but unless there's a huge difference, are unlikely to close their accounts and haul themselves across town to get one-half per cent more. However, the bond trader making investments around the world has to put the money somewhere, and just has to look at his computer screen to determine who pays the best rate.

## WHY CASH UNIT TRUSTS PAY MORE

A cash unit trust lets you act – and earn interest – like the big boys.

Legal & General's Stephen Abbott, whom we met earlier discussing financial planning, says of the Legal & General's cash fund:

'We deposit our money in banks and building societies, just like you do. Except we earn a higher interest rate, thanks to our ability to make larger deposits.' The sales brochure for Legal & General's cash fund 'Cash Trust' bears this out:

### Where your money goes:

*All the money invested in the Legal & General Cash Trust will normally be placed [deposited] overnight on short-term deposit with a number of major banks and building societies who have a minimum credit rate of 'AA' in the name of our Trustee to ensure that you enjoy maximum security of your money.*

*Investments deposited May–July 1996*

| | |
|---|---|
| Bank of Montreal | Lloyds |
| Bank of Scotland | Midland |
| Barclays | NatWest |
| Bradford & Bingley | North West Securities |
| Deutschebank Morgan Grenfell | West Deutschebank |
| Halifax | |

*Source:* Cash Trust brochure, Legal & General (Unit Trust Managers) Limited.

Fidelity's Cash Fund (see Figure 9.8), which is the largest cash fund in the country, says in its brochure that they manage to achieve these high interest rates by 'bulk purchasing power'. Fidelity 'combines the savings of thousands of investors which is deposited with at least five banks who will pay much higher interest rates than you could hope to secure as an individual saver'. Finally, Fidelity says that its Cash Fund earns a AAA rating from Moody's rating service. 'AAA' is the highest measure of credit quality and Fidelity states that 'No UK bank or building society currently has such a high rating.'

Another reason that the cash funds can pay a higher rate of interest than instant access bank or building society accounts is that, by

## Fig 9.8 Fidelity Cash Builder Fund

### Fidelity Cash

Fidelity Investment Services, Oakhill House, 130 Tonbridge Road, Tonbridge, Kent TN11 9DZ.

Information: Telephone - 01732 361 144    Dealing - 0800 414 161

**Fund Objective:**
To produce as high a yield as possible commensurate with a proper degree of security through investment in cash & near cash instruments.

# micropal

## Fund Analysis

### MONEY MARKET
#### Q003 Fidelity Cash

| Micropal Cumulative Performance - to 30th September 1996 | | | | | |
|---|---|---|---|---|---|
| Performance Period | 6 Months | 1 Year | 3 Years | 5 Years | 10 Years |
| Fund Performance | +2.1% | +4.3% | +12.6% | +27.0% | |
| Sector Average | +1.4% | +3.6% | +11.8% | +25.8% | |
| Best Performing Fund | +2.3% | +4.7% | +14.0% | +27.5% | |
| Fund Performance / Sector Average Performance | | | | | |
| Worst Performing Fund | -4.9% | -1.8% | +7.6% | +22.6% | |

(Offer-bid, net income reinvested)

| | | | | |
|---|---|---|---|---|
| Top Quartile | | | | |
| Second Quartile | | 14/28 | 10/25 | 7/17 |
| Third Quartile | 15/28 | | | |
| Bottom Quartile | | | | |

| Micropal Star Rating ™ | |
|---|---|
| ⭐ ⭐ ⭐ ⭐ ⭐ | |
| **Performance** | **Volatility** |
| +12.6% | +0.0 |
| 10/25 | 1/25 |

| Micropal 6 Month Indicators |
|---|
| Fund Performance |
| ⇧ **2.1%** |
| Fund Relative to Sector |
| ⇧ **0.1%** |
| Fund Relative to UK SAVINGS 2500+ |
| ⇧ **1.1%** |

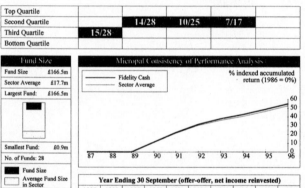

| Fund Size | |
|---|---|
| Fund Size | £166.5m |
| Sector Average | £17.7m |
| Largest Fund: | £166.5m |
| Smallest Fund: | £0.9m |
| No. of Funds: 28 | |

■ Fund Size
□ Average Fund Size in Sector

**Micropal Consistency of Performance Analysis**

— Fidelity Cash
— Sector Average

% indexed accumulated return (1986 = 0%)

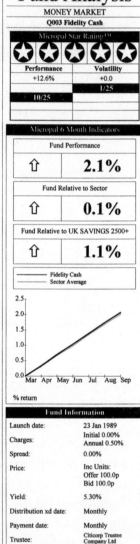

— Fidelity Cash
— Sector Average

% return

| Year Ending 30 September (offer-offer, net income reinvested) | | | | | | | | | | |
|---|---|---|---|---|---|---|---|---|---|---|
| | 1987 | 1988 | 1989 | 1990 | 1991 | 1992 | 1993 | 1994 | 1995 | 1996 |
| Performance of Fund (%) | | | | 11.1 | 9.9 | 7.7 | 4.7 | 3.6 | 4.2 | 4.3 |
| Performance of Sector (%) | | | 8.8 | 10.7 | 9.6 | 7.5 | 4.4 | 3.4 | 4.1 | 4.3 |
| Perf. of Micropal UT Total (%) | 46.8 | -18.1 | 27.6 | -20.7 | 26.8 | -3.9 | 40.8 | 4.2 | 10.0 | 12.8 |
| UK SAVINGS 2500+ (%) | 7.4 | 6.1 | 8.3 | 9.6 | 8.5 | 6.1 | 3.7 | 2.9 | 3.1 | 2.3 |
| UK Retail Price Index (%) | 4.2 | 5.9 | 7.6 | 10.9 | 4.1 | 3.6 | 1.8 | 2.2 | 3.9 | 1.2 |

| | 1987 | 1988 | 1989 | 1990 | 1991 | 1992 | 1993 | 1994 | 1995 | 1996 |
|---|---|---|---|---|---|---|---|---|---|---|
| Top Quartile | | | | | 5/11 | 4/17 | | | | |
| Second Quartile | | | | 3/4 | | | 10/21 | 9/25 | 10/26 | |
| Third Quartile | | | | | | | | | | 16/28 |
| Bottom Quartile | | | | | | | | | | |

| Micropal Rolling Period Analysis | 1987 | 1988 | 1989 | 1990 | 1991 | 1992 | 1993 | 1994 | 1995 | 1996 |
|---|---|---|---|---|---|---|---|---|---|---|
| Highest 12 monthly return: **11.1%** | % return | | | offer-offer, net income reinvested | | | | | | |
| Lowest 12 monthly return: **3.6%** | | | | | | | | | | |
| Average 12 monthly return: **6.7%** | | | | | | | | | | |

| Fund Information | |
|---|---|
| Launch date: | 23 Jan 1989 |
| Charges: | Initial 0.00%<br>Annual 0.50% |
| Spread: | 0.00% |
| Price: | Inc Units:<br>Offer 100.0p<br>Bid 100.0p |
| Yield: | 5.30% |
| Distribution xd date: | Monthly |
| Payment date: | Monthly |
| Trustee: | Citicorp Trustee Company Ltd |
| PEP Available: | No |
| Minimum Investment: | £1000 |
| Regular Savings: | £50 per month |

**To subscribe: Micropal Publications / Micropal Ltd  Tel: 0181 741 4100  Fax: 0181 741 0939**

© **Micropal Publications / Micropal Ltd 1996**

*Source: Micropal.*

pooling the money from thousands of savers, they are fairly certain that all the savers won't come to the fund for money at once. Hence, they can deposit the money for longer periods of time with the banks and earn a higher interest rate. While if you redeem some funds, they'll pay you with available funds without having to break a time deposit. Thus, you receive the benefits of tying up your funds – without having to tie up your funds.

A cash fund is altogether different from the funds called 'money market' offered by banks and the building societies. Remember the story above about the asset and liability committee, which decides interest rates paid to depositors? This does not exist at the fund management company. Instead, the interest earned on the fund is simply a result of the investments chosen by the fund manager of the unit trust. Thus, if the deposit made by the cash unit trust is earning, say, 5 per cent, then the annual and other charges are deducted, and you, the fund holder, is paid what is left. Accordingly, the interest rate paid by a cash fund is more likely to fluctuate along with the market, as opposed to the building society or bank which uses a committee to decide how much to pay.

## PICKING A CASH FUND

Most unit trust cash funds charge no initial fee. Most have annual fees of one-half of one per cent. The initial investment amount is usually £1,000. Unfortunately, because cash funds usually invest in securities which have less than five years before maturity, they do not meet the guidelines for PEP investments and cannot be used with a PEP.

Figure 9.9 shows a list of the ten largest cash funds, with the current rates, fees and minimum investments. When choosing a cash fund, I suggest that the easiest solution is to choose the fund where you already have existing unit trust holdings. The interest rate differential isn't that great from one fund to the next – except if the fund management company weighs it down with fees. If you don't already have a fund management company, choose from the list in Figure 9.9

or refer to the magazines which list unit trust performances, such as *What Investment?*, *Money Management*, or *Money Observer.* Secondly, choose one that has no upfront charges.

Look at the spread, which contains the initial charge and the 'other bit' expenses. Make sure the annual fees are no more than one-half of 1 per cent.

**Fig 9.9  Ten largest cash funds**

| Fund | Return 1 year | Return 3 years | Minimum | Initial charge | Spread | Annual charge |
|------|------|------|------|------|------|------|
| Fidelity cash | 4.33% | 12.57% | £1,000 | 0.00% | 0.00% | 0.50% |
| Prudential cash | 3.54% | 10.88% | £1,000 | 0.00% | 0.48% | 0.50% |
| Perpetual money | 4.59% | NA | £1,000 | 0.00% | 0.00% | 0.50% |
| Mercury cash | 4.53% | 13.02% | £1,000 | 0.00% | 0.00% | 0.50% |
| UTD. friendly | 4.08% | 11.02% | £1,000 | 0.00% | 0.00% | 0.75% |
| Gartmore cash | 4.43% | 12.08% | £1,000 | 0.00% | 0.00% | 0.50% |
| Scot. Amicable max income | 2.03% | 11.58% | £5,000 | 2.50% | 2.54% | 0.50% |
| M&G treasury | 4.66% | 14.02% | £5,000 | 0.00% | 0.16% | 0.60% |
| Five Arrows cash port. | −1.84% | NA | £1 | 0.00% | 3.99% | NA |
| Midland money market | 4.43% | 12.87% | £1,000 | 0.00% | 0.00% | 0.50% |
| Average | 3.48% | 12.26% | £1,700 | 0.25% | 0.72% | 0.54% |
| | | | | | | |
| UK savings £2,500+ | 2.25% | 8.52% | £2,500 | – | – | – |

*Source: Micropal Expert, 30 September 1996.*

| We discuss bond funds in Chapter 10. |
|---|

Unlike bond funds and equity funds, the distinction between management styles is not all that important for cash funds. Choose a fund which is convenient.

The cash fund should be used only for money you desire instant access to. If you're willing to tie up your money a little longer, for your medium-term needs, then we step into the world of bond funds. Bond funds generally pay higher interest rates, and are potentially more profitable.

# SUMMARY

- Cash funds are a home for your emergency money as you can get immediate access.

- Cash funds typically pay around one per cent more over comparable immediate-access accounts at banks and building societies.

- Cash funds cannot be held in a PEP.

Before investing:
- verify no initial charge

- fund pays no more than 0.50 per cent in annual management charges.

# INVESTING FOR INCOME: THE SAFER ROUTE

# THE WHOLE FINANCIAL PLAN

'Unit trusts are sexy,' says Jeff Prestridge, personal finance editor for the *Financial Mail on Sunday*. (He's the first person I've spoken to who believes this.) 'People buy unit trusts – and PEPs – on an ad-hoc basis.' He believes they should be invested in only in conjunction with a firm understanding of your financial needs.

Jamie Berry, an independent financial advisor oriented towards investments, adds, 'Too often investors view each PEP in isolation instead of thinking of them as part of an overall portfolio.'[1] We'll learn of Berry's views later in Chapter 17.

'PEPs aren't going to save you, if you lose your job or if you have a heart attack.' Prestridge, who holds a financial planning certificate, writes every week about new products, new abuses, and new ways of financial planning. He says that most people think of equities when they think of unit trusts. 'Some people should not even be considering unit trusts', because of their financial situation.

Along these lines, he believes the recently introduced Corporate Bond PEP has done 'a world of good', by adding another investment possibility with lower volatility characteristics than equities.

In this chapter, we discuss first where bonds fit in with your financial strategy. Second, we discuss what a bond is and where its price comes from. We'll discover there are different sorts of income-producing securities with different return and volatility characteristics. Next, we step into the world of gilts and fixed-interest unit trusts, where we focus on three large PEP-able corporate bond unit trusts to pick up the three key factors for assessing bond funds.

# WHERE THEY FIT

The savings sergeant from the last chapter, M&G's Roger A. Jennings, says, 'You need something that keeps pace with inflation, and provides a little more.' Bonds offer that little bit more.

We focus now on the middle region of your financial portfolio, the medium-term, which we've defined as three to five years. In such a period, you're willing to risk a small amount in capital, in exchange for a higher income.

Before you invest in an income-producing fund, make sure it's not an equity fund, dressed up to look like a bond fund, which could prove to be a wolf in grandma's clothes. In my research, I discovered often it is not clear whether the investment is based in equities or in fixed-interest-type instruments. If you invest in an equity fund, even one that pays out a high level of income, this has different volatility characteristics from a bond fund. This chapter is dedicated to pointing out where the bond fund's income comes from.

**Fig 10.1 Timing class of investments**

| Timing class | Investment | Return | | Volatility |
|---|---|---|---|---|
| Short-term | Cash | Lowest | 4.7% | Least |
| **Medium-term** | **Bonds** | **Medium** | **7.3%** | **Medium** |
| Long-term | Equity | Highest | 12.8% | Highest |

These investments can be useful for paying school fees, if due within five years. Similarly, if you're saving up for the down payment on a house or flat, this is the source. If you're less definite about your plans, but feel you want part of your funds in a relatively safe vehicle, yet earning higher interest than is available through your bank or a cash fund, a bond fund is your money's home.

If absolute certainty is needed, you may consider TESSAs or postal accounts which offer competitive tax-free rates. However, as economists say, there's no such thing as a free lunch. Any time you get certainty, you give up something, such as the ability to get your funds without paying a penalty or some other restriction, or earn a lower rate.

## THE CHOICE BEGINS

It's getting near the end of the year, you've procrastinated, and now it's time to PEP. You turn to the Chase de Vere's *PEP Guide*, BESt Investments *Portfolio Advice*, Allenbridge Group's *PEP Talk* brochure, *Money Management, What Investment?* (or one of the other documents produced during the PEP season) to discover the following three yields:[2]

| Fairy tale funds | Advertised yield |
|---|---|
| Three Little Piggies: | 8.90 per cent |
| Big, Bad Wolf: | 8.48 per cent |
| Little Red Riding Hood: | 7.62 per cent |

Which do you choose? (The fairy tale funds are real funds, the identity of which will be revealed at the end of the chapter.)

The choice couldn't be more important, especially if you depend on the income for monthly living expenses. Unfortunately, the answer is not straightforward and will require a bit of sleuthing to understand what you're in for.

In the 1930s, authors C. L. Rosenheim and C. O. Merriman complained that in 'flexible trusts there are less obvious ways of increasing the apparent yield and they have not in all cases been eschewed'.[3] Unfortunately, those 'less obvious ways' are back again. I'll show you where they show up.

> '... it is not just a matter of choosing the best yield.'

The first key feature, as Joanna Slaughter states in her excellent book, *A Guide to Investment Trusts and Unit Trusts*, is: 'Never forget the general rule, the higher the yield, the greater the risk.'[4] Slaughter provides us with the first clue about how to compare unit trusts promising income. We will come back over and over again to this key aspect.

You need to understand the yield, concretely, to sort out the advertisements. Because, as you've ascertained by now, it is not just a matter of choosing the best yield. In fact, because the yield is what is relied upon to convince you of the worthiness of this unit trust over that, this chapter is devoted to understanding the yield.

## YOU'RE A BOND TRADER

Bonds are loans made to the public. Typically, bonds are issued at 'par', which means £100. At the end of a bond's life, the total amount originally paid – the total face value of the bond – is paid back to the holders. Over the bond's life, interest payments are made, called 'coupon payments' or 'coupons'. The rate appearing on the coupon is the interest rate the issuer of the bond, BP, Tesco, the government, and so on, will pay.

Bonds issued by the government are called 'gilt-edged securities' or just 'gilts'. Bonds issued by companies, which pay a fixed rate of interest are called 'fixed-interest'. Bonds can also be issued with varying rates of interest, though they too are lumped together with the fixed-interest instruments for unit trust purposes. A debenture is a bond issued with a secured interest in some specified portion of the company's assets. A general bond has an unspecified interest in the company's assets in the event of a default on the part of the issuer. A debenture has a legally determined claim on specific company assets. For that reason, all other things being equal, a debenture is less risky than a general bond, and pays a slightly lower interest rate.

There are two other kinds of instruments which may be held by gilt and fixed-interest unit trust investments: convertibles and preferred shares. A convertible is a general purpose bond issued by the company, which can also be converted into equity of the company on a predetermined basis. You can think of it as a straight bond with an option attached to it: the option gives you the right, not the obligation, to convert into shares of the company.

Convertible shares are bonds or loan stock issued by companies that are convertible into equity by a predetermined formula. A convertible becomes valuable if the shares of the company perform well. On the other hand, if the shares never perform well enough to make it worthwhile to convert, you still have the interest payments from the bond portion of the convertible. Again, all other things being equal, a convertible will pay a lower rate of interest than the straight debt. Further, because of the equity-related link through the convertibility option, convertibles are more volatile than straight debt, but less volatile than equities in the same company.

For example, at this writing, News Corp's 15-year convertibles are yielding 6 per cent, while gilts with the same maturity offer 8 per cent. While the gilts will never default, there is some possibility that a non-governmental company would default, hence, you would expect the yield on the non-government security to be higher. Yet, we see that it's not. Instead, the value of the option, the ability to convert the debt to equity, is high enough to increase the price of the News Corp security such that the yield is lowered.

Finally, a gilt and fixed-interest unit trust can invest in preferred shares. Preferred shares are probably the most volatile of the three generic types of fixed-interest products but less so than company shares. Preferred shares pay a fixed, and sometimes rising, rate of interest (called 'dividends' because they arise from shares). If the company were to default, holders of preferred shares follow holders of secured and unsecured debt.

Preferred shares never become due. That is, there is no maturity date. Hence, for analytical purposes, the interest dividends are assumed to continue for eternity and there is no redemption of the principal.

In some instances, preferred shares are convertible into ordinary shares.

As Joanna Slaughter explains, 'The funds that provide the highest immediate income are those that invest in gilts and corporate bonds, followed by those that have fixed-interest securities, like convertible shares and preference shares.'[5]

## THE SIMPLEST YIELD

You're a bond trader. The most basic element of a bond is the yield. The yield at its simplest is the income received divided by the amount invested:

$$\text{Yield \%} = \frac{\text{Income received}}{\text{Amount invested}} = \frac{£5}{£100} = 5\%$$

When you see an interest rate quoted for a bank or building society, this formula applies. This is often referred to as simple interest, because it is not a result of any compounding.

If the investment is held for two years, and the interest is paid at the end of each year, the amount you had at the end of the second year would be greater than the two years of £5 each. Instead, you would receive 5 per cent or £5 on £100 for the first year, and then you would earn 5 per cent on the compounded amount, £105, from the first year:

| | |
|---|---|
| Original investment: | £100.00 |
| First year's interest: (5% of £100) | £5.00 |
| Second year's interest: (5% of £105.00) | £5.25 |
| Total over two years: | £110.25 |

In this instance, the simple interest rate equals the interest rate if you held the investment until it matured, two years in our example.

# YIELD TO MATURITY

However, if you leave your bank and go into the marketplace, you'll find bonds issued by the government and corporations. These securities, when issued, work on a similar premise as the bank or building society: they guarantee to pay you, usually twice a year, a fixed rate of interest until they mature. The primary difference between the bank deposit and the marketplace bond is that in the marketplace, the price of the original investment can change.

For example, if the government offered 20-year bonds at 5 per cent; the government would pay you 2½ per cent twice a year for the next 20 years. At the conclusion of the 20 years, you would receive back your original investment. In this case the coupon rate, 5 per cent, is the same as the yield to maturity, 5 per cent. Yield to maturity refers to the effective rate of interest you'll earn if you hold the bond until the original payment amount is returned.

Original price → 5% over 20 years, twice per year + Original payment (Yield to maturity = 5%)

Now a lot can happen over 20 years.

The most important thing that will happen is that the market level of interest rates will change. You often hear a comment like this, that interest rates will change. There's not one single interest rate. Instead, commentators are referring to the whole lot, which tend to move in swells like an ocean. There are always low rates and high rates. When a storm hits, the low rates are likely to move higher and the high rates even higher.

To go back to the 20-year government bond, if the swell hits and all rates move up, the government doesn't come back to you and say, 'Right, rates are higher now, we'll agree to pay you 10 per cent instead of 5 per cent.' The coupon rate remains fixed on the bond you bought for the remaining life of the bond.

Instead, the price of the bond falls. Rates are higher now. Buyers in the marketplace say, 'Why should I pay the original payment price for a bond which pays only 5 per cent, when I could go somewhere else and get 10 per cent?' The market adjusts by lowering the price. You would still get 20 years of semi-annual 5 per cent payments plus the original payment back at the end of 20 years. But the price of the bond is lowered to make 20 years of semi-annual payments plus original payment equate with the 10 per cent yield to maturity in the marketplace today.

New lower price → 5% over 20 years, twice per year + Original payment
(Yield to maturity = 10%)

The reverse holds as well. If rates drop to 2½ per cent from 5 per cent, and you have an obligation that enables you to receive 20 years of semi-annual 5 per cent payments, the price of the bond increases to reduce the overall yield to maturity of the bond:

New higher price → 5% over 20 years, twice per year + Original payment
(Yield to maturity = 2½%)

## THE IMMUTABLE TRUTHS

- If rates go up, the price of the bond goes down (see Figure 10.2).
- Ignore the coupon or simple interest rate: Yield to maturity is what's important.
- The longer the maturity, the higher the rate, the higher the price volatility.

**Fig 10.2  Yield to maturity vs price**

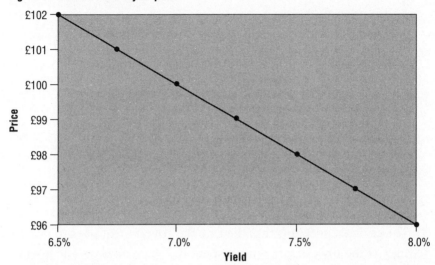

*Note:* The chart makes it appear as if the relationship between rates increases and price decreases is a straight one-to-one relationship: interest rates increase 1 per cent causing a drop of £2 in price. This will only be the case under very specific situations. In reality it is not a straight line, but curved slightly, and will change depending on the level of the rate.

The state of interest rates reflects many, many different factors, not the least of which is the amount of government borrowings, inflation, the borrowings of foreign governments, the price of oil, and sometimes, it seems the price of tea in China. A company looking for longer-term funding than the money market can offer will enter the bond market. The primary distinction between bonds and money market instruments is the time to maturity. That is, money market instruments and bonds are both loans made to governments or companies, with the main difference being that bonds are paid back over a longer time period.

As a consequence, because there is a greater likelihood that market interest rates will change over the term of the loan (or bond), the market price of the bond could change. This is the great kernel of information about bonds: because there is a possibility that the interest rates will change – and therefore the price of the bond, bonds tend to have higher interest rates than money market securities. Accordingly, the interest rate paid on longer-term bonds will usually be higher than interest paid on money market instruments (see Figure 10.3).

**Fig 10.3 Yield to maturity**

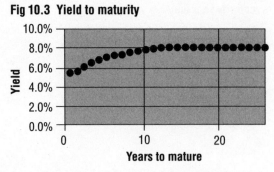

Source: *Financial Times*, UK Gilts Prices, 17 September 1996, p. 30.

- **Risky bonds, risky price.**

The critical concept is that the rate the government pays to borrow money is the lowest rate with respect to credit quality. The government will never default on its obligations. Hence, the credit quality of the government sets a standard. Every other issuer of debt is more likely to default on its obligation, and therefore has to pay a higher rate of interest to investors to compensate for this added burden. Blue-chip companies will pay only one-half of one per cent more for debt of similar maturity as gilts, whereas riskier companies could pay 1 per cent, 2 per cent, 3 per cent or more than government debt of a similar maturity. The same general principle holds; the worse the credit quality of the company, the higher the rate, and the more volatile the price.

Combining these two concepts: length of maturity and credit quality, we find the following relationship: all other things being equal, the longer the maturity and the worse the credit quality, the higher the yield (see Figure 10.4).

# INSIDE A BOND UNIT TRUST

We need to investigate four items to assess the prospects for dividends and the yield to maturity for these unit trusts:

- the type of securities: gilts, corporate debt, convertible debt, preference;

**Fig 10.4 Relationship between credit quality, time to maturity and yield**

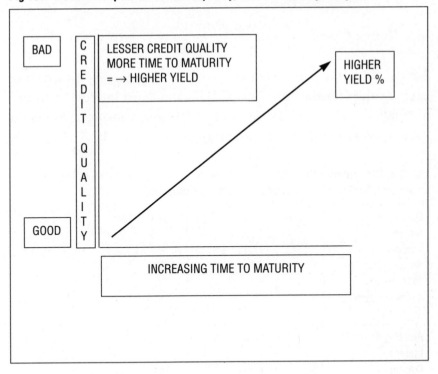

- the average maturity of the bonds held in the fund: one, five, ten, 15, 20 years;
- the credit quality of the securities in the fund;
- and, of course, the charges.

Answers to these questions will fuel a much better understanding of why the rate is as high or low as it is.

## PERFORMANCE COMPARISON

As we saw earlier, the simple yield is to divide the investment by the annual income paid:

$$\text{Yield \%} = \frac{\text{Income received}}{\text{Amount invested}} = \frac{£5}{£100} = 5\%$$

For a unit trust, this is known as the running yield.

$$\text{Running yield} = \frac{\text{Unit trust dividends}}{\text{Unit trust bid price}} = \text{Unit trust yield \%}$$

Let's look at the gross annual income and beginning and ending capital values for Barclays Unicorn Gilt and Fixed Interest Fund and a building society 90-day account with gross income, which to simplify, is assumed not to be reinvested (see Figure 10.5).

**Fig 10.5  Performance Comparison: Barclays Unicorn Gilt and Fixed Interest Fund vs Building Society 90-Day notice account (figures gross)[6]**

| Unit Trust | 12/90 | 12/91 | 12/92 | 12/93 | 12/94 | 12/95 | Gain |
|---|---|---|---|---|---|---|---|
| Income | | 82 | 80 | 78 | 74 | 73 | 386 |
| Capital | £1,000 | £1,035 | £1,113 | £1,269 | £1,095 | £1,171 | £171 |
| Simple yield | | 8.2% | 8.0% | 7.8% | 7.4% | 7.3% | |
| Total annual average return | | | | | | | 9.3% |

| Building Society | 12/90 | 12/91 | 12/92 | 12/93 | 12/94 | 12/95 | Gain |
|---|---|---|---|---|---|---|---|
| Income | | 114 | 87 | 51 | 45 | 45 | 342 |
| Capital | £1,000 | £1,000 | £1,000 | £1,000 | £1,000 | £1,000 | £0 |
| Simple yield | | 11.4% | 8.7% | 5.1% | 4.5% | 4.5% | |
| Total annual average return | | | | | | | 6.1% |

On an average annual basis, the bond unit trust paid 9.3 per cent, of which 6.7 per cent was in income and 2.5 per cent was capital appreciation, whereas the building society paid 6.1 per cent in yield and 0 per cent in capital appreciation. Notice also that a 90-day savings rate was used, not a five-year lock-up rate. The £1,000 invested in the Barclays fund paid £36 or 3.6 per cent commission, plus charges upfront.

Grant Phillips, former managing director of unit trusts for Barclays, pointed out to me that with such a yield advantage over banks, Barclays Unicorn Gilt and Fixed Interest Trust has gained a 20 per cent share of the market (see Figure 10.6). He says it is designed for people in their late 40s and upwards who are looking at a finite source of income from their working years.

## Fig 10.6  Barclays Unicorn Gilt and Fixed Interest Unit Trust

### Barclays Unicorn Gilt & FI

Barclays Unicorn Ltd, Head Office, Gredley House, 11 Broadway, Stratford, London E15 4BJ.

Information: Telephone - 0181 534 5544   Dealing - -

**Fund Objective:**
To provide a high income from a managed portfolio investing in sterling Fixed Interest Securities including British Government Stocks consistent with security of capital. UCITS.

# micropal

## Fund Analysis

### UK GILT & FIXED INTEREST
**A011 Barclays Unicorn Gilt & FI**

| Micropal Cumulative Performance - to 30th September 1996 | | | | | |
|---|---|---|---|---|---|
| Performance Period | 6 Months | 1 Year | 3 Years | 5 Years | 10 Years |
| Fund Performance | +3.2% | +5.4% | +10.9% | +48.0% | +120.9% |
| Sector Average | +2.3% | +4.7% | +8.1% | +42.7% | +116.9% |
| Best Performing Fund | +8.3% | +12.7% | +20.9% | +105.8% | +188.9% |
| Fund Performance | | | | | |
| Sector Average Performance | | | | | |
| Worst Performing Fund | -1.8% | -0.9% | +1.2% | +21.9% | +91.2% |

(Offer-bid, net income reinvested)

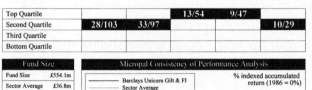

| | | | | | |
|---|---|---|---|---|---|
| Top Quartile | | | 13/54 | 9/47 | |
| Second Quartile | 28/103 | 33/97 | | | 10/29 |
| Third Quartile | | | | | |
| Bottom Quartile | | | | | |

**Fund Size**

| | |
|---|---|
| Fund Size | £554.1m |
| Sector Average | £36.8m |
| Largest Fund | £554.1m |
| Smallest Fund | £0.2m |
| No. of Funds | 104 |

■ Fund Size
□ Average Fund Size in Sector

### Micropal Consistency of Performance Analysis

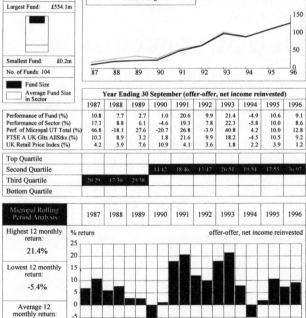

— Barclays Unicorn Gilt & FI
— Sector Average

% indexed accumulated return (1986 = 0%)

| Year Ending 30 September (offer-offer, net income reinvested) | | | | | | | | | | |
|---|---|---|---|---|---|---|---|---|---|---|
| | 1987 | 1988 | 1989 | 1990 | 1991 | 1992 | 1993 | 1994 | 1995 | 1996 |
| Performance of Fund (%) | 10.8 | 7.7 | 2.7 | 1.0 | 20.6 | 9.9 | 21.4 | -4.9 | 10.6 | 9.1 |
| Performance of Sector (%) | 17.3 | 8.8 | 6.1 | -4.6 | 19.3 | 7.8 | 22.3 | -5.8 | 10.0 | 8.6 |
| Perf. of Micropal UT Total (%) | 46.8 | -18.1 | 27.6 | -20.7 | 26.8 | -3.9 | 40.8 | 4.2 | 10.0 | 12.8 |
| FTSE A UK Glts AllStks (%) | 10.3 | 8.9 | 3.2 | 1.8 | 21.6 | 9.9 | 18.2 | -4.5 | 10.5 | 9.2 |
| UK Retail Price Index (%) | 4.2 | 5.9 | 7.6 | 10.9 | 4.1 | 3.6 | 1.8 | 2.2 | 3.9 | 1.2 |
| Top Quartile | | | | | | | | | | |
| Second Quartile | | | | 14/42 | 18/46 | 13/47 | 26/51 | 19/51 | 17/55 | 36/97 |
| Third Quartile | 20/29 | 17/30 | 29/38 | | | | | | | |
| Bottom Quartile | | | | | | | | | | |

| Micropal Rolling Period Analysis | 1987 | 1988 | 1989 | 1990 | 1991 | 1992 | 1993 | 1994 | 1995 | 1996 |
|---|---|---|---|---|---|---|---|---|---|---|

| | |
|---|---|
| Highest 12 monthly return: 21.4% | |
| Lowest 12 monthly return: -5.4% | |
| Average 12 monthly return: 8.2% | |

% return    offer-offer, net income reinvested

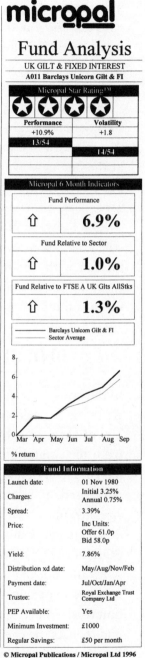

### Micropal Star Rating™

★★★★

| Performance | Volatility |
|---|---|
| +10.9% | +1.8 |
| 13/54 | |
| | 14/54 |

### Micropal 6 Month Indicators

**Fund Performance**

⇧  **6.9%**

**Fund Relative to Sector**

⇧  **1.0%**

**Fund Relative to FTSE A UK Glts AllStks**

⇧  **1.3%**

— Barclays Unicorn Gilt & FI
— Sector Average

Mar Apr May Jun Jul Aug Sep

% return

### Fund Information

| | |
|---|---|
| Launch date: | 01 Nov 1980 |
| Charges: | Initial 3.25% Annual 0.75% |
| Spread: | 3.39% |
| Price: | Inc Units: Offer 61.0p Bid 58.0p |
| Yield: | 7.86% |
| Distribution xd date: | May/Aug/Nov/Feb |
| Payment date: | Jul/Oct/Jan/Apr |
| Trustee: | Royal Exchange Trust Company Ltd |
| PEP Available: | Yes |
| Minimum Investment: | £1000 |
| Regular Savings: | £50 per month |

© Micropal Publications / Micropal Ltd 1996

*Source: Micropal*

157

You'll note from the yearly yields on the original invested capital that the fixed-interest fund reflected what the market was paying, whereas the building society account reflected the decisions of interest-rate deciding committees. Clearly, the interest-rate deciding committee reflects the market, but it also reflects the commercial realities of the ebb and flow of competition in the banking world.

The other key fact to recognise is that the £1,000 in the building society account always remained at £1,000; whereas the £1,000 in the unit trust first paid a commission of £36 and its value fluctuated, in the one negative year for bonds, the price went down by 14 per cent; over the five years, however, the value increased 2.5 per cent. Time heals all wounds.

John Kelly, Barclays Investments Manager, explained that in 1994, when interest rates went up as bond prices went down, 'we communicated with our investors to make them understand with clarity what the situation in the market was'. He believes that 'the test is not when conditions are fair, but instead, when the storm hits'.

## DEDUCTING EXPENSES FROM CAPITAL

In the last few years, another little angle has worked its way into the reporting of yields which is perfectly legal, perfectly justifiable, and downright despicable. The annual manager's charge can be deducted from the capital of the fund at the fund manager's discretion. This has the effect of increasing the running yield – the yield that you'll see advertised, and decreasing the yield from capital. The amount is not sizeable, but if you're making your decision on the basis of, say, half a percentage point, and one fund does deduct from capital and the other doesn't, you're not really comparing like with like.

At the bottom line, deducting the expenses from capital – as opposed to income – has the effect of increasing the tax slightly on the unit trust. Hence, it is bad on two counts: it increases the yield slightly and reduces the overall performance of the fund. Yes, we're only talking about a very small fraction of a per cent, but it's not a good thing.

Equity funds can choose to take expenses out of capital, instead of income, as well (see Figure 10.7).

**Fig 10.7 Effects of deducting annual management charges from income and from capital**

---

**Annual management charge from income**

Dividends – management charge / Capital

$$\frac{£5.00 - £1.00}{£100.00} = \frac{£4.00}{£100.00} = 4.00\%$$

Reported running dividend yield = 4.00%

**Annual management charge from capital**

Dividends / Capital – management charge

$$\frac{£5.00}{£100.00 - £1.00} = \frac{£5.00}{£99.00} = 5.05\%$$

Reported running dividend yield = 5.05%

---

# THE INGENIOUS LINK

The more important interest rate, the yield to maturity, takes into account an estimate of the entire amount paid out over the life of the investment.

For unit trusts, this is referred to as the 'redemption yield': what you would receive if you waited until redemption of the securities held within the fund.

The difference between these two yields will tell you a lot. If the redemption yield is the same as the running yield, you've got nothing to worry about. If the redemption yield is significantly lower than the running yield, this suggests that the unit trust gilt and fixed-interest fund has bought bonds at a premium, i.e., paid more for them than will be paid back at redemption. This suggests that the capital value of the fund will decrease with time.

If the running yield is less than the redemption yield, this suggests the opposite, that the capital value will increase with time.

This all links together in a very ingenious way. IFA Clive Scott-Hopkins of Towry Law, who has been a unit trust investor for over 35 years, says, 'People, especially retired people, should look at the total return [redemption yield].' He makes the point, 'If I throw a pound coin on the table, is it an income coin or a capital gain coin?' His point is that a gain is a gain and a loss is a loss, regardless of its source, income or capital gain.

'Income' is the dividends paid out of the fund while 'capital gain' is the appreciated price of the fund. The difference, of course, is that the income can be sent out to you via a cheque, whereas the capital gain is realised when you finally sell some units.

We can adapt this concept of the yield from dividends, capital gains or losses, and the total return.

**Cash:**

$$\text{Dividend} + \text{capital gain (or loss)} = \text{total return}$$

**%:**

$$\text{Running yield} + \text{capital yield} = \text{redemption yield}$$

Figure 10.8 gives a list of some large gilt and fixed-interest funds with their income or running yields, and their gross redemption or yields to maturity.

### Fig 10.8  Yields reported for some large corporate bond funds

|  | Income yield | Redemption yield |
|---|---|---|
| Abtrust Fixed Interest | 9.80% | 10.20% |
| Barclays Unicorn Gilt & Fixed Interest* | 7.83% | 8.04% |
| Clerical Medical Extra Income Trust | 7.70% | 7.50% |
| Fidelity Moneybuilder Income | 8.00% | 7.40% |
| HTR Preference & Bond | 8.50% | 8.50% |
| M&G Gilt & Fixed Interest | 7.60% | 7.40% |
| NatWest Extra Income Trust | 7.40% | 7.40% |
| Prolific Corp. Bond PEP | 6.40% | 6.40% |
| TSB High Income PEP | 7.20% | 6.90% |
| Virgin Income | 7.80% | 7.20% |

\* Barclays data at 14 November 1996; all others November 1995.
*Source:* 'Altered States, Survey of Corporate Bond PEPs' by Pauline Skypala, *Money Management*, February 1996, pp. 24–28.

We go back to the fairy tale funds and find that something very interesting emerges; originally, there was a 1.28 per cent difference between the high- and low-yielding fund whereas, on a total return basis, the difference is slightly more than one-third of a per cent, only 0.39 per cent (see Figure 10.9).

The second outstanding difference is the re-ordering of funds: Three Little Piggies actually moved to the lowest position from the highest, once the potential loss to capital was included in the review.

**Fig 10.9  Fairy tale funds**

| Fund[7] | Running yield | | Capital yield | | Redemption yield |
|---|---|---|---|---|---|
| Big, Bad Wolf | 8.48% | + | (1.06%) | = | 7.42% |
| Little Red Riding Hood | 7.62% | + | (0.47%) | = | 7.15% |
| Three Little Piggies | 8.90% | + | (1.87%) | = | 7.03% |

The conclusion: look to the redemption yield or the yield to maturity when reviewing funds.

Of our three funds, the Big Bad Wolf and Little Red Riding Hood deduct the management charge from the income and dividends of the fund directly, while the third deducts it from capital. This partly explains the large variation between the yield from income and the redemption yield for the Three Little Piggies, which takes into account this charge to capital.

> '... with unit-trust income-generating investments, there is some possibility that your capital will be reduced.'

Simply stated, you must take into account that with unit trust income-generating investments, there is some possibility that your capital will be reduced.

## WHAT'S IN THE PORTFOLIO?

From the bond traders' immutable truths we also know that the type of holdings, the length to maturity, and the credit quality of the portfolio directly influences the yield, the price, and future of the portfolio.

Unfortunately, the extent of each of these key aspects is not clearly laid out in the unit trust brochures. You'll have to ferret these aspects out via looking at the brochures, looking at the name of the fund, and comparing yields with existing yields in the marketplace.

### The first clue: read what they give you

The brochure for the largest gilt and fixed interest fund, Barclays Unicorn Gilt and Fixed Interest Trust, (which has the undeserving acronym of BUGFIT) described the objectives as:

> to provide a high income from a managed portfolio investing in sterling
> fixed interest securities, including British Government stocks, *consistent
> with the security of capital.*[8]

We find that this fund invests only in loans or debt. The investments manager for BUGFIT, John Kelly, says that 'because we're associated with a bank (Barclays), we're on the cusp between savers and investors. We have deliberately built a safe fund, which is massively diversified. We have a cash buffer and government bonds. We don't want investors to be disappointed.'

Another example is provided by Virgin Income, another large gilt and fixed-interest fund. Its objective is as follows:

> Your money is used to buy units in the Virgin Income trust, 45 per cent of
> which is invested in Gilts, tracking the FT Actuaries 5-15 Year Gilt Index.
> 55 per cent is evenly spread across 22 corporate bonds, issued by some
> of the top UK companies.[9]

Finally, we look at GT's High Yield Fund:

> To achieve a high and stable income together with long-term capital
> growth from a portfolio consisting primarily of fixed interest securities
> issued by UK companies including convertible loan stocks and
> debentures.
>
> from *Micropal*

This last fund invests in convertible debt which can be switched to equity. Typically, it will pay a lower interest rate than a similarly structured non-convertible debt. The ability or option to convert the debt into shares could be valuable. Hence, companies which issue convertible debt need not pay as high an interest rate, because they offer the potentially valuable equity option.

Mr Paul Reed, manager of the high-yielding Abtrust Fixed Interest Fund states that over 70 per cent of his fund is invested in convertibles, with the remainder invested in bonds and preference shares. 'Convertibles stand up on their yield and have a bit of an equity kicker,' he says.[10]

We turn back to BUGFIT. Explaining a divergence from the index, the Scheme Particulars explain that:

> the performance of the Trust [was driven lower than the index] ... because of the comparatively long maturity position ...[11]

Later the brochure describes:

> a disappointing performance from utility issues caused long-dated un-secured bonds to underperform as the market became wary of credit implications of corporate activity.

Thus, we discover that the utility issues were long-dated, meaning that they had a long maturity date. We also discover that:

> the market became wary of credit implications.

Presumably, this means the prices of some bonds in the portfolio diminished (and the yield increased).

This description is better than most. I wish the fund management company were more upfront about the maturity and credit aspects of their portfolios. You can find out if you ring up the portfolio man-ager, and sometimes the client helplines will know the answer. It's more likely you'll have to do a little sleuthing, e.g., spend ten minutes reading the brochure.

Professional rating agencies give credit ratings to bonds and occasionally to the funds themselves. These ratings traditionally are a series of gradings, such as A or AA or AAA or A1 or A1–. I always have to look up what the grading means. I haven't seen too many references to the actual letters, unless it's AAA. If you see these gradings, ask the client helpline or your IFA what they mean. Some-times, what is held out as a high rating is nothing of the sort.

## The second clue: look at the name

Some funds describe their maturity aims in the name of the fund. The maturity aim means how long the average bonds in the portfolio have until they become due.

For example:

- Mercury Long-Dated Sterling Bond
- Whittingdale Short-Dated Gilt

- Fidelity Long Gilt
- Commercial Union Prestige Portfolio Trust Long Gilt
- Burrage Short-Dated Gilt

Unfortunately, there aren't many like this.

Similarly, if the fund calls itself the 'high, extra, lotta income yield fund', it must do something to attract this extra yield. This extra something is either to extend the maturity of the bonds or buy bonds of a lesser credit quality.

You'll note in Figure 10.10, that most of the funds with the name suggesting a higher yield have indeed a higher yield. However, six of the 15 funds listed do not have that higher yield, despite their name. This only proves that you need to look deeper to understand the potential income of the fund.

**Fig 10.10  UK gilts and fixed-interest funds with names promising higher yields (ranked by current yield)**

| Fund Name | Yield | Size £ millions |
|---|---|---|
| Eagle Star Extra Income | 8.04% | 7.5 |
| GT High Yield | 7.87% | 15.2 |
| INVESCO High Income Investment | 7.79% | 10.3 |
| Lloyds Bank High Interest | 7.57% | 76.1 |
| Clerical Medical Extra Income | 7.35% | 92.7 |
| Allied Dunbar Extra Income | 7.32% | 20.1 |
| Gartmore Extra Yield | 7.29% | 15.1 |
| Henry Cooke High Yield | 7.25% | 8.3 |
| S&P High Income | 7.22% | 42.6 |
| NatWest Extra Income | 7.07% | 79.3 |
| Cazenove High Income Pref. | 7.04% | 26.7 |
| Royal Bank of Scotland High Yield | 7.03% | 50.6 |
| Guardian Extra Income | 7.02% | 6.4 |
| **Median of all 86 UK gilt and fixed-interest funds** | **6.97%** | **4.1** |
| BWD High Yield | 6.84% | 0.95 |
| Tilney High Yield | 6.69% | 13.1 |
| NPI High Income Bond | 6.60% | 8.7 |
| Hambros High Provider | 6.50% | 2.4 |
| Sun Alliance High Income Provider | 6.33% | 69.3 |
| Scot Equitable Extra Income | 6.28% | 0.30 |

Source: Micropal Expert, 30 September 1996.

Look at the summary descriptions of the fairy tale funds in Figure 10.11.

**Fig 10.11 Summary descriptions of fairy tale funds**

| Name | Objective | Investments | Maturity | Credit Quality |
|---|---|---|---|---|
| **Big, Bad Wolf**<br>Gilt & fixed-interest | high income, consistent with security of capital | sterling fixed-interest securities | no mention | some British Government Stocks |
| **Little Red Riding Hood**<br>Income | to provide level of income slightly above gilt-edged securities | gilts and corporate bonds | 5–15 yrs for gilts; no mention of corporate bonds | 22 top-credit rated companies |
| **Three Little Piggies**<br>High Yield | High income/capital growth | UK fixed-interest: convertible, loans stocks, debenture | no mention | high credit standing |

## Third clue: where the money is invested

Another source of yield difference is whether the bonds are UK-oriented or internationally-oriented. You'll see names like sterling bonds or global bonds, which will tell you where managers selects bonds for your portfolio.

> '... by increasing the spread of investments, you diminish the likely volatility of the returns.'

I can't make a blanket statement about which funds are likely to be more volatile or which will pay the highest yields. When you buy into an internationally diversified portfolio, the fund can benefit or can suffer from variations in interest rates in different countries and from currency fluctuations.

Now, before you say, 'I'm not investing in anything with the possibility of currency fluctuations', remember that by increasing the spread of investments, you diminish the likely volatility of the returns. You'll need to look carefully at where the global bond fund invests your money, whether it's in Russian-rouble notes or German notes or D-Mark bonds; as my example suggests, where the money is invested makes a world of difference.

## The final clue: the yield

The final clue about the stability of the income and capital of the fund is the yield itself. Remember Figure 10.4, which suggested that longer maturity combined with lower credit quality results in a higher yield? In evaluating the yield of any fund, look to other comparable yields. How much are straight three-year, five-year, ten-year, and 20-year gilts yielding? This information can be obtained from the *Financial Times*, and from other newspapers. Alternatively, simply look at how much your bank is offering for similar-term investments. Or look at how much National Savings accounts are offering.

Ask the fund manager or your IFA for the simple and redemption yields on the fund; get the fund management company to send you a list of comparable funds with running and redemption yields from an outside source like *Micropal*: if you rely on the in-house brochure, you can bet good money that it will make its own fund look good.

The idea is to compare the yield promised by the funds with what the rest of the marketplace is doing. You will be with this investment probably for five years or more. It's worth your while to take 15 minutes to understand its policies. Furthermore, the aims of all the funds sound admirable: solid income, capital preservation, high yields. Nothing you can argue with. Yet, the proof is in the pudding. Look at the yield. How does it compare? If the fund is investing in short-term gilts, the least volatile, highest credit quality around, is the 12-month return the same as low quality, long-dated junk bonds?

This need not be a time-consuming exercise.

You'll note in the list of Income-producing bond funds listed in Figure 10.12 that the yields are fairly closely grouped, ranging mainly from 6.0 per cent to 8.91 per cent. The funds with no yield hold zero coupon bonds, which make no interest payments – the gain on a zero-coupon bond occurs at maturity. I've also listed returns for the previous 12 months, taking into account the initial charge and the extra bit spread, and the dividends after tax. Note, once again, the wide variation in returns.

**Fig 10.12 Income-producing bond funds: fund yields and 12-month return, ranked by yield**

| Gilt and fixed interest, UK sector | Running yield | Prior 12 months return, after expenses, dividends, and tax |
|---|---|---|
| Abtrust Fixed Interest | 8.91% | 12.70% |
| Thornton Preference | 8.80% | 4.48% |
| HTR Preference & Bond | 8.30% | 6.53% |
| Britannia | 8.28% | 5.60% |
| Eagle Star Extra Income | 8.04% | −0.04% |
| **20-Year Gilt** | 8.00% | – |
| INVESCO Gilt & Fixed Interest | 7.99% | 5.64% |
| CU PPT Preference Shares | 7.99% | 1.82% |
| GT High Yield | 7.87% | 3.57% |
| INVESCO High Income Investment | 7.79% | 4.61% |
| Barclays Unicorn Gilt & Fixed Interest | 7.78% | 5.44% |
| Perpetual PEP Bond | 7.68% | 5.09% |
| Fidelity Money Builder | 7.61% | 9.08% |
| M&G Corporate Bond | 7.60% | 9.55% |
| Edinburgh Preferred High Income | 7.60% | 2.38% |
| **10-Year Gilt** | 7.60% | – |
| Schroders Gilt & Fixed Int. | 7.58% | 4.63% |
| Lloyds Bank High Interest | 7.57% | 6.79% |
| Prolific Preference & FI | 7.50% | 1.45% |
| UTD Friendly Fixed Int. | 7.47% | 0.83% |
| Murray Acumen Reserve | 7.43% | 8.26% |
| Sun Life of Canada BD & G | 7.35% | <12 months results |
| Clerical Med. Extra Income | 7.35% | 2.25% |
| Allied Dunbar Extra Income | 7.32% | 7.33% |
| Gartmore Extra Yield | 7.29% | 5.19% |
| Legal & General Fixed Interest | 7.29% | 3.72% |
| Five Arrows UK Fixed Int. Portfolio | 7.28% | 3.80% |
| Aberdeen Gilt Income | 7.26% | 7.26% |
| Henry Cook High Yield | 7.25% | 1.38% |
| S&P High Income | 7.22% | 4.91% |
| CCM Fixed Interest | 7.21% | 7.03% |
| Murray Corporate Bond | 7.15% | 6.49% |
| Fidelity Long Gilt | 7.11% | 8.64% |
| M&G Gilt & Fixed Int. | 7.10% | 8.96% |
| KB Bond Income | 7.09% | 6.66% |
| NatWest Extra Income | 7.07% | 2.51% |

| Gilt and fixed interest, UK sector | Running yield | Prior 12 months return, after expenses, dividends, and tax |
|---|---|---|
| St. James Pl Corp. Bond | 7.06% | 4.96% |
| Cazenove High income Ptfl. | 7.04% | 9.19% |
| Std. Life Premier Income | 7.04% | 3.14% |
| Scot. Amicable Corp Bond | 7.03% | 5.14% |
| Royal Bk. Scot. High Yield | 7.03% | 1.57% |
| Guardian Extra Income | 7.02% | 5.09% |
| Canlife Bond | 7.00% | 3.20% |
| Sovereign Controlled Performance | 7.00% | 2.61% |
| Guinness Flight Corp. Bond | 6.98% | 4.53% |
| Abbey Gilt & Fixed Interest | 6.96% | 2.22% |
| **5-Year Gilt** | 6.90% | – |
| Midland Corp. Bond | 6.86% | <12 months results |
| BWD High Yield Bond | 6.84% | 6.78% |
| Norwich Sterling Bond | 6.82% | 4.93% |
| KB Gilt Yield | 6.82% | 3.43% |
| Framlington Gilt | 6.79% | 6.06% |
| TSB Premier Income | 6.78% | 4.44% |
| Virgin Income | 6.72% | 10.13% |
| Whittingdale Sterling Bond | 6.70% | 2.68% |
| Tilney High Yield | 6.69% | 5.48% |
| BG Bond | 6.69% | 3.37% |
| Hill Samuel Gilt & FI Income | 6.68% | 4.11% |
| Std. Lf. Gilt & Fixed Interest | 6.63% | 3.14% |
| Woolwich Corp. Bond | 6.60% | <12 months results |
| NPI High Income Bond | 6.60% | 1.77% |
| Prudential Premier Income | 6.58% | 2.99% |
| NatWest UK Gilt & Fixed Int. | 6.50% | 5.04% |
| Hambros High Provider | 6.50% | 4.53% |
| Legal & General Gilt | 6.50% | 2.82% |
| Burrage Short Dated Gilt | 6.41% | 5.68% |
| Mercury Long Dated Stg. Bond | 6.37% | 2.32% |
| Sun Alliance High Income Bond | 6.33% | <12 months results |
| Scot. Equitable Extra Income | 6.28% | 2.61% |
| Canlife Gilt & Fixed Interest | 6.26% | 2.34% |
| Midland Gilt & Fixed Interest | 6.16% | 4.05% |
| AIB Corp. Bond | 6.14% | 4.56% |
| CU PPT Long Gilt Portfolio | 6.10% | <12 months results |
| Singer & Fried. Preferred Income | 6.06% | 5.37% |
| Mercury Government Sec. | 6.02% | 5.23% |
| Whittingdale Gilt Income | 6.00% | 3.90% |
| CIM Community Income | 5.93% | 3.87% |

| Gilt and fixed interest, UK sector | Running yield | Prior 12 months return, after expenses, dividends, and tax |
|---|---|---|
| Allied Dunbar Govern. Securities | 5.88% | 2.15% |
| Eagle Star UK Pref. & FI | 5.81% | 1.25% |
| AXA Equity & Law Gilt & FI | 5.77% | 1.92% |
| Fidelity Strategic Income | 5.71% | 4.69% |
| Guardian Gilt & Fixed Int | 5.55% | 1.20% |
| Alliance & Leicester Income | 5.52% | <12 months results |
| Norwich Gilt & Convertible | 5.10% | 4.92% |
| Abbey Capital Reserve | 4.80% | 5.36% |
| UTD Friendly Index-Linked Gilt | 1.30% | −0.93% |
| Whittingdale Short Dated Gilt | 0.01% | 5.16% |
| Exeter Zero Preference* | 0.00% | 2.94% |
| Whittingdale Gilt Growth | 0.00% | 2.25% |

* Fund pays no income currently.
*Source: Micropal Expert*, 30 September 1996.

## THE INEVITABLE CHARGES

Charges will affect your performance. The range of charges for gilt and fixed-interest funds is less than for equity funds: from 6.8 per cent to 0 per cent for initial charges. Running a bond fund is not as difficult as an equity fund. Jason D. Hollands of BESt Investments, an IFA firm specialising in investments, concurs that the charges are 'probably most important for fixed-interest investments'. Pay as little as possible.

The range of annual charges is 1.5 per cent to 0.25 per cent. The cheapest fund charges one quarter of one per cent, while the most expensive charge six times as much.

## THE END OF THE FAIRY TALE

Let's unveil the three funds in our make-believe story (Figure 10.13).

We find that the running yield, the yield you see in the newspaper bears little or no relationship to what your total return on the fund is likely to be. While any fund can perform very well or very poorly, based on the fund management company and the individual

**Fig 10.13 Ending the fairy tale[12]**

| Fund | Running yield | Redemption yield | Last yr return | Spread* | Annual charge | Source** capital, income |
|---|---|---|---|---|---|---|
| **Big, Bad Wolf:** **Barclays Unicorn** **Gilt & Fixed Interest** | 8.48% | 7.42% | +5.4% | 3.39% | 0.75% | Income |
| **Little Red Riding Hood:** **Virgin Direct** **Income** | 7.62% | 7.15% | 10.1% | 0.00% | 0.70% | Income |
| **Three Little Piggies:** **GT** **High Yield** | 8.90% | 7.03% | +3.6% | 5.39% | 1.00% | Capital |

\* The spread is what you pay upfront and includes the initial charge.
\*\* Details if annual management charge is paid out of income or capital. Annual charge paid out of capital increases reported running yield and decreasing capital return.

managers' skill, often there are elements which will give you a clue as to the likely performance.

We saw many of those ingredients:

- the kind of investments;
- the average maturity of the holding;
- the volatility of the underlying securities.

These all affect the potential volatility of gilt and fixed-interest unit trust funds.

## PERSONAL EQUITY PLANS

The Personal Equity Plan now accept bonds as a qualifying investment. This breathed new life into unit trusts offering corporate bonds, preference shares, and convertibles. Between 1995 and 1996, when bonds were allowed to be included in PEPs, the growth in the gilt and fixed income sector amounted to 33 per cent, up £721 million.[13] *What Investment?* magazine said these 'can potentially bring greater balance to PEP portfolios'.[14]

Anne Davis, marketing director at Fidelity, says that corporate bond PEPs 'help investors bridge the gap' between cash funds and equity funds in volatility and return. *Money Observer* made the same observation, 'the main reason for the enthusiasm for corporate bond PEPs is the fact that they are a useful investment stepping stone for traditional building society savers, providing them with a bridge between savings deposits and stock market investments'.[15]

For a bond to qualify to be held in a PEP, it must have an average maturity of greater than five years. Debbie Harrison, in her exacting study on PEPs, *Good PEPs Guide*, says, 'The government is partly responsible for the potential volatility of corporate bond PEPs because it insists that qualifying bonds must have at least five years to run before maturity. This,' she explains, 'directs capital towards the long-term needs of industry (an underlying motive for introducing corporate bond PEPs) but at the same time forcing the fund to take on the risk of volatility of capital.'[16]

## REFERENCES

[1] 'Decide on a strategy then work on a shortlist,' by Helen Pridham, *Investors Chronicle*, 6 December 1996, p. 47.

[2] Data from 1 October 1996, 'Corporate Bond Peps', *PEP Talk*, Allenbridge Group, 1996.

[3] *Unit Trusts and How They Work* by C. L. Rosenheim and C. O. Merriman, London: Sir Isaac Pitman & Sons, Ltd., 1937, p. viii.

[4] *A Guide to Investment Trusts & Unit Trusts* by Joanna Slaughter, Pitman Publishing, 1996, p. 105.

[5] Ibid., p. 105.

[6] 'Survey: Corporate Bond Peps' by Pauline Skypala, *Money Management*, February 1996, p. 23.

[7] Data from 1 October 1996, 'Corporate Bond Peps', *PEP Talk*, Allenbridge Group, 1996.

[8] *Managers' Report*, Barclays Unicorn Gilt and Fixed Interest Income Trust, Barclays Unicorn, July 1996, p. 3.

[9] The Virgin Income PEP, Virgin Direct Personal Financial Services Ltd., October 1996.

[10] 'How Reed puts his formula to work' by Joanna Slaughter, *Money Observer*, October 1996, p. 22.

[11] *Managers' Report*, Barclays Unicorn Gilt and Fixed Interest Income Trust, Barclays Unicorn, July 1996, p. 3.

[12] Data from 1 October 1996, 'Corporate Bond Peps', *PEP Talk*, Allenbridge Group, 1996.

[13] Trust Update, Sector Growth, *Money Management*, February 1996, p. 68.

[14] 'Of Extra Interest', in *A Practical Guide to Tax-Free Savings*, Volume 6, p. 42.

[15] 'Abtrust leads the pack in race for high income,' by Joanna Slaughter, *Money Observer*, October 1996, p. 21.

[16] *Good PEPs Guide* by Debbie Harrison (London: Pitman Publishing), 1996, p. 81.

# SUMMARY

- Bonds are medium-term, medium-volatility investments.

- Gilt and fixed-interest unit trusts generally provide greater income than equity investments.

- When interest rates rise, bond prices decrease and vice versa.

- The longer the time for the bond to become due, the higher the income and the higher the volatility.

- Be careful about the yield advertised in the paper.

- The running yield is the interest paid on your investment.

- The redemption yield is the interest paid plus any potential gain or loss in principal.

Before you invest:

- find out the redemption yield and running yield

- check out the annual management charge and the spread.

# Chapter 11

# THE RULES
# OF THE
# EQUITY GAME

In the *Financial Times* we read that, 'A second wave of extreme nervousness about the vulnerability of Wall Street hit European stock markets yesterday driving UK stocks lower.' The next day, thank goodness, 'benign economic news [inflation figures gave no cause for concern] lifted UK equities'.[1]

The market, of course, consists of millions of investors. To read the daily market reports, you would think that these millions of investors sit with their eyes and ears firmly tuned in to every single economic and political event of even slight import, ready to buy or sell. This of course does not happen. But it does raise the question: how do you know in what and when to invest?

Of Anthony Bolton, Fidelity Funds Special Situations portfolio manager, who has obtained long-term, stellar, consistent performance, James Morton writes, 'first and foremost, he is looking for unfashionable and undervalued stocks'.[2]

Neil Woodford, senior fund manager at Perpetual, on the Perpetual High Interest and Income Funds (combined size: £1,600 million): 'We focus on undervalued stocks wherever they are. We can go to small companies, if small companies look good; we can go to the Footsie Blue Chips, if that's attractive; we can go to recovery shares. We're fundamentally focused, we don't use technical charts.'

> '. . . how do you know in what and when to invest?'

Former *Investors Chronicle* editor Michael Brett summarises by saying, 'The aim of investment analysts and managers and of commentators in the financial press is to find companies which are undervalued relative to their growth prospects.'[3]

There are as many ways to make money as to lose it. This and the next five chapters, Chapters 11 to 16, examine the task of picking a winning equity unit trust. Our aim, as before, is to break the analysis down to the relevant pieces: the various investment styles and geographic choices, where the return comes from, the volatility

**Fig 11.1 Timing class of investments**

| Timing Class | Investment | Return | | Volatility |
|---|---|---|---|---|
| Short-term | Cash | Lowest | 4.7% | Least |
| Medium-term | Bonds | Medium | 7.3% | Medium |
| **Long-term** | **Equity** | **Highest** | **12.8%** | **Highest** |

associated with the performance, the magical elixir of consistency, and the fund management company. We'll determine what the past can and cannot teach us. In the meantime, note that the investment with the highest return – 12.8 per cent – and highest volatility is equity, in the long-term timing class (see Figure 11.1).

## HOW DO *YOU* PICK A UNIT TRUST?

In my research into the topic, I asked key players in the unit trust investment management business, 'How do you pick a unit trust?', and then remained quiet. The next section is spent listening to how the experts responded.

I spent a good part of one afternoon talking with Gartmore's Duncan Trinder who has been, he says, 'in the City a long, long time'. He managed funds for Bankers Trust and presently manages one of the larger UK growth funds, Gartmore's British Growth Fund. I asked Trinder what investors should consider when looking at a fund. He replied:

- Make sure the fund manager doesn't have other commitments and is the only one responsible for stock selection.
- Make sure the fund size is manageable.

There's much controversy about the effect of fund size on performance. Everyone has an opinion, but the facts are not clear.

At this point in our discussion, Brian O'Neill joined us. O'Neill, a portfolio manager and director of Gartmore, manages the European Selected Opportunities Fund for Gartmore which aims to 'achieve the highest possible capital growth from an actively managed portfolio of European investments'.

O'Neill suggested that, 'Investors should try to get behind the numbers.' For example, 'If it's a small companies fund, investors should know the extra risk they're taking on.' He went on to say

> 'There's much controversy about the effect of fund size on performance.'

that the UK market is fairly mature. To outperform the market over the long-term, for fund managers to beat the index, 'you've got to stay away from the UK and the US', because these are over-researched markets. 'To outperform, you've got to go to Europe, which is not as efficient.' ('Efficient' in this context means well-researched and followed by many analysts and investors.) He concluded, 'An investor should seek consistency and a balanced approach', between growth and value. He complains that the industry is too fashion-driven. 'Everyone wants to identify the new idea.'

I next spoke to Clive Boothman, managing director for unit trusts for Schroders and chair of the industry group, The Association of Unit Trusts and Investment Funds (AUTIF). With solid credentials, he's engaging and thoughtful with a boyish appearance that hides his 14 years in the business. His responses were reasoned. The first step is to know thyself, before plunging headfirst into the market.

'First,' he said, 'look for a fund that fits your lifestyle, one that suits your personal risk profile.'

Then, he said, 'Go through a checklist,' be methodical about it. He said the first stop on your checklist should be past performance, 'which is easy to tabulate, it's easy to objectify'.

He pointed out that, 'If you pick the stellar performer in any one year, it's possible that that one won't do so well in the following year.' He said, 'Investors should be aware of what factors made it perform well in the past' – are those factors still present today to offer the possibility of good performance in the future?

'Is the good team still in place?' he asked rhetorically, referring to the portfolio managers.

His next comment echoed what virtually everyone I spoke to in the industry said about selecting a fund. He said, 'Investors should choose a fund sponsored by a fund manager which has a reputation for that particular style of fund.' Some fund management companies have reputations for performance or for income or for specialities. We'll look at how to address this issue, in the chapter on evaluating a fund management company.

Further, he described a difference in portfolio management policies, using his house, Schroders, and Perpetual as examples of two extremes. He said, 'Perpetual has stellar fund managers who are responsible themselves for performance. They attract good managers.'

'Schroders,' on the other hand, 'has committees with economists that put together lots of information.' The Schroders asset allocation committee decides the current fund policies and then give their managers specific directions about how to invest. Boothman says that their portfolio managers 'only exercise their judgements consistent with the guidelines'.

'If we find a manager isn't performing consistently with his particular market and mandate, we'll take a closer look at his investments.' He warns investors to be cautious in switching out of a fund, and indeed practises what he preaches, 'You shouldn't lose faith too soon unless there's good reason. You have to ask yourselves, as we do, "why do these people still deserve this confidence". Sometimes we make a change. It's rare, but we do.'

Roger Cornick, marketing director at Perpetual, concurs with Boothman about Perpetual's fund management style. Cornick said, 'We've always sought the best managers. People come here for managerial freedom,' he added. 'We have a formal agreement with our managers, that basically says they will achieve the fund's objectives. We set up a benchmark, and then keep track of it frequently. If the manager is outperforming his benchmark each month, we examine his record very closely – he could be taking on excessive risk. If he is consistently underperforming his benchmark, we try to understand why. We keep pressure off,' he said seriously, 'but we keep monitoring.'

Perpetual's Cornick echoes Schroders' Boothman in his suggestions about picking the right unit trust:

- 'Above all else, look for consistency.'
- 'This month's high-flyer, you should stay away from. Where British press, investors, and advisors get confused is when they look at one-year returns. People should be investing over a lifetime. Look for the one with a long, consistent record.'
- 'A good fund house picks up good press,' he suggests to investors in search of a fund management company. Given Perpetual has achieved incredible publicity and a reputation as a house with top performance, it's not a surprise that he suggests this.

Another important filter in choosing a fund is the fund management company itself. Cornick says, 'Investors above all else are choosing "confidence and trust".' He says Perpetual have tried to provide this for its investors.

Cornick suggests following a negative screen to narrow down fund management companies: 'Which ones wouldn't I choose?'

- 'Don't look at funds without a certain critical mass.' (Meaning look to larger fund management companies with the resources to support research and administration.)
- 'Look at all funds sponsored by the house and if no funds are in the top quartile,' look elsewhere.
- 'Do you feel comfortable with the fund management companies still on the list?'
- Finally: 'Do you like banks or life assurance companies?' Cornick asks with a smile, given the reputation of banks and life assurance companies in the performance tables.

He raises a good point. The prime business of banks and life assurance companies is not unit trust fund management. However, I would suggest you take a hard look at the performance and strengths of the fund management companies – all of them. For instance, Barclays Bank is among the largest fund management company and has the largest gilt and fixed interest fund, Barclays Unicorn Gilt and Fixed Interest, whose performance we looked at in Chapter 10.

Engaging Mary Blair, director of product development at Threadneedle Asset Management, joins the growing chorus of consistency, explaining that the 'The investor must first know what he wants. Look at consistency over three and five years. Make sure the fund is consistently top quartile. Look at the fund management and the house management.' She suggests 'You've got to make sure there's consistency across the Group. A big house achieves economies of scale, they can deal better.' But, she implies, the small houses can be just as successful.

'Is there any one investment style which is better or worse than the others?' I asked her.

'No, any style can work.'

She complains that in the unit trust industry, 'There's a real tendency to use long words just to confuse you.' She counsels new investors 'to learn, learn to get the jargon, learn to look at the performance tables'. She warns, 'Stay away from the short-term performance literature.'

'There's always a fund *du jour*,' adds Mercury unit trust division managing director, Richard Royds. Royds said they'd recently changed their measurement system. 'Fund managers are told not to compete with other fund managers [which is encouraged by the monthly publication of league tables], and instead, we gave them a target to beat the FTSE by 2 per cent.' He stated that performance had really improved and allowed Mercury's fund managers to be more 'contemplative about investing' instead of chasing after the unit trust sector league tables.

Paul Calkin, an IFA who manages the firm his father started in 1964, is very involved in analysing and recommending unit trusts. He recommends the following list.

- **Regular consistent performance:** 'We want to make sure it's not a flash in the pan.'
- **Fund manager:** 'Technically solid?'
- **Cash flow position:** 'Is money flowing into fund?'
- **Fund size:** 'If fund gets too large, it's too hard to handle.'

## THE FINAL LIST

There are some general characteristics which should be known about any fund before investment. These begin to form a checklist. Unfortunately, I cannot give you a right or wrong answer for how these items are checked. The idea is to give you a feel for the fund, how it is being managed.

There are several messages from the above comments, which form the basis of our checklist. See the box on page 182 for the checklist, then we'll go about showing you the technique to monitor.

---

### Equity investor's checklist

**1** Investor, know thyself:
- Develop shortlist of appropriate risk-rated investment areas.

**2** Choose a consistently performing unit trust:
- Come up with shortlist of funds.
- How much money is in the fund, relative to others in its sector and relative to a year ago?
- Has the fund manager changed recently?
- What is the style of the fund and its volatility?

**3** Look at the fund management company:
- Come up with shortlist.
- Do they have many top-performing funds?
- How large are they?
- Do they have a parent with deep pockets.
- What's their reputation?

**4** Invest

---

# IT BEGINS WITH STOCKMARKET PRICES

Before stepping into the first 'narrowing-down topic, the type of unit trust, we take a short look at some of the basics of stockmarket pricing and evaluation.

Equities refers to the shares of stock that own a company. The term 'equities' is synonymous with 'company capital' and 'shares'. Typically, the firm begins by private contributions from the entrepreneur and a small group of friends in exchange for shares of ownership. As the firm grows, it raises additional money from outside investors. When the entrepreneur can no longer raise money from people he or she knows, the company goes public, and agrees with an underwriting firm to sell a portion of ownership to public investors.

After the company has gone public, the original shareholders can sell their shares to others. They sell these shares usually through an exchange, such as the London Stock Exchange or the New York Stock Exchange. In some instances, these shares can be sold between stockbrokers and not over an exchange.

The key ingredient here is that the shares can be sold by the original shareholders to others, who in turn can sell these shares to others. There is no limit to the number of times these shares can be sold.

Each day, in newspapers, you find voluminous prices of securities, printed in extremely small typefaces. These prices reflect the hopes, aspirations, bets, hedges, and financing means of modern society. Some say that security prices are random; yet, the amount of blood, sweat, and tears expended on these prices is far from random.

There are many means of evaluating the price, which is typically done in relation to the price of other similar securities. Professor Jeremy J. Siegel in his *Stocks for the Long Run*, says, 'Most financial advisors rely on the fundamental building blocks of stock value – dividends and earnings – to direct their market decisions.' Unlike other investments, such as art, which has the benefit that you can admire it on the wall, the only reason shares have value is 'because of the potential cash flows, called dividends, which a stockholder expects to receive from her share of the ownership of the firm.'[4]

Professor Siegel says that 'The value of any asset [share price] is determined by the discounted value of all future expected cash flows.'[5]

The theoretical concept behind valuing a share price is as follows:

| Share | =Dividend | Dividend | Dividend | ...Share Price when |
|-------|-----------|----------|----------|---------------------|
| Price | *Next Year* | *in 2 years* | *in 3 years* | *...sold in the future* |
| Today | 1 yr interest factor | 2 yr interest factor | 3 yr interest factor | Interest factor when sold |

Obviously, it is very difficult to work out what something will be worth in the future? However, the equation is a basic one from which all ratios used to estimate value are derived.

So, the main means of evaluating shares is to look at the growth potential for the company. Growth in earnings per share is what fuels the share price. A fast-growing company is likely to have a fast-growing share price. You would rather have more profits growing faster than fewer profits growing more slowly, as would the rest of the market. Accordingly, the price of rapidly growing companies advances faster than those of slow-moving tortoises.

The growth-oriented investor aims to discover those companies whose fast-growing earnings will be recognised by the market; ergo, the shares advance faster than the average share.

The statistic capturing this information is the price/earnings (P/E) ratio, which gives a snapshot of the growth prospects of the company; it is less complex than the formula for calculating the theoretical value of a share, hinted at by Professor Siegel. This is the number one statistic used by investment specialists around the world to value securities. It's quick, easy to understand, and translates across languages. It is so familiar that sometimes it is just called the multiple, short for the multiple of price to earnings.

Figure 11.2 gives the share prices and price/earnings ratios of four bank shares chosen at random on one day in December 1996.

**Fig 11.2  Share prices and price/earnings ratios of four bank shares on 12 December 1996**

| Bank | Price | Price/earnings ratio |
|------|-------|----------------------|
| Lloyds | 419 | 17.7 |
| Bank of Scotland | 288 | 10.6 |
| Barclays | 1028.5 | 11.2 |
| NatWest | 666 | 9.5 |
| **Finance industry average** | — | **13.4** |

Source: Financial Times, 12 December 1996, p. 44.

You can see by Lloyds' high P/E ratio that the market views its growth prospects higher than for the industry in general and for the other three companies as well. The other approach is to view the other three banks' lower ratios as signalling greater value.

In a related fashion, fast-growing companies tend to pay lower or no dividends, preferring instead to conserve their capital for future growth instead of cash dividend payouts. Alternatively, slower growth companies, those with lower P/E ratios do pay out more of their earnings in dividends. Hence, lower growth companies tend to have stocks with higher income payouts. Hence, as we'll see, the two key words in the unit trust market are 'growth' and 'income' or 'value'.

That's the theory. There are many, many more exceedingly complicated variants of the above ratios. The basic concepts are simple: if it looks as if the company is growing faster than other companies, this is a 'growth' situation. Conversely, if the market values the earnings of one company lower than other similar shares, then this is said to be a 'value' opportunity.

Neil Woodford, a senior fund manager at Perpetual in charge of its High Income Fund, said that he was always on the lookout for undervalued situations, be they growth or value stocks.

In *The Warren Buffet Way*, the story of America's richest and most famous investor, Buffet 'admits that years ago, he participated in this intellectual tug-of-war. Today he thinks the debate between these two schools of thought is nonsense. Growth and value investing are joined at the hip,' says Buffet. 'Value is the discounted present value of an investment's future cash flow; growth is simply a calculation used to determine value.'[6]

## MANAGEMENT STYLES

Equity unit trust funds are broadly categorised as either 'actively' or 'passively' managed. 'Active management' is where the fund manager picks shares that he believes will increase. When he no longer believes there is potential for growth, he sells those shares to buy others with more potential.

The other major category is called 'passive management' and refers to a fund investment manager who buys shares in a stock market index, such as the *Financial Times* Stock Exchange Index of 100 large shares (the so-called 'Footsie') or the FTSE All-Share Stock Index. The aim is not to beat the index, but, instead to track right along with the index. This has become very popular in recent years. The fund manager in this instance has very complicated technical issues to deal with, but the one issue he doesn't deal with is choosing shares that are undervalued.

This chapter continues with a discussion of active stock-picking, which is the basis of the majority of unit trusts. In Chapter 15, we examine index-tracking.

# BEGINNING TO NARROW IT DOWN

To help you narrow your search, the industry divides funds into categories that broadly describe the aims of the fund. First, we find a style description: income funds (which would be classified as the 'value' funds), growth funds, or growth and income. Secondly, there is a geographic component, UK, Europe, North America, and so on. There is a size classification, smaller companies.

Unit trust funds come in many varieties, yet, at the end of the day, the fund manager usually lines up on one side or the other of the value/growth divide.

On the other hand, there are many recovery or special situations funds. These funds would fall firmly in the value camp, those that pick undervalued situations.

## Gartmore's British Growth Fund

Duncan Trinder's style is at odds with that of many of his younger brethren. He runs Gartmore's British Growth Fund, which despite its classification as an equity growth fund, looks more like a value-oriented fund (see Figure 11.3). Indeed, the *Financial Times* noted that his was more a 'cautious' growth fund (their words). The article's author claimed that even though the fund's volatility was about average, the returns were above average, suggesting that 'superior management was at work'.[7]

As we looked out on the Monument, facing Gartmore's offices in the City, Trinder said his fund's goals were to:

- consistently beat the market;
- provide liquidity to investors at all times (which means that you can sell out of the fund without affecting the price of the fund);
- minimise the volatility of the fund.

He explained his hypothesis to achieve these aims: 'a focused list of large companies'. He said that he didn't want to 'get into a redemption problem with small caps', that is, to have trouble selling smaller capitalised shares when no market-maker is willing to offer a sensible price for them.

The aim of his fund is 'to provide investors with long-term capital growth by investing in a carefully selected range of leading UK equities'.

## Fig 11.3 Gartmore British Growth

### Gartmore British Growth

Gartmore Broker Unit Trusts, Gartmore House, PO Box 65, 16-18 Monument Street, London EC3R 8QQ.

Information: Telephone - 0171 782 2000   Dealing - 01277 264 421

**Fund Objective:**
To provide investors with long-term capital growth by investing in a carefully selected range of leading United Kingdom equities.

| Micropal Cumulative Performance - to 30th September 1996 | | | | | |
|---|---|---|---|---|---|
| Performance Period | 6 Months | 1 Year | 3 Years | 5 Years | 10 Years |
| Fund Performance | +0.0% | +9.1% | +24.7% | +72.3% | |
| Sector Average | +1.3% | +10.7% | +32.2% | +71.7% | +177.0% |
| Best Performing Fund | +17.0% | +36.7% | +71.0% | +143.8% | +325.7% |
| Fund Performance / Sector Average Performance | | | | | |
| Worst Performing Fund | -6.4% | -1.7% | +6.8% | +2.4% | +59.6% |

(Offer-bid, net income reinvested)

| | 6 Months | 1 Year | 3 Years | 5 Years | 10 Years |
|---|---|---|---|---|---|
| Top Quartile | | | | | |
| Second Quartile | | | | 47/126 | |
| Third Quartile | 108/159 | 90/152 | | | |
| Bottom Quartile | | | 104/137 | | |

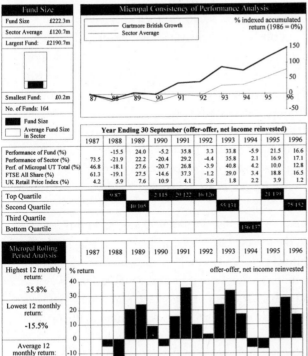

| Fund Size | | Micropal Consistency of Performance Analysis |
|---|---|---|
| Fund Size | £222.3m | |
| Sector Average | £120.7m | |
| Largest Fund: | £2190.7m | |
| Smallest Fund: | £0.2m | |
| No. of Funds: | 164 | |

Gartmore British Growth — Sector Average

% indexed accumulated return (1986 = 0%)

| Year Ending 30 September (offer-offer, net income reinvested) | | | | | | | | | | |
|---|---|---|---|---|---|---|---|---|---|---|
| | 1987 | 1988 | 1989 | 1990 | 1991 | 1992 | 1993 | 1994 | 1995 | 1996 |
| Performance of Fund (%) | | -15.5 | 24.0 | -5.2 | 35.8 | 3.3 | 33.8 | -5.9 | 21.5 | 16.6 |
| Performance of Sector (%) | 73.5 | -21.9 | 22.2 | -20.4 | 29.2 | -4.4 | 35.8 | 2.1 | 16.9 | 17.1 |
| Perf. of Micropal UT Total (%) | 46.8 | -18.1 | 27.6 | -20.7 | 26.8 | -3.9 | 40.8 | 4.2 | 10.0 | 12.8 |
| FTSE All Share (%) | 61.3 | -19.1 | 27.5 | -14.6 | 37.3 | -1.2 | 29.0 | 3.4 | 18.8 | 16.5 |
| UK Retail Price Index (%) | 4.2 | 5.9 | 7.6 | 10.9 | 4.1 | 3.6 | 1.8 | 2.2 | 3.9 | 1.2 |

| | 1987 | 1988 | 1989 | 1990 | 1991 | 1992 | 1993 | 1994 | 1995 | 1996 |
|---|---|---|---|---|---|---|---|---|---|---|
| Top Quartile | | 9/87 | | 2/115 | 29/122 | 16/126 | | | 21/139 | |
| Second Quartile | | | 10/105 | | | | 55/131 | | | 75/152 |
| Third Quartile | | | | | | | | | | |
| Bottom Quartile | | | | | | | 136/137 | | | |

| Micropal Rolling Period Analysis | 1987 | 1988 | 1989 | 1990 | 1991 | 1992 | 1993 | 1994 | 1995 | 1996 |
|---|---|---|---|---|---|---|---|---|---|---|
| Highest 12 monthly return: 35.8% | | | | | | | | | | |
| Lowest 12 monthly return: -15.5% | | | | | | | | | | |
| Average 12 monthly return: 12.3% | | | | | | | | | | |

% return | offer-offer, net income reinvested

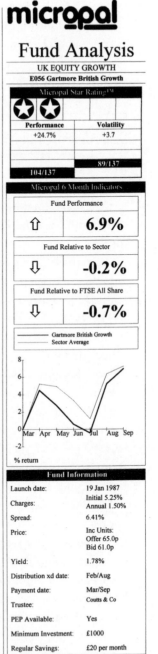

# micropal

# Fund Analysis

**UK EQUITY GROWTH**

**E056 Gartmore British Growth**

| Micropal Star Rating™ | |
|---|---|
| Performance | Volatility |
| +24.7% | +3.7 |
| 104/137 | 89/137 |

**Micropal 6 Month Indicators**

| Fund Performance |
|---|
| ⇧ **6.9%** |

| Fund Relative to Sector |
|---|
| ⇩ **-0.2%** |

| Fund Relative to FTSE All Share |
|---|
| ⇩ **-0.7%** |

Gartmore British Growth — Sector Average

% return

**Fund Information**

| | |
|---|---|
| Launch date: | 19 Jan 1987 |
| Charges: | Initial 5.25% Annual 1.50% |
| Spread: | 6.41% |
| Price: | Inc Units: Offer 65.0p Bid 61.0p |
| Yield: | 1.78% |
| Distribution xd date: | Feb/Aug |
| Payment date: | Mar/Sep |
| Trustee: | Coutts & Co |
| PEP Available: | Yes |
| Minimum Investment: | £1000 |
| Regular Savings: | £20 per month |

*Source: Micropal*

The first thing he did when he took over the fund in 1989 was to reduce the holdings in the portfolio from 100 shares to 25. He believes that 'it is extremely difficult for a fund manager to follow 200 companies when everything is changing'. Today, the fund's total value is £222 million, one of the largest funds in the UK Equity Growth sector. However, as the market strained to new heights Trinder's fund held back: falling from a first quartile rank in 1994 to a third quartile ranking by 1996.

## Schroder UK Equity Fund

Among the largest, most consistent performers in the growth and income category is Schroder UK Equity Fund (see Figure 11.4). £50 a month for the last ten years, totalling £6,000, would equal £12,742 today. I became aware of this fund via the BRUT technique which captures consistent high performers.

From these strong results, I rang up Philip Hardy, portfolio manager and requested ten minutes of his time. About three-quarters of an hour later, I realised I had met a man who lives and breathes stocks.

Mr Hardy's fund is one of the largest available today, £888 million, while the average fund in the equity growth and income category is £137 million. When Mr Hardy took over managing this fund, it was worth a mere £60 million. Because of strong, consistent performance, he continues to attract substantial new money from investors each year.

How good has the performance been? Each of the last five years, his fund has ranked in the top quartile of funds. Total five-year performance has been 90 per cent, including fees and taxes, whereas the average fund in the sector has performed at only 62 per cent: two-thirds of the Schroder UK Equity Fund level.

Mr Hardy's fund maintains a portfolio of about 90 stocks. Hardy says he always stays invested with the top ten UK stocks in size and as a general rule, maintains the same weighting in his fund as in the overall market. He gives an example: 'British Petroleum makes up 4 per cent of the market, so I'll aim to keep 4 per cent of the fund in BP.' At various times, depending on his outlook, he'll increase or decrease the weighting of these stocks relative to the market. He says that the top ten companies make up 26 per cent of the market.

His aim, like almost all portfolio managers I spoke with, is 'to beat the market consistently and to be among the top quartile of funds in the sector'. Unlike many portfolio managers, though, he has been able to achieve this goal.

## Fig 11.4  Schroder UK Equity

### Schroder UK Equity

Schroder Unit Trusts, Senator House, 85 Queen Victoria Street, London  EC4V 4EJ.

Information: Telephone - 0800 526 535    Dealing - 0800 526540

**Fund Objective:**
To achieve capital growth through investment in UK equities.

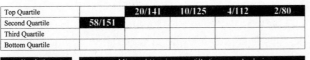

| Micropal Cumulative Performance - to 30th September 1996 | | | | | |
|---|---|---|---|---|---|
| Performance Period | 6 Months | 1 Year | 3 Years | 5 Years | 10 Years |
| Fund Performance | +1.8% | +12.0% | +37.1% | +89.6% | +281.2% |
| Sector Average | +1.3% | +8.3% | +27.4% | +61.6% | +189.5% |
| Best Performing Fund | +8.6% | +17.2% | +44.9% | +95.2% | +431.0% |
| Fund Performance ▮ Sector Average Performance ▯ | | | | | |
| Worst Performing Fund | -10.7% | -7.7% | +6.8% | +27.1% | +111.7% |

(Offer-bid, net income reinvested)

| | | 20/141 | 10/125 | 4/112 | 2/80 |
|---|---|---|---|---|---|
| Top Quartile | | | | | |
| Second Quartile | 58/151 | | | | |
| Third Quartile | | | | | |
| Bottom Quartile | | | | | |

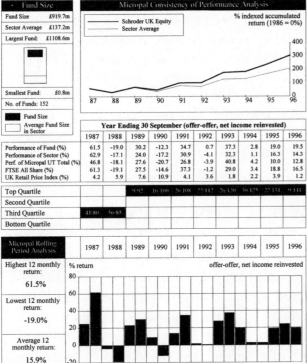

| Fund Size | |
|---|---|
| Fund Size | £919.7m |
| Sector Average | £137.2m |
| Largest Fund | £1108.6m |
| Smallest Fund | £0.8m |
| No. of Funds: 152 | |

**Micropal Consistency of Performance Analysis**

Schroder UK Equity / Sector Average
% indexed accumulated return (1986 = 0%)

**Year Ending 30 September (offer-offer, net income reinvested)**

| | 1987 | 1988 | 1989 | 1990 | 1991 | 1992 | 1993 | 1994 | 1995 | 1996 |
|---|---|---|---|---|---|---|---|---|---|---|
| Performance of Fund (%) | 61.5 | -19.0 | 30.2 | -12.3 | 34.7 | 0.7 | 37.3 | 2.8 | 19.0 | 19.5 |
| Performance of Sector (%) | 62.9 | -17.1 | 24.0 | -17.2 | 30.9 | -4.1 | 32.3 | 1.1 | 16.3 | 14.3 |
| Perf. of Micropal UT Total (%) | 46.8 | -18.1 | 27.6 | -20.7 | 26.8 | -3.9 | 40.8 | 4.2 | 10.0 | 12.8 |
| FTSE All Share (%) | 61.3 | -19.1 | 27.5 | -14.6 | 37.3 | -1.2 | 29.0 | 3.4 | 18.8 | 16.5 |
| UK Retail Price Index (%) | 4.2 | 5.9 | 7.6 | 10.9 | 4.1 | 3.6 | 1.8 | 2.2 | 3.9 | 1.2 |

| | 1987 | 1988 | 1989 | 1990 | 1991 | 1992 | 1993 | 1994 | 1995 | 1996 |
|---|---|---|---|---|---|---|---|---|---|---|
| Top Quartile | | | 9/92 | 16/100 | 26/108 | 22/112 | 26/120 | 30/125 | 22/131 | 9/141 |
| Second Quartile | | | | | | | | | | |
| Third Quartile | 41/80 | 56/85 | | | | | | | | |
| Bottom Quartile | | | | | | | | | | |

| Micropal Rolling Period Analysis | 1987 | 1988 | 1989 | 1990 | 1991 | 1992 | 1993 | 1994 | 1995 | 1996 |
|---|---|---|---|---|---|---|---|---|---|---|
| Highest 12 monthly return: 61.5% | | | | | | | | | | |
| Lowest 12 monthly return: -19.0% | | | | | | | | | | |
| Average 12 monthly return: 15.9% | | | | | | | | | | |

offer-offer, net income reinvested

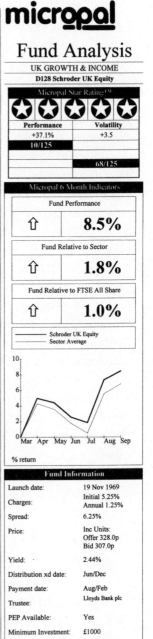

*Source: Micropal*

He explains that by not holding these large shares, you could be significantly affected when the market moves and you miss out.

The rest of the portfolio is constructed from a top-down and bottom-up approach. I would label this 'opportunistic'. He evaluates the economy and the current situation to determine which sectors are likely to benefit from, say, low-inflation, low-interest-rate, strong-growth economy, as we are experiencing at the time of writing.

For the medium-sized companies, he says it is 'key to take a contrarian approach. We don't chase companies which have already had big run-ups. You have to be brave because you can never get in at the absolute bottom.' But if a company's shares have been lying dormant for five, six, or seven years, he'll take a close look. In these situations, he believes there's going to be some activity as the market re-examines its assumptions. He says that sometimes you see shares that have been subject to continued selling over the years as investors give up on them. He says, everyone who's going to sell, has sold.

'Finally, at some point, there's so much value in these shares.' His voice picks up in excitement. 'Everyone's saying, 'I've had enough . . . I'm throwing in the towel.' Hardy adds, that if he can see positive trends developing, then he'll buy. 'But you have to be brave,' he adds. 'If you're looking at the bottom of the market, with high yields, they're almost paying you to hold the stock,' he says, noting the pure value approach of buying high-yielding stocks, which, by definition, have low prices.

He doesn't like to have uninvested cash lying around. He believes investors pay him to remain fully invested. Occasionally, though, he sits on cash for up to three days, clearly not the technique of the long-term market timer.

## NO RETURN WITHOUT RISK

Each style of stock selection generates a different return as demonstrated by the five-year average annual return chart (see Figure 11.4). Clearly, if there was nothing more involved, you would pick the highest returning category, UK Smaller Companies. But no return is without risk and this second, complementary, aspect must be taken into consideration. We turn, in the next chapter, to the volatility component.

## Fig 11.5 Five year average annual returns by sector

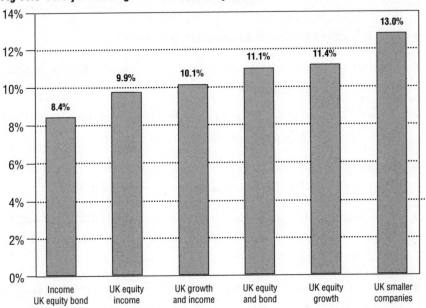

Source: Money Management, November 1996.

## REFERENCES

1 'Wall St fear factor returns to haunt Footsie' by Steve Thompson, *Financial Times*, 12 December 1996, p. 46.
2 *Investing with the Grand Masters* by James Morton (London: Pitman Publishing, 1997), p. 47
3 *How to Read the Financial Pages* by Michael Brett (London: Century Limited), 4th ed., 1995, p. 119.
4 *Stocks for the Long Run* by Jeremy J. Siegel (Burr Ridge, Illinois: Richard D. Irwin Publishers, Inc., 1994), p. 65.
5 Ibid., p. 66.
6 *The Warren Buffet Way: Investment Strategies of the World's Greatest Investor* by Robert G. Hagstrom, Jr. (New York: John Wiley & Sons, Inc., 1994), p. 95.
7 'A sector in need of facts,' by John Cuthbert, *Financial Times Weekend*, 19–20 February 1994, p. 25.

# SUMMARY

- Equities refers to shares of ownership in companies.

- Equities provide the highest return – coupled with the highest volatility.

- Growth unit trusts offer potential for higher capital gains, but don't generally pay much in income.

- Income or value unit trusts provide higher current income but also offer potential of capital gains.

- Most equity unit trusts are actively managed: fund managers decide to buy or sell shares based on his or her view on future direction of company shares.

- Passive fund managers never makes a decision about a stock's potential; they buy shares to track an index.

Before you invest in equity unit trusts:

- invest only your long-term funds

- get all the available documents from the fund management company.

# Chapter 12

# VOLATILITY'S THE NAME OF THE GAME

Premier Investment's team gained notoriety with Morgan Grenfell, and unit trust investor fame, when they accurately assessed the growing volatility of Morgan Grenfell's European Growth Fund. About six months prior to parent Deutsche Bank's £180 million injection into the European Growth Fund to make up for irregularities, Premier noticed that the fund's volatility had grown dramatically. Jonathan Fry, a Premier Investment director, rang up Morgan Grenfell to ask why the volatility had increased; they stonewalled him. Premier, in exasperation, cashed in £800,000 worth of European Growth units of client funds. Afterwards, he says that he was treated coolly by Morgan Grenfell.

Brian O'Neill, the portfolio manager of Gartmore's European Selected Opportunities Fund, whom we met in Chapter 11, pulls out a chart depicting the monthly trend of his fund versus the European Growth Fund. While the performance of the competitor's fund was stronger, the zigs and zags of the European Growth Fund was considerably pronounced. He says of the Morgan Grenfell's European Growth's investment manager, 'He's taking big bets. Investors should be aware of this.'

The key was following the volatility (see Figure 12.1). The fund was performing quite well, too well, in fact; volatility had advanced substantially. The one-year return was nearly double the sector average and, right before the news broke, the volatility had increased to more than twice the sector average. Risk and return go hand in hand. The message is, pay attention to the volatility figures, readily available. They must be compared with other funds in the same league.

You can't examine return without considering the flip side, volatility. If a share didn't go up or down, you would say that it had no return and no volatility. If the share can go up – return – then it can also go down – negative return. Volatility is a good thing. Usually

**Fig 12.1 Morgan Grenfell European Growth Fund: return and volatility comparison**

|  | FT S&P Index Europe ex UK | Morgan Grenfell European Growth |
|---|---|---|
| Annual Average Return | 26% | 49% |
| Annual Volatility | 6% | 16% |

Source: Micropal from Premier Investments data from 1 May 1995 to 1 May 1996.

194

'risk' refers to the likelihood that the investment can go in only one direction – down. Nobody complains about positive volatility. We cherish equities when they move up, and condemn them when they move down. But it is all part of the same package: stocks move up and stocks move down.

> 'You can't examine return, the potential gains you make, without considering the flip side, volatility.'

In this chapter, we assess two kinds of volatility: the monthly volatility which results in any market-based investment and the potential for fraud, an unquantifiable risk. At the conclusion of Chapter 11, we saw a list of UK equity unit trust sectors and their returns (Figure 11.4). This is looking at only one side of the equation; you need consider the other side: the likelihood that you'll earn the return promised by the average return. And, as we've seen all along, return and volatility need to fit snugly into your overall financial scheme.

## THE UNQUANTIFIABLE RISK

Philip Robinson, chief operating officer of the Investment Management Regulatory Organisation (IMRO), says an investor's best weapon against devious business practices is to be informed. He says, 'If it looks too good to be true, it probably is.' IMRO serves as the industry's self-policing body.

> '. . . by understanding the way the unit trust business works, the potential rewards, and the potential volatility in unit prices, you can guard against the unexpected.'

Investors should ring IMRO's Ombudsman 'whenever they feel something isn't right'. IMRO's chief source of questionable business practices is investors calling to complain. The more understanding the investor has of what he or she should and should not expect, the less likely it is that fraud will be perpetrated. Thus by understanding the way the unit trust business works, the potential rewards, and the potential volatility in unit prices, you can guard against the unexpected.

Robinson says, 'People need to ask the right questions', and

# IMRO Dos and Don'ts*

- **Don't** deal with a firm that is not authorised. They are committing a criminal offence. If you lose your money, you will not be covered by a compensation scheme.

- **Don't** buy investments offered in unsolicited telephone 'cold calls', or let sales people pressurise you into buying investments. Ask for information in writing before you decide, and make sure you understand before you invest. If you are still concerned, seek professional advice.

- **Don't** invest in something you don't understand. Get advice.

- **Don't** assume that the person giving you advice is impartial. Ask if the person is a tied agent or an Independent Financial Advisor (IFA). Tied agents may only recommend the products of the company that employs them, whereas an IFA may recommend any company's products.

- **Don't** assume that you will definitely get your money back. Examine carefully any investment which offers a set return. Make sure you understand what is being offered, and on what terms.

- **Do** be sceptical of promises of quick profits or unusually high returns. High returns usually mean high risk.

- **Do** consider your attitude towards risk. Different investments carry different degrees of risk. Would it matter to you if the value of your investment fell?

- **Do** consider what you are trying to achieve. To keep pace with inflation? To make your money grow as much as possible? Also think about how long you can afford to tie-up your money. Most investments are designed to be held for the medium- or long-term.

- **Do** read all the investment literature, particularly the small print.

- **Do** look at the charges. Are they reasonable? Are they comparable to other similar firms' offers?

- **Do** remember that past investment performance is no guarantee of future returns.

- **Do** keep copies of all correspondence and literature.

- **Do** keep notes of all discussions you have with a firm.

\* Investor Dos and Don't – available on IMRO's website at www.imro.co.uk.
IMRO public enquiries available on 0171-390 5777.
IMRO Ombudsman available on 0171-796 3065.
Investors Compensation Scheme information available on 0171-628 8820.

suggests reading IMRO's list of dos and don'ts (see box). You'll find them remarkably like many of the suggestions in this book.

The other type of risk, the monthly volatility of investments, is much more addressable.

## HOW RISK-AVERSE ARE YOU?

I visited IFA Pascal Matic of the Unit Trust Advisory Service (UNITAS), in the heart of winter in Scunthorpe, where I was warmly welcomed into his office and house. I am very impressed by Matic's demeanour, professionalism, and his newsletter (P. A. Matic, UNITAS (01724) 849481). The newsletter is a good source of unit trust information, including unit trust manager shifts. Before the interview began, he asked about my risk attitude and gave me these choices:

- **very conservative**
- **conservative**
- **medium risk**
- **speculative.**

'Speculative,' I said.

He then asked me about my current holdings, which consist of an internationally diversified unit trust mixture of index-tracking and stock-picking funds.

He asked, with a puzzled look on his face: 'I thought you said you were "speculative"?'

'Well, to some people, this would probably reflect a speculative portfolio. OK, mark me down as "medium risk".'

All along I've tried not to use the word 'risk' because it only accentuates the negative, while ignoring the positive. In fact, I'd rather you consider only the time available for investment, short-, medium-, and long-term as this is something you have some control over, whereas volatility is a result of your choices, not affected by your choices.

In fact, his question, though typical, was incorrect. Had he said, 'How much are you willing to invest adventurously with your short-term, day-to-day funds?' I would have said, 'Not at all.' Had he posed the same question about my long-term savings, I would have said, 'Yes, that's how I propose to invest my long-term funds.'

> 'The real question is, "How much volatility can you shoulder for your different timing classes of funds?"'

I think that the question 'How risk-averse are you?', by the choice of words, begs the question. The real question is, 'How much volatility can you shoulder for your different timing classes of funds?'

The answer, probably for everyone, is:

- short-term: *not at all*
- medium-term: *some*
- long-term: *a lot.*

## GETTING HOLD OF VOLATILITY

Jonathan Fry, an investment director of Premier Investments, simplifies why volatility is important: 'Volatility is the zigs and zags in performance.' He says within any investment class, you want to balance high returns with low volatility. The reason for choosing a less volatile fund within any given sector is that when you decide to sell, it will vary less from its long-term growth trend than would a fund which is more volatile.

Consider two funds (see Figure 12.2): the first, Steady as She Goes, moves up over two years at an annual average rate of 12 per cent per year (or 1 per cent per month). The second fund, No Risk No Gain, grows by half that rate, 6 per cent per year (or 0.5 per cent per month) for the first year, but increases to 18 per cent (1.5 per cent per month) for the second year. In both instances, your £1,000 would have grown to £1,270 at the end of two years, through compounding.

Fig 12.2 Two funds: Same performance, different volatility

| Fund Name | Initial value | 1st year growth | Each month | 1st year end value | 2nd year growth | Each month | 2nd year end value |
|---|---|---|---|---|---|---|---|
| Steady as She Goes | £1,000 | 12% | 1% | £1,127 | 12% | 1% | £1,270 |
| No Risk No Gain | £1,000 | 6% | 0.5% | £1,062 | 18% | 1.5% | £1,270 |

The monthly results for the same funds are shown in Figure 12.3, and depicted graphically in Figure 12.4. Note that the fund with the varying performance has results that increase at a faster rate during the second year.

From the graph in Figure 12.4, we can derive the chart showing monthly returns for each of the 24 months (see Figure 12.5). You'll note that Steady moves along at 1 per cent per month (12 per cent annually) whereas No Risk, No Gain moves along at a slower rate and then bumps up to the higher rate. Keep in mind that the two-year performance of both funds is exactly the same. However, Steady moves up steadily, whereas No Risk No Gain drags along until the surprise performance causes it to move at a faster clip.

Steady shows no variability of returns, month after month, 1 per

**Fig 12.3 Two funds: monthly results**

|        |     | Steady as She Goes £1,000 | Monthly increase | No Risk No Gain £1,000 | Monthly increase |
|--------|-----|--------------------------|------------------|------------------------|------------------|
| Year 1 | Jan | £1,010 | 1.0% | £1,005 | 0.5% |
| Year 1 | Feb | £1,020 | 1.0% | £1,010 | 0.5% |
| Year 1 | Mar | £1,030 | 1.0% | £1,015 | 0.5% |
| Year 1 | Apr | £1,041 | 1.0% | £1,020 | 0.5% |
| Year 1 | May | £1,051 | 1.0% | £1,025 | 0.5% |
| Year 1 | Jun | £1,062 | 1.0% | £1,030 | 0.5% |
| Year 1 | Jul | £1,072 | 1.0% | £1,036 | 0.5% |
| Year 1 | Aug | £1,083 | 1.0% | £1,041 | 0.5% |
| Year 1 | Sep | £1,094 | 1.0% | £1,046 | 0.5% |
| Year 1 | Oct | £1,105 | 1.0% | £1,051 | 0.5% |
| Year 1 | Nov | £1,116 | 1.0% | £1,056 | 0.5% |
| Year 1 | Dec | £1,127 | 1.0% | £1,062 | 0.5% |
| Year 2 | Jan | £1,138 | 1.0% | £1,078 | 1.5% |
| Year 2 | Feb | £1,149 | 1.0% | £1,094 | 1.5% |
| Year 2 | Mar | £1,161 | 1.0% | £1,110 | 1.5% |
| Year 2 | Apr | £1,173 | 1.0% | £1,127 | 1.5% |
| Year 2 | May | £1,184 | 1.0% | £1,144 | 1.5% |
| Year 2 | Jun | £1,196 | 1.0% | £1,161 | 1.5% |
| Year 2 | Jul | £1,208 | 1.0% | £1,179 | 1.5% |
| Year 2 | Aug | £1,220 | 1.0% | £1,196 | 1.5% |
| Year 2 | Sep | £1,232 | 1.0% | £1,214 | 1.5% |
| Year 2 | Oct | £1,245 | 1.0% | £1,232 | 1.5% |
| Year 2 | Nov | £1,257 | 1.0% | £1,251 | 1.5% |
| Year 2 | Dec | £1,270 | 1.0% | £1,270 | 1.5% |

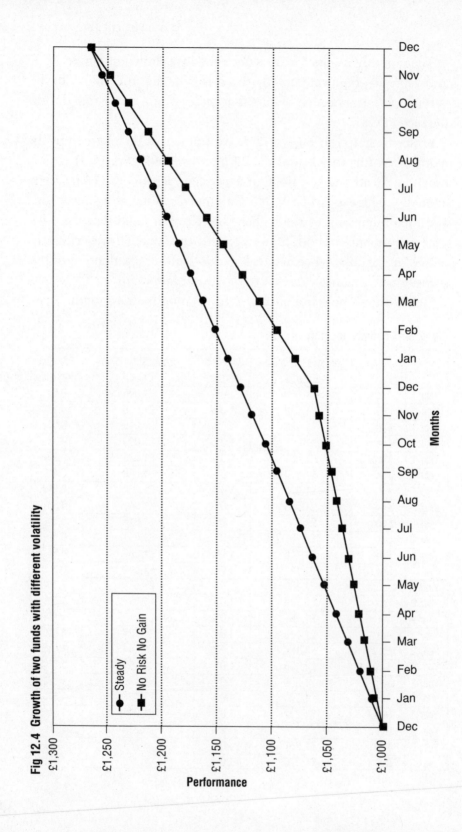

**Fig 12.4 Growth of two funds with different volatility**

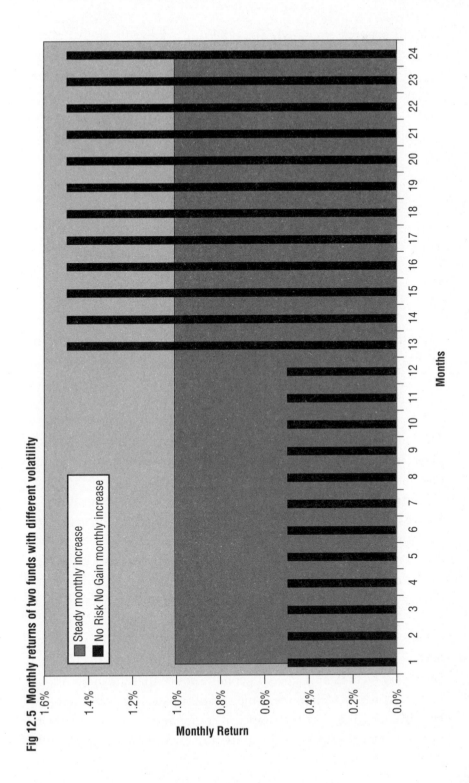

**Fig 12.5 Monthly returns of two funds with different volatility**

Legend:
- Steady monthly increase
- No Risk No Gain monthly increase

Monthly Return axis: 0.0%, 0.2%, 0.4%, 0.6%, 0.8%, 1.0%, 1.2%, 1.4%, 1.6%

Months axis: 1, 2, 3, 4, 5, 6, 7, 8, 9, 10, 11, 12, 13, 14, 15, 16, 17, 18, 19, 20, 21, 22, 23, 24 cent (12 per cent annually). The other fund does vary in its returns, 0.5 per cent (6 per cent annually) to 1.5 per cent (18 per cent annually). Thus, the returns from No Risk No Gain can vary by 1 per cent per month (or 12 per cent annually). The volatility of this fund is expressed as 0.5 per cent per month (see Figure 12.6).

**Fig 12.6  No Risk No Gain: volatility**

|  | Monthly | Annually |
|---|---|---|
| Greatest gain | 1.5% | 18% |
| Lowest gain | 0.5% | 6% |
| Difference | 1.0% | 12% |
| Volatility* | 0.5% | 6% |

* This is also called the standard deviation, if you remember back from your statistics, which is the average or typical or *standard* variation from the average.

Typically, volatility is expressed in monthly terms; how much you might expect the return to vary in a given month. Investors think in annual, not monthly, terms. The average return is 12 per cent, but it varies up or down by 6 percentage points.

Thus, we have established a precise measure of a fund's volatility. The monthly investment pattern, encouraged by the monthly savings plans offered by most fund management companies, also reduces volatility.

Premier has worked out the classifications of volatility shown in Figure 12.7. Fry, who says he is 'passionate about performance and volatility', says 'looking at it statistically challenges your preconceived notions'. I have added my own time-periods associated with each class. These volatility classifications were calculated in exactly the same manner as outlined above, and then grouped according to ranking.

Some comments about the table in Figure 12.7. Notice that international equity income unit trusts are in a lower volatility class than UK equity income unit trusts. Secondly, notice that the international unit trusts tend to fall in the same volatility category as the companion UK unit trust, e.g., international equity and bond unit trusts are in the same category as UK equity and bond unit trusts. Another

**Fig 12.7 Premier volatility rating table**

| Volatility grade | Investment | Time-orientation |
|---|---|---|
| 1 | Short-dated gilts | short |
| 1 | Bank and building society deposits | short |
| 1 | Cash unit trusts | short |
| 2 | Medium-dated gilts | medium |
| 2 | International fixed-interest unit trusts | medium |
| 2 | UK gilt and fixed-interest unit trusts | medium |
| 2 | Long-dated gilts | medium |
| 3 | International equity and bond unit trusts | long |
| 3 | UK equity and bond income | long |
| 3 | Fund of fund unit trusts | long |
| 3 | International equity income unit trusts | long |
| 3 | UK equity and bond unit trusts | long |
| 3 | Financial and property | long |
| 4 | Europe equity unit trusts | long |
| 4 | UK equity income unit trusts | long |
| 4 | UK growth and income | long |
| 5 | International equity growth | long |
| 5 | North America equity unit trusts | long |
| 5 | UK equity growth unit trusts | long |
| 5 | UK smaller company unit trusts | long |
| 5 | Investment trust unit trusts | long |
| 6 | Far East including Japan unit trusts | long |
| 6 | Japan equity unit trusts | long |
| 7 | Commodity and energy unit trusts | long |
| 7 | Emerging markets unit trusts | long |
| 7 | Far East excluding Japan unit trusts | long |

*Source:* Premier Investments from *Micropal* data.

broad generality is that investment trust units – those unit trusts which invest solely in investment trusts are higher up on the volatility scale than other UK and internationally diversified unit trusts.

Figure 12.8 gives a detailed listing of return and volatility characteristics of funds which hold UK securities. You'll note the increases in return are matched by increases in volatility. The final two columns depict the range you might expect the fund to vary within.

For example, the UK growth and income fund has enjoyed a 10 per cent per year average return. However, the monthly swings imply that investors might endure a decrease of 12.1 per cent, or enjoy an increase of 12.1 per cent per year from the anticipated average

**Fig 12.8  Returns, volatility and likely return ranges UK unit trust sectors**

| AUTIF sector | Lower return range | Average annual return | Upper return range | Monthly average volatility | Annual average volatility |
|---|---|---|---|---|---|
| Money market | 4.4% | 5% | 5.0% | 0.1% | 0.4% |
| UK gilt and fixed interest | 0.4% | 7% | 14.3% | 2.0% | 6.9% |
| UK equity and bond income | −1.7% | 8% | 18.4% | 2.9% | 10.1% |
| UK equity income | −1.8% | 10% | 21.7% | 3.4% | 11.8% |
| UK growth and income | −2.0% | 10% | 22.2% | 3.5% | 12.1% |
| UK equity and bond | 0.3% | 11% | 21.8% | 3.1% | 10.7% |
| UK equity growth | −1.1% | 11% | 23.9% | 3.6% | 12.5% |
| UK smaller companies | 0.6% | 13% | 25.5% | 3.6% | 12.5% |

growth. Thus, the range for this fund would average 10 per cent per year, swinging between a loss of −2.1 per cent (10 per cent −12.1 per cent) and 22.1 per cent (10 per cent + 12.1 per cent). Thus, with this information, you can better understand the potential volatility between different investment sectors. For example, you'll note that the equity and bond sector had higher returns than growth and income, coupled with lower volatility limits.

Let's say, after reading the premier volatility rating table in Figure 12.7 and the list of ranges in Figure 12.8, you decide to pursue an investment in the second least volatile of the long-term investments: Grade 4. You decide to invest in one of following categories:

- UK equity income (87 funds)
- UK growth and income (146 funds)
- European equity unit trusts (122 funds)

This gives a total of 354 grade 4 volatility unit trust funds. That's a pretty large list to begin with, but it is better than the 1,600 funds available. We'll use these as our examples as we move on to the next step. Chapter 13 establishes which unit trusts are consistent performers.

# SUMMARY

- Volatility or risk is zigs and zags an investment takes as it moves upward.

- Unit trust sectors can be ranked according to their volatility:

| | |
|---|---|
| *Lowest volatility* | |
| Cash | Cash |
| Bonds | Gilt and fixed interest |
| Equities/Bonds | UK equity and bond income |
| Equities | UK income |
| Equities | UK growth and income |
| Equities | UK equity and bond |
| *Highest volatility* | |
| Equities | UK growth |
| Equities | UK smaller companies |

Before you invest:

- compare the volatility for the unit trust you're considering versus others in the same sector.

# Chapter 13

# CONSISTENCY, CONSISTENCY, CONSISTENCY

'Too many investors select a common stock fund based solely on its [recent] past performance record,' complains John Bogle, founder of the third-largest US unit trust company, Vanguard. He decries unit trust advertisements common on both sides of the Atlantic: 'The record provided by the fund sponsor is usually a chronicle of championship results for one or more of its funds, carefully selected and accompanied by braggadocio about being the top-performing fund for some particular period.' This erroneous focus is exacerbated as 'reports by the financial press typically lionise the portfolio managers who had the "best" records (i.e., achieved the largest gains) during the previous quarter or year or even longer. This myopic focus on past performance is not helpful.' He argues that this singular emphasis on performance proves an unprofitable path.[1]

Yet, if not past performance, then what? Jason D. Hollands of BESt Investments complains about the weekly citation of one- and five-year performance figures. The newspapers 'show the five year picture which hides the details,' he says. 'Investors should treat those figures with caution. We use historical performance as a first filter. We then create a list of funds that have consistently outperformed.' Every single investment professional with whom I spoke about picking the right unit trust said, 'Go for consistency.' Consistency adds depth to the performance measure, it means performing well but consistently. The industry standard for a 'good' fund is, generally, a fund which performs in the top quartile as compared with other funds in its league. The aim is to choose a fund which year-in, year-out is consistently a top performer.

I will provide you with an easy-to-use technique for isolating consistently top-performing unit trusts. It takes about five minutes to isolate the funds, and then that's when the work begins. In this chapter, first we will look inside a top performing fund. We will then begin describing the nuts and bolts of picking a consistently top-performing unit trust. We use as our example the medium-risk long-term investment categories chosen in Chapter 12 (see page 204). We describe the secondary criteria of winnowing the top performers and look at a

> 'Consistency adds depth to the performance measure, it means performing well, but consistently.'

means of volatility-testing the chosen funds. Finally, we look for the holy grail of unit trusts, the single best statistic which captures the return-consistency characteristics of each and every unit trust. First, a story.

# INSIDE A CONSISTENT PERFORMER

Ever since this project began, I have religiously reviewed most personal finance and unit trust-tracking magazines. One fund name kept coming up on the performance lists: Prolific Technology. I never saw any articles about Prolific Technology. Yet, month after month, I'd always find Prolific Technology's fund among the top five.

Then, I completed my analysis of consistent top performers described above, and not surprisingly, Prolific Technology bubbled to the top. Enough of this mystery. I called up Prolific and arranged to meet the manager of the technology fund, Alan Torry.

Torry started with Prolific 26 years ago at the age of 22 in 1970. An earlier investment director of a predecessor organisation was the famed economist John Maynard Keynes, whom, their brochures claim, 'eschewed "short-termism" as costly and short-sighted'.

However, as you'll see shortly, Mr Torry's policy is extremely short-term oriented. Yet, he has managed to achieve spectacular long-term investment results.

Figures 13.1 to 13.4 give the data from *Money Management*[2] which raised my interest.

In 1982, Prolific and Torry launched the Prolific Technology unit trust. Prolific, at this time, also brought out the Prolific North American, which he still runs.

**Fig 13.1  Value of £1,000 invested, after paying commission (reinvesting dividends)**

| Fund | 1 year | 2 years | 3 years | 5 years |
|------|--------|---------|---------|---------|
| Prolific Technology | £1,666 | £1,755 | £2,161 | £5,479 |
| Rank in sector | 2 | 1 | 1 | 1 |
| Avg fund in sector | £1,065 | £1,008 | £1,392 | £2,038 |

**Fig 13.2 Returns and volatility: Prolific Technology vs average international fund**

|  | Prolific Technology | Avg intl fund |
|---|---|---|
| 5-year total return | 447.9% | 103.9% |
| 5-year average return | 40.5% | 15.3% |
| Monthly volatility | 5.6% | 3.4% |

Over the years, he's brought in two other managers to run the Prolific Technology unit trust. Now he is back fully running the portfolio. 'It's 100 per cent time consuming, . . . you can't let the portfolio sit idly.' Whether it will keep up this first-rate performance is a question for the future investors.

He says he owns 100 to 120 stocks at any time, with only a few making up more than 1 per cent of the portfolio. 'With technology stocks,' he explains, 'you need to have more than just a few different types. Individuals or diversified portfolio managers will only own a few, and then when one drops, say, 40 per cent on a day, it scares them to death, they chuck in the towel, sell quickly, and abandon the sector. You need to take a portfolio approach [that is, to own shares in many different kinds of companies] so the big drops don't devastate your portfolio.'

And owning so many volatile shares does take a toll, in a certain sense. The volatility of his fund is the highest by far of any fund in the International Growth sector. We'll spend much time focusing on risk, volatility, and how to make sure the volatility is sensible for your investment attitude and portfolio.

The toll it takes is that his fund is only £95 million. This is larger than the average in the sector; yet, it is not as large as its performance warrants. He explains, 'UK investors are perpetually nervous about technology stocks and American stocks [which are approximately 70 per cent of his portfolio]. We accept that we'll be a volatile fund; we're always trying to ride the next wave.' The volatility is part of strategy; he says any one stock doesn't find a home for very long in his portfolio, except a few tried-and-true technology stocks. 'Over the next decade, there's not a better place to be than technology stocks.'

# Fig 13.3 Lump sum investment of £1,000*: Prolific Technology vs various indices

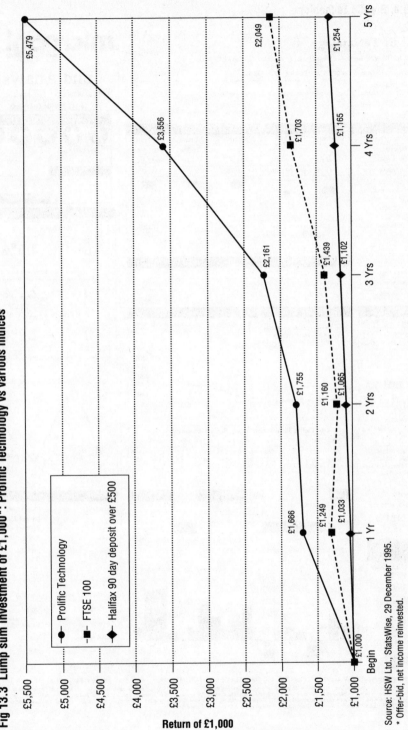

**Return of £1,000**

Legend:
- ● Prolific Technology
- ■ FTSE 100
- ◆ Halifax 90 day deposit over £500

Source: HSW Ltd., StatsWise, 29 December 1995.
* Offer-bid, net income reinvested.

## Fig 13.4 Prolific Technology

# Prolific Technology

Prolific Unit Trust Managers, Walbrook House, 23 Walbrook, London EC4N 8LD.

Information: Telephone - 0171 280 3700   Dealing - 0800 592 487

**Fund Objective:**
To provide capital appreciation from companies in high technology industries.

### Micropal Cumulative Performance - to 30th September 1996

| Performance Period | 6 Months | 1 Year | 3 Years | 5 Years | 10 Years |
|---|---|---|---|---|---|
| Fund Performance | -1.7% | +14.7% | +116.5% | +326.3% | +531.0% |
| Sector Average | -3.6% | +6.4% | +24.6% | +75.4% | +152.4% |
| Best Performing Fund | +5.1% | +35.3% | +116.5% | +326.3% | +531.0% |

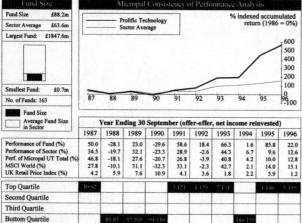

| | | | | | |
|---|---|---|---|---|---|
| Fund Performance | | | | | |
| Sector Average Performance | | | | | |
| Worst Performing Fund | -18.3% | -17.0% | -15.4% | +34.9% | +38.2% |

(Offer-bid, net income reinvested)

| | | | | | |
|---|---|---|---|---|---|
| Top Quartile | 39/162 | 6/159 | 1/139 | 1/129 | 1/62 |
| Second Quartile | | | | | |
| Third Quartile | | | | | |
| Bottom Quartile | | | | | |

### Fund Size

| | |
|---|---|
| Fund Size | £88.2m |
| Sector Average | £63.6m |
| Largest Fund: | £1847.6m |

| | |
|---|---|
| Smallest Fund: | £0.7m |
| No. of Funds: 163 | |

■ Fund Size
□ Average Fund Size in Sector

### Micropal Consistency of Performance Analysis

— Prolific Technology
— Sector Average

% indexed accumulated return (1986 = 0%)

87 88 89 90 91 92 93 94 95 96

### Year Ending 30 September (offer-offer, net income reinvested)

| | 1987 | 1988 | 1989 | 1990 | 1991 | 1992 | 1993 | 1994 | 1995 | 1996 |
|---|---|---|---|---|---|---|---|---|---|---|
| Performance of Fund (%) | 50.0 | -28.1 | 23.0 | -29.6 | 58.6 | 18.4 | 66.3 | 1.6 | 85.8 | 22.0 |
| Performance of Sector (%) | 34.5 | -19.7 | 32.1 | -23.3 | 28.9 | -2.6 | 44.3 | 6.7 | 9.6 | 12.6 |
| Perf. of Micropal UT Total (%) | 46.8 | -18.1 | 27.6 | -20.7 | 26.8 | -3.9 | 40.8 | 4.2 | 10.0 | 12.8 |
| MSCI World (%) | 27.8 | -10.1 | 31.1 | -32.3 | 33.1 | -2.3 | 42.7 | 2.1 | 14.0 | 15.1 |
| UK Retail Price Index (%) | 4.2 | 5.9 | 7.6 | 10.9 | 4.1 | 3.6 | 1.8 | 2.2 | 3.9 | 1.2 |

| | 1987 | 1988 | 1989 | 1990 | 1991 | 1992 | 1993 | 1994 | 1995 | 1996 |
|---|---|---|---|---|---|---|---|---|---|---|
| Top Quartile | 16/62 | | | | 3/121 | 1/129 | 7/134 | | 1/146 | 5/159 |
| Second Quartile | | | | | | | | | | |
| Third Quartile | | | | | | | | | | |
| Bottom Quartile | | 81/85 | 92/101 | 94/110 | | | | 116/139 | | |

### Micropal Rolling Period Analysis

| | 1987 | 1988 | 1989 | 1990 | 1991 | 1992 | 1993 | 1994 | 1995 | 1996 |
|---|---|---|---|---|---|---|---|---|---|---|

| | |
|---|---|
| Highest 12 monthly return: 85.8% | |
| Lowest 12 monthly return: -29.6% | |
| Average 12 monthly return: 24.7% | |

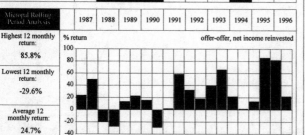

% return

offer-offer, net income reinvested

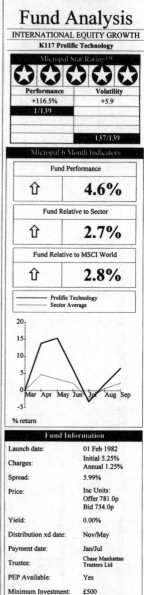

# micropal

## Fund Analysis

### INTERNATIONAL EQUITY GROWTH
#### K117 Prolific Technology

#### Micropal Star Rating™

★ ★ ★ ★ ★

| Performance | Volatility |
|---|---|
| +116.5% | +5.9 |

1/139

137/139

#### Micropal 6 Month Indicators

| Fund Performance | |
|---|---|
| ⇧ | **4.6%** |

| Fund Relative to Sector | |
|---|---|
| ⇧ | **2.7%** |

| Fund Relative to MSCI World | |
|---|---|
| ⇧ | **2.8%** |

— Prolific Technology
— Sector Average

Mar Apr May Jun Jul Aug Sep

% return

### Fund Information

| | |
|---|---|
| Launch date: | 01 Feb 1982 |
| Charges: | Initial 5.25% Annual 1.25% |
| Spread: | 5.99% |
| Price: | Inc Units: Offer 781.0p Bid 734.0p |
| Yield: | 0.00% |
| Distribution xd date: | Nov/May |
| Payment date: | Jan/Jul |
| Trustee: | Chase Manhattan Trustees Ltd |
| PEP Available: | Yes |
| Minimum Investment: | £500 |
| Regular Savings: | £50 per month |

*Source: Micropal*

He refuses to invest in start-up, venture-capital type situations; instead, he chooses companies which have existing products and have demonstrated some ability to sell these products. His fund is composed, in general, of three types of securities:

1 Software/networking;
2 Communications companies;
3 Healthcare: biotechnology, medical equipment, and software companies analysing health care data;
4 Semiconductors.

## THE NUTS AND BOLTS

So far we have identified the broad-risk categories of funds which we are interested in: European growth, UK growth and income, and UK equity income. Buy the magazine *Money Management* or *What Investment?*, or any other magazine which lists unit trust performance by investment category.

> *Money Management:*
> 0171-896 2525
> *What Investment?:*
> 0171-638 1916

These magazines portray the value today of £1,000 invested one year ago, two years ago, three years ago, and five years ago. For example, £1,000 invested in the Schroder UK Equity Fund a year ago would today be worth £1,121. This technique takes into account initial fees, other initial charges, and the basic rate tax paid on dividends.

The rankings within the sector or league are also reported. If the fund performed in the top quartile during the period under examination, it will be bold-faced to highlight its good performance. The Schroder fund's one-year performance was 20th out of 141, ranked in the 14th percentile (20/141 = 14 per cent), and was printed in bold face.

These are called league tables, as they group together all funds with broadly similar objectives, e.g., UK growth and income. At the bottom of the table, you'll find averages for all funds in that particular league.

The listings shown in Figure 13.4 appeared in the UK growth and income league table from *Money Management*. I spent literally ten minutes and selected funds consistently appearing in the top quartiles over one, two, three, and five years.

These are funds which have proven themselves year after year after year of selecting stocks which are going to outperform the market and holding them in their portfolios. These are the managers who are most adroit. Note these chosen funds can go down in value. Indeed, in 1994, the average UK growth and income fund lost 7.2 per cent. Hence, if a fund lost less than 7.2 per cent, it performed better than the average.

In 1995, a great year, the average UK growth and income fund earned 20 per cent while the top quartile funds returned at least 22 per cent.

---

### The Buying the Right Unit Trust (BRUT) technique

The BRUT technique to isolate winners is:

1 In the five-year category, circle the bold-faced top quartile funds.

2 Circle the bold-faced top quartile funds in the three-year category, only if you circled them in the five-year category.

3 Choose the top quartile two-year funds, again only the top quartile performers in the three- and five-year categories.

4 In the one-year category, choose the top quartile funds that were top quartile funds in the two-, three-, and five-year categories.

---

The box shows you how to use the consistency technique to find a short-listed group of top performers across five years. There's a little more work to determine if there was one spectacular year, and four mediocre ones, and we'll examine that shortly.

Ignore the ten-year category – the fund manager and fund philosophy might have changed over such a long time. Ignore the one-month and six-month categories as they may be too dependent on short-term success, and aren't necessarily representative of the longer-term performance.

Ignore top performers which haven't been around five years. There are always a few funds that meet the stringent BRUT top quartile criteria. Why look to a fund without as long a record, given there are other funds that undoubtedly will have been around for five years?

If the fund manager has a stellar track record at another fund and fund management company, you may want to consider his new fund. I go back to my original point, though. Because you can always find a fund in a particular sector with at least a five-year record, why choose the unproven fund?

Using the criteria specified above, I have reprinted sections from the UK growth and income sector to get a list of consistent performers. I've printed the first ten, and then bold-faced the consistent high performers along with a few others (see Figure 13.4).

Note that at the bottom of the table is the relevant index for comparing the actual funds with a common benchmark.

The one-, two-, three-, and five-year performance take into account the initial and other bit fees paid. This is referred to as a offer-to-bid basis; that is, it is assumed that you'll pay the initial and other bit fee in the offer price and receive the bid price when you sell. It assumes all dividends are reinvested net of basic rate tax. This is the most commonly used technique.

Funds can be reported on two other bases:

- **Offer-to-offer:** uses the beginning price to buy units and the ending price to buy units.
- **Bid-to-Bid:** uses the beginning price to sell units and the ending price to sell units.

These last two methods ignore the initial fees, and thus, are useful for comparing performance alone.

I completed the same exercise for the UK equity income and European equity fund sectors and came up with a shortlist of highly consistent funds (see Figure 13.5).

## Fig 13.4 Picking consistent performers: UK growth and income sector

| UK growth and income | One year | Rank | Two years | Rank | Three years | Rank | Five years | Rank |
|---|---|---|---|---|---|---|---|---|
| Abbey General | 1,058 | 113 | 1,321 | 22 | 1,314 | 36 | 1,660 | 41 |
| Abbey Natl UK Grth | 1,077 | 93 | – | – | – | – | – | – |
| AES UK General | 1,122 | 18 | 1,369 | 4 | 1,356 | 15 | – | – |
| Allied Dunbar Accumulator | 1,083 | 79 | 1,283 | 51 | 1,267 | 69 | 1,605 | 57 |
| Allied Dunbar Asset Value | 1,084 | 76 | 1,259 | 72 | 1,254 | 80 | 1,558 | 70 |
| : | : | : | : | : | : | : | : | : |
| : | : | : | : | : | : | : | : | : |
| Barclays Unicorn Trustee | 1,083 | 81 | **1,315** | **25** | **1,294** | **52** | **1,728** | **20** |
| **Barclaytrust Investment** | **1,148** | **5** | **1,345** | **9** | **1,357** | **14** | **1,771** | **16** |
| Baring Portfolio | 1,030 | 130 | 1,120 | 126 | 1,141 | 123 | 1,560 | 69 |
| : | : | : | : | : | : | : | : | : |
| : | : | : | : | : | : | : | : | : |
| Canlife Growth | 1,092 | 62 | 1,293 | 44 | 1,334 | 23 | 1,721 | 21 |
| **Cazenove UK Equity** | **1,132** | **10** | **1,339** | **11** | **1,436** | **2** | **1,873** | **6** |
| CF John Siddal Inc & Gwth | 979 | 139 | 996 | 130 | – | – | – | – |
| : | : | : | : | : | : | : | : | : |
| : | : | : | : | : | : | : | : | : |
| Colonial Mutual Cap | 1,107 | 38 | 1,263 | 69 | 1,261 | 75 | 1,555 | 74 |
| **Credit Suisse Growth Port** | **1,118** | **21** | **1,330** | **15** | **1,449** | **1** | **1,924** | **3** |
| Com Un PPT UK & Genl | 1,097 | 52 | 1,319 | 23 | 1,356 | 16 | 1,661 | 40 |
| : | : | : | : | : | : | : | : | : |
| : | : | : | : | : | : | : | : | : |
| Gartmore UK Equity Income | 1,068 | 101 | 1,253 | 77 | 1,218 | 96 | 1,643 | 47 |
| **Gartmore UK Index** | **1,154** | **3** | **1,366** | **5** | **1,407** | **4** | **1,811** | **8** |
| Govett FTSE Mid-250 Index | 1,075 | 95 | 1,251 | 79 | 1,292 | 53 | – | – |
| : | : | : | : | : | : | : | : | : |
| : | : | : | : | : | : | : | : | : |
| Govett UK Safeguard | 1,019 | 133 | 1,185 | 115 | – | – | – | – |
| **Guardhill** | **1,121** | **19** | **1,358** | **8** | **1,398** | **7** | **1,751** | **17** |
| Halifax Accumulation | – | – | – | – | – | – | – | – |
| : | : | : | : | : | : | : | : | : |
| : | : | : | : | : | : | : | : | : |
| PM Income & Growth | 1,061 | 110 | 1,245 | 86 | 1,287 | 55 | **1,856** | **7** |
| **Prolific UK Blue Chip** | **1,144** | **8** | **1,371** | **2** | **1,423** | **3** | **1,949** | **2** |
| Prudential Equity | 1,080 | 86 | 1,277 | 55 | 1,277 | 61 | 1,563 | 68 |
| : | : | : | : | : | : | : | : | : |
| : | : | : | : | : | : | : | : | : |
| Save & Prosper UK Gth & Inc | 1,069 | 99 | 1,266 | 65 | 1,275 | 62 | 1,434 | 106 |
| **Schroder UK Equity** | **1,121** | **20** | **1,334** | **14** | **1,371** | **10** | **1,896** | **4** |
| Scot Amicable UK Equity Inc | 1,087 | 72 | 1,250 | 80 | 1,192 | 108 | 1,658 | 42 |
| : | : | : | : | : | : | : | : | : |
| : | : | : | : | : | : | : | : | : |
| Ave/total | 1,083 | 141 | 1,258 | 131 | 1,274 | 125 | 1,616 | 112 |
| FTSE A ALL-SHARE | 1,165 | | 1,383 | | 1,431 | | 1,822 | |

*Source: Money Management, November 1996.*

## Fig 13.5 Consistent performers: UK equity income and European equity funds

| | Fund size | Yield | Six month | Rank | One year | Rank | Two year | Two rank | Three year | Three rank | Five year | Five rank | Ten year | Ten rank | Five year average % | Ten year average % | Volatility |
|---|---|---|---|---|---|---|---|---|---|---|---|---|---|---|---|---|---|
| **UK EQUITY INCOME** | | | | | | | | | | | | | | | | | |
| Britannia Higher Yield | 145 | 3.9% | 1,030 | 7 | 1,151 | 3 | 1,382 | 3 | 1,419 | 4 | 1,988 | 4 | – | – | 14.7% | – | 3.8% |
| BWD UK Equity Income | 2.9 | 3.8% | 1,035 | 4 | 1,144 | 6 | 1,299 | 12 | 1,434 | 3 | 1,734 | 16 | – | – | 11.6% | – | 3.4% |
| CU PPT Equity Income | 55 | 4.5% | 1,040 | 3 | 1,146 | 4 | 1,322 | 8 | 1,344 | 11 | 1,736 | 15 | 3,874 | 5 | 11.7% | 14.5% | 3.8% |
| Eagle Star UK High Income | 177 | 3.7% | 1,022 | 15 | 1,092 | 16 | 1,273 | 16 | 1,296 | 17 | 1,746 | 13 | 4,086 | 1 | 11.8% | 15.1% | 3.5% |
| GT Income | 172 | 4.1% | 1,015 | 26 | 1,154 | 2 | 1,350 | 4 | 1,466 | 2 | 2,273 | 2 | 3,819 | 6 | 17.8% | 14.3% | 3.3% |
| Jupiter Income | 283 | 4.3% | 1,023 | 14 | 1,170 | 1 | 1,530 | 1 | 1,709 | 1 | 2,749 | 1 | – | – | 22.4% | – | 3.6% |
| Lazard UK Income | 81 | 5.0% | 1,018 | 21 | 1,109 | 9 | 1,395 | 2 | 1,410 | 5 | 1,819 | 8 | 4,030 | 3 | 12.7% | 14.9% | 3.6% |
| Mercury Income | 95 | 4.2% | 1,029 | 9 | 1,118 | 7 | 1,323 | 7 | 1,331 | 13 | 1,739 | 14 | 3,204 | 12 | 11.7% | 12.4% | 3.7% |
| Prolific High Income | 447 | 4.2% | 1,004 | 46 | 1,091 | 17 | 1,283 | 14 | 1,290 | 19 | 1,794 | 9 | 3,200 | 14 | 12.4% | 12.3% | 3.1% |
| Schroder Income | 341 | 4.9% | 1,012 | 32 | 1,112 | 8 | 1,271 | 18 | 1,302 | 16 | 1,860 | 6 | 3,446 | 8 | 13.2% | 13.2% | 3.5% |
| Sun Alliance Equity Income | 47 | 5.1% | 1,010 | 37 | 1,093 | 13 | 1,278 | 15 | 1,291 | 18 | 1,758 | 12 | – | – | 11.9% | – | 3.7% |
| Average/total all funds | 136 | 4.7 | 1,001 | 90 | 1,059 | 88 | 1,213 | 83 | 1,227 | 80 | 1,606 | 78 | 2,920 | 59 | 9.8% | 11.2% | 3.4% |
| Benchmark: FTSE 100 | | 0.0% | 1,069 | | 1,127 | | 1,306 | | 1,302 | | 1,508 | | 2,541 | | 8.6% | 9.8% | 3.5% |
| **EUROPEAN EQUITY** | | | | | | | | | | | | | | | | | |
| Allied Dunbar European Grth | 28 | 10.0% | 1,002 | 26 | 1,214 | 9 | 1,496 | 5 | 1,671 | 9 | 2,443 | 5 | – | – | 19.5% | – | 3.6% |
| Baring Europe Select | 94 | 0.8% | 1,037 | 6 | 1,323 | 2 | 1,592 | 2 | 1,995 | 1 | 2,227 | 14 | 2,716 | 15 | 17.4% | 10.5% | 3.6% |
| Friends Provident European Growth | 191 | 0.0% | 1,001 | 29 | 1,188 | 14 | 1,469 | 6 | 1,645 | 10 | 2,199 | 16 | – | – | 17.1% | – | 2.9% |
| Gartmore European Select Opportunities | 122 | 0.0% | 989 | 51 | 1,154 | 26 | 1,464 | 7 | 1,765 | 4 | 2,344 | 7 | 2,731 | 12 | 18.6% | 10.6% | 3.1% |
| INVESCO European Grth | 63 | 0.0% | 1,016 | 18 | 1,219 | 6 | 1,508 | 4 | 1,727 | 7 | 2,546 | 4 | 2,580 | 21 | 20.5% | 9.9% | 4.1% |
| INVESCO Euro Small Cos | 60 | 0.0% | 1,019 | 17 | 1,289 | 3 | 1,522 | 3 | 1,829 | 3 | 2,380 | 6 | 2,719 | 14 | 18.9% | 10.5% | 3.5% |
| Jupiter European | 22 | 0.6% | 1,056 | 3 | 1,361 | 1 | 1,683 | 1 | 1,909 | 2 | 2,746 | 2 | – | – | 22.4% | – | 3.5% |
| Mercury European Growth | 258 | 0.1% | 1,036 | 7 | 1,185 | 17 | 1,328 | 25 | 1,481 | 24 | 2,078 | 25 | 2,413 | 26 | 15.8% | 9.2% | 3.2% |
| Metropolitan Eurogrowth + | 25 | 0.1% | 1,029 | 9 | 1,190 | 13 | 1,350 | 20 | 1,472 | 28 | 2,065 | 26 | – | – | 15.6% | – | 3.3% |
| Schroder Euro Smaller Cos | 54 | 0.2% | 994 | 43 | 1,218 | 4 | 1,425 | 9 | 1,753 | 5 | 2,191 | 17 | – | – | 17.0% | – | 2.9% |
| Average/Total all funds | 89 | 0.9% | 984 | 127 | 1,115 | 126 | 1,272 | 120 | 1,404 | 117 | 1,913 | 110 | 2,435 | 61 | 13.7% | 9.1% | 3.3% |
| Benchmark: FT & S&P Europe excluding UK | – | 0.0% | 1,021 | – | 1,161 | – | 1,371 | – | 1,450 | – | 2,053 | – | 2,424 | – | 15.5% | 9.3% | 3.4% |

We've narrowed down 1,600 funds to 29 funds in our selected volatility category. Any one of these funds would be fine to invest in: remember, they showed up consistently, year after year as top performers.

We now have the tools to look a little further into performance calculation. As we saw before you'll typically see performance reported

Whitechurch Securities Ltd of Bristol uses an extremely similar technique to rank funds based on quarterly volatility and consistency, instead of annually. Keen Seager, Whitechurch managing director, says, 'the risk/consistency ratings are designed to be used as an important tool to monitor the performance of funds you hold and to assess potential purchases'. (Copies of *The Whitechurch Pedigree Investment Ratings Service* are available by calling 0800 374413).

as the value of £1,000 invested over varying time periods: if you had bought £1,000-worth of units in the Schroder UK Equity Fund, one of the top performing funds, one year ago, you would have £1,121 today. Had you invested £1,000 in the same fund two years ago, you would have £1,334 today.

| Value £1,000 after | 1 year | 2 years | 3 years | 5 years |
|---|---|---|---|---|
| Schroder UK Equity | £1,121 | £1,334 | £1,371 | £1,896 |

With a little maths, you can figure out how much the investment grew in each of the preceding years. For example, if you bought £1,000 a year ago, you would have earned £121 over the year. Similarly, if you bought two years ago, your total return would be £334. The difference between the one year return, £121, and the two-year return, £334, is £213. Thus, the investment earned £121 in the most recent years and £213 in the year preceding that.

| 2 years | 1 year | Difference |
|---|---|---|
| £1,334 | £1,121 | £213 |
| (£1000) | (£1000) | |
| £334 | £121 | £213 |

Thus, you can calculate the gain straight off the page by subtracting, say, the two-year figure from the three-year figure:

| Value £1,000 after | 1 year | 2 years | 3 years | 5 years |
|---|---|---|---|---|
| Schroder UK Equity | £1,121 | £1,334 | £1,371 | £1,896 |
| Gain | £121 | £213 | £37 | £525 |

Now, you can see very clearly what has happened with this fund: great year five years ago, fairly good years last year and before, and then a bad year three years ago. Using this information, your next step would be to look at other funds, especially three years ago, to find out whether the drop occurred across the market or if this fund was unique.

We prepare the same analysis for the average fund in the sector and for the FTSE All-Share Index (found at the bottom of the league table in Figure 13.4):

|  | Begin | Year 1 | Year 2 | Year 3 | Year 5 |
|---|---|---|---|---|---|
| **Sector Average:** | | | | | |
| Cumulative | £1,000 | £1,083 | £1,258 | £1,274 | £1,616 |
| Each Year | £0 | £83 | £175 | £16 | £342 |
| **FTSE A ALL-SHARE:** | | | | | |
| Cumulative | £1,000 | £1,165 | £1,383 | £1,431 | £1,822 |
| Each Year | £0 | £165 | £218 | £48 | £391 |

We discover that in the third year, both the fund-sector average and the overall index increased just marginally.

Clive Boothman, managing director of Schroders, said, 'I don't think much of the league tables, because if you're doing the best in one year, you look very good for all five years.' He continued, 'I prefer discrete one-year absolute numbers.' If it's good for Mr Boothman, who has responsibility for monitoring performance over his funds and making portfolio manager recommendations, it must be worthwhile to explore.

You might have been fooled if you saw an advertisement that said:

---

**The BIG GROWTH Fund**
Top gainer in one-year category
62 per cent gain over five years
award-winning fund

---

But once you looked underneath the figures, you'd see that the performance was inconsistent. The 'Underlying Value' fund is more worthwhile to you because of its consistent returns.

|  |  |  | Annual |
|---|---|---|---|
|  | 1 year | 5 years | average return |
| **Big growth** | £1,616 | £1,616 | 10 per cent |
| **Underlying value** | £1,213 | £1,616 | 10 per cent |

Which do you choose? Both funds returned the same over five years, and you're a long-term investor, so you wouldn't make a decision based on the short-term results.

It's fairly obvious from the example above that for the Big Growth Fund, all the gain came in the most recent year. Here are the underlying figures to calculate performance for individual years.

|  | Begin | Year 1 | Year 2 | Year 3 | Year 5 |
|---|---|---|---|---|---|
| Big Growth growth cumulative | £1,000 | £1,616 | £1,616 | £1,616 | £1,616 |
| Each year | £0 | £616 | £0 | £0 | £0 |
| Underlying value cumulative | £1,000 | £1,123 | £1,246 | £1,370 | £1,616 |
| Each year | £0 | £123 | £123 | £123 | £246 |

I realise the maths to complete this exercise may be a little tedious; if you don't want to do this, call the fund management company, and ask them to send you the Managers' Report or a *Micropal* summary sheet, detailing each year's performance.

Unfortunately, the real world isn't as simple as hypothetical examples. I've chosen two funds from the UK growth and income sector to offer another comparison of the discrete year analysis (see Figure 13.6). One of the funds, the Schroder UK Equity Fund passed our test as a consistent high performer; the second fund, Global Asset Management's UK Diversified (GAM), performed well five years ago and has a great volatility of returns.

> 'Unfortunately, the real world isn't as simple as hypothetical examples.'

As you can see, the five-year annual average returns are fairly close together: 13.2 per cent versus 12.2 per cent. However, the volatility figures are different: the lower the volatility, the more consistent are the returns. You can see this graphically in the chart in Figure 13.7. The GAM fund dropped 12 per cent one year and then shot up 50 per cent the following year. The Schroder's fund, on the other hand, followed the general

**Fig 13.6 UK growth and income sector: comparison of two funds' return and volatility over five years**

|  | Five-year annual average return | Volatility |
|---|---|---|
| Schroder UK Equity | 13.2% | 3.5% |
| Global Asset Management UK Diversified | 12.2% | 4.1% |
| Sector Average | 9.9% | 3.5% |

**Fig 13.7  Annual performance 92–96: selected funds vs average growth and income sector**

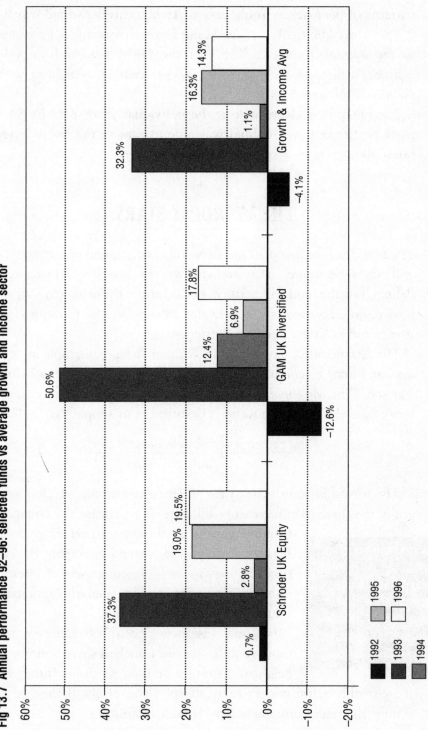

patterns of the market. You'll note in 1992, Schroder's fund was up 0.7 per cent, admittedly not much, but better than losing 4.1 per cent as the average fund did. The year the GAM fund did so well, Schroder's did less well, up only 37 per cent as compared with GAM's 50 per cent.

The message is clear: look at the individual year's data to get a truer picture of how the fund was able to achieve the returns they boast about.

## THE *MICROPAL* STARS

The holy grail for investors has been long sought, and unfortunately, will never be found. That statistic will be one which concretely defines how the fund will perform in the future. Unfortunately, all we have to go on is the past. As indicated by our analysis above, performance and volatility equals consistency.

The Sharpe ratio, developed by William Sharpe, is simple in concept and aims to combine the return calculation with the volatility statistic. (The *Micropal* Star system uses a similar means to characterise funds.) The Sharpe Ratio is beautiful in its simplicity:

$$\frac{\text{Total return less risk-free interest rate}}{\text{Volatility}}$$

The reason for subtracting the risk-free interest rate, which is generally the three-month treasury bill rate, is to release the equation from the general level of interest rates currently. If rates are high, you would anticipate returns from equities to be high; conversely, if interest rates are low you would similarly anticipate returns from equities to be low.

> 'The message is clear: look at the individual year's data to get a truer picture of how the fund was able to achieve the returns they boast about.'

In some instances, portfolio managers use more volatile securities, such as share options, to heighten the return on their portfolio. If they get it right, the return will increase sharply; conversely, if they get it wrong, the return plummets. This is high volatility.

**Fig 13.8 Medium/long-term volatility category: top consistent performance ranked by size**

| Sector | Fund name | Fund size | 5 year average % | Vola- tility | Micropal stars |
|---|---|---|---|---|---|
| UK growth and income | Schroder UK Equity | 919.7 | 13.6% | 3.5% | ***** |
| UK equity income | Prolific High Income | 446.7 | 12.4% | 3.1% | **** |
| UK equity income | Schroder Income | 340.6 | 13.2% | 3.5% | **** |
| UK equity income | Jupiter Income | 282.9 | 22.4% | 3.6% | ***** |
| UK growth and income | Guardhill | 276.6 | 11.9% | 3.5% | ***** |
| European equity | Mercury European Growth | 257.7 | 15.8% | 3.2% | **** |
| UK growth and income | Gartmore UK Index | 216.4 | 12.6% | 3.5% | **** |
| European equity | Friends Provident Euro. Grth. | 190.6 | 17.1% | 2.9% | ***** |
| UK equity income | Eagle Star UK High Income | 176.6 | 11.8% | 3.5% | **** |
| UK equity income | GT Income | 172.3 | 17.8% | 3.3% | ***** |
| UK equity income | Britannia Higher Yield | 144.6 | 14.7% | 3.8% | ***** |
| European equity | Gartmore European Select Ops. | 122.3 | 18.6% | 3.1% | ***** |
| UK growth and income | Prolific UK Blue Chip | 109.3 | 14.3% | 3.6% | ***** |
| UK equity income | Mercury Income | 95.2 | 11.7% | 3.7% | **** |
| European equity | Baring Europe Select | 94.3 | 17.4% | 3.6% | ***** |
| UK equity income | Lazard UK Income | 81.4 | 12.7% | 3.6% | ***** |
| European equity | INVESCO European Growth | 63.2 | 20.5% | 4.1% | **** |
| European equity | INVESCO Euro Small Cos. | 60.2 | 18.9% | 3.5% | ***** |
| UK equity income | CU PPT Equity Income | 55.3 | 11.7% | 3.8% | **** |
| European equity | Schroder Euro Smaller Cos. | 53.5 | 17.0% | 2.9% | ***** |
| UK equity income | Sun Alliance Equity Income | 46.8 | 11.9% | 3.7% | **** |
| UK growth and income | Credit Suisse Growth Port. | 41.2 | 14.0% | 3.7% | ***** |
| UK growth and income | Barclaytrust Investment | 32.7 | 12.1% | 3.6% | **** |
| UK growth and income | Cazenove UK Equity | 30 | 13.4% | 2.9% | ***** |
| European equity | Allied Dunbar European Growth | 28.3 | 19.5% | 3.6% | ***** |
| European equity | Metropolitan Eurogrowth Plus | 25.1 | 15.6% | 3.3% | **** |
| European equity | Jupiter European | 21.8 | 22.4% | 3.5% | ***** |
| UK equity income | BWD UK Equity Income | 2.9 | 11.6% | 3.4% | ***** |

*Note: Micropal* stars: ***** = best return/volatility trade-off; * = worst return/volatility trade-off.
*Source: Micropal Expert,* 30 September 1996.

Fortunately, you don't have to go through these mechanics to determine a consistency ratio. Instead, the unit trust data provider, *Micropal,* from whom I've obtained many statistics in this book, has created a star-rating system ranging from one star, the funds with the worst return relative to the volatility, to five stars, indicating the best return relative to the volatility of the fund. This measurement system can provide results that may not appear right at first glance because, for example, a low-performing fund coupled with a even lower volatility. This suggests that the fund manager has chosen shares with average performance coupled with low volatility. Figure 13.8 (on p. 223) lists the *Micropal* star ratings for the consistent funds we chose earlier in this chapter, along with their returns and volatility.

## PUTTING IT ALL TOGETHER

There are several keys to picking a unit trust. First, go for performance. Second, go for low volatility. These two items wrapped together are called 'consistency', and is your best insurance that you get what you pay for. The other point I tried to illustrate is you can't just trust the performance number selectively chosen to advertise the fund. Buy one of the industry magazines with a table depicting performance. Go through the analysis, and choose 20 or so funds for your consideration. Out of this select group of funds, choose the fund management company you trust.

Chapter 14 discusses fund management companies.

### REFERENCES

[1] 'How to Select a Common Stock Mutual Fund', *Bogle on Mutual Funds* by John C. Bogle (Burr Ridge, Illinois: Richard D. Irwin Publishers, Inc., 1994), p. 77.

[2] Year-end 1995: 'Unit Trust Statistics: International Growth', *Money Management*, February 1996, p. 77.

# SUMMARY

- Consistent performance is what the risk-minimising investor seeks.

- Consistent performance is strong returns coupled with relative lower volatility, over five years.

- Consistent top performance is defined as the top quartile of yearly performance as compared with other funds in the same category.

Before you invest:

- use the BRUT technique (Buying the Right Unit Trust): in a unit trust category, choose only those funds in the top performance quartile in each of the last five years

- choose only those funds with *Micropal* Star ratings of four or five

- from this select group, look at the fund management company and choose the one with the lowest charges and volatility.

# KEEPER OF
# THE VAULT

Perpetual Investment's Roger Cornick: 'In building a brand, there's nothing magic about fund products, except you can't see them. They are invisible and intangible but extremely important to people. We offer clients "confidence and trust".'

Anybody who's looked at a financial magazine or newspaper's personal finance section in the last few years couldn't help but see Perpetual's brand-image: a monumental snow-capped mountain. The idea came to Cornick while skiing in France. Perpetual selected this particular mountain, Anna Dablam, which is located north of Mount Everest, because of its grandeur and dominance.

Today, beside the mountain, you'll see a raft of awards which Perpetual has won from various fund-rating sources. This message is exemplified by all the fund management company's advertising: rest easy, and when you awake, your garden will have grown.

> 'There's nothing more important than the security of your money; yet naïve investors often fall prey to their own unachievable hopes.'

Market studies show that people must have confidence and trust in the fund management company with whom they're placing their savings and investments. Consequently, the various fund management companies capitalise on this human requirement. In the United States, the fund management companies advertise with pictures of families and sons and daughters. The implication is clear: 'invest with us, and your family will be safe and secure'.

Richard Royds, managing director of unit trusts at Mercury, says there are four things which trigger an investor's investment decision:

- performance
- charges
- reputation of the fund management company
- service.

We've spent considerable time on the first two topics which are measurable. We move now into a less tangible, yet nonetheless important, area.

There's nothing more important than the security of your money; yet naïve investors often fall prey to their own unachievable hopes. I believe there are three characteristics you desire in a fund management company. You need to form a picture about the fund management company before investing. Only if you feel comfortable should you invest. See Figure 14.1 for my criteria.

**Fig 14.1 Criteria for choosing a fund management company**

| Fund competence | Why? | How? |
| --- | --- | --- |
| Administratively competent and proper | Easy to work with | Personal experience |
| Financial strength | Confidence | Size/IFA recommendation |
| Strong fund management | Trust | Awards<br>Check with Regulators |

If the unit trust company advertises enough, you're bound to see their name. Banks send you PEP adverts. Assurance companies send you adverts. Creating name recognition is just a matter of spending enough money. There is some acknowledgement that the performance of unit trusts sponsored by banks is lacking. This isn't universal; but the issue becomes one of focus. Banks aren't investment experts. If you perform the analysis suggested in Chapter 13, and one of your bank's funds appears on your shortlist, by all means consider it. However, just recognising a bank's name, which is likely, is no guarantee that the fund will appear in the top quartile of performance.

While recognising the name of the fund management company certainly isn't a bad sign, there's more to it than recognising the name. After all, everyone knew the name of Barings, that very large, very old, very recognisable bank.

## ADMINISTRATIVE COMPETENCE MEANS
## 'EASY TO WORK WITH'

I've invested with various fund management companies in continental Europe, the UK, and America. In some instances, transferred money was lost in the morass of bank transfers, funds weren't sent as requested, share amounts were incorrectly calculated, brochures weren't sent, and so on. There are an incredible amount of things which can go administratively wrong, yet not necessarily result in money losses. Instead, you could undergo an administrative nightmare in trying to straighten up your affairs.

Administrative aptitude is one of the key reasons I'll choose a certain fund management company. That's why I urge you to make a shortlist of potential funds in which to invest, and then call up the fund management company. How long does it take before your phone call is answered? Ask them to send you information on the particular fund, the brochure about all their funds, and the scheme particulars.

> 'Because there are so many funds, if you don't like something about the fund management company ... you can go somewhere else.'

The last one is important. The scheme particulars is a drab, little, legally required document. Most people don't ask for it as I determined in doing research for this book. Some of the client helplines didn't even know what the scheme particulars were. This is the small print. Here's where it tells you the deal underlying your potential unit trust purchase.

Ask for all this information to be sent to you.

See how long it takes for you to receive it. Is your name spelt properly? Did they send you all the information you asked for? If they promise to follow up with a question, do they? These administrative details are more important than you think. Your first impressions of the fund management company are important

It's not a proven fact, but, probably your experience on the telephone is indicative of all your further dealings with the fund management company. Because there are so many funds, if you don't like something about the fund management company – bad telephone manners, unresponsive, not informative – you can go somewhere else.

The bad service in the telephone unit could be indicative of bad administration, bad fund management, and overall sloppy administration. The two most important days to you, administratively, are when you send in your funds, and when you sell out and request your funds. You certainly don't want any inefficiency at this time. You've got enough to worry about.

Push on to the next fund management company.

# DOES SIZE EQUAL STRENGTH?

A second means of developing confidence in the fund management company is to look at the size of the fund management company. A list of the largest fund management companies is given in Figure 14.2. Inevitably, this will change by the time you read this. There are some 160 fund management companies. However, if you choose a fund from the analysis in Chapter 13 you've never heard of or your IFA recommends a fund, call up the fund management company and ask how large they are and if anybody owns the firm.

You'll often find that fund management companies you've never heard of are owned by gigantic banks or insurance companies or other financial services companies.

Investing with a firm with large resources means just that. They're a large institution to which many have entrusted their wealth. While you are offered a degree of financial protection by the Investor Protection Scheme with IMRO, you don't want to have to get embroiled with the Regulator fighting to get your money back.

The list in Figure 14.2 shows fund management groups in terms of how much they have in unit trusts. Clearly, some quite large groups, such as Credit Suisse, one of the world's largest banks, are low down on the list because the size of the actual unit trust funds they manage is not as great as some of the other fund management companies.

Large fund management companies have the financial where-withal to support extensive research and to develop broad talent. Small fund management companies may be more innovative and creative. Which is better? It largely depends on your own inclinations. My only point is not to discard a fund management company out of hand because you've never heard of it.

We turn back to our list of consistent performers in Chapter 13 (Figure 13.4) to look at the fund management companies which sponsor these funds. Figure 14.3 gives our list of selected top per-forming–consistent funds along with the fund management company and size.

## Fig 14.2 Largest fund management companies

| Fund management company | 1995 £ millions | 5-year growth | Fund management company | 1995 £ millions | 5-year growth |
|---|---|---|---|---|---|
| Schroders | 8,858.4 | 652% | Newton | 825.7 | 3,889% |
| M&G | 8,017.2 | 108% | Old Mutual | 819.0 | 390% |
| Gartmore | 5,465.5 | 371% | Canada Life | 812.7 | 513% |
| Mercury | 4,657.2 | 291% | | | |
| Perpetual | 4,391.1 | 1,192% | Abtrust | 773.4 | 310% |
| Barclays | 4,101.8 | 125% | Framlington | 769.6 | 77% |
| Allied Dunbar | 3,521.8 | 55% | Eagle Star | 737.2 | 289% |
| Standard Life Trust | 3,417.9 | −24% | Scottish Mutual | 649.1 | 88% |
| Fidelity | 3,390.2 | 106% | Royal Life | 637.9 | 7% |
| Save & Prosper | 3,265.4 | 68% | Refuge | 634.5 | 214% |
| | | | Guardian | 629.9 | 79% |
| Prudential | 2,236.7 | 118% | Lincoln | 624.4 | 124% |
| Friends' Provident | 1,972.8 | 647% | CIS | 621.3 | 1,290% |
| Morgan Grenfell | 1,774.2 | 730% | Scottish Equitable | 605.9 | 45% |
| Hill Samuel | 1,682.7 | 86% | | | |
| Henderson Touche Remnant | 1,647.9 | 20% | Kleinwort Benson | 602.6 | −4% |
| TSB | 1,646.4 | 6% | Commercial Union | 567.2 | 189% |
| Abbey Life | 1,597.3 | 138% | Standard Life Fund | 563.6 | 8,571% |
| Norwich | 1,594.2 | 173% | PDFM | 562.4 | 1,880% |
| Legal & General | 1,559.1 | 164% | Royal London | 549.4 | 361% |
| AXA Equity & Law | 1,529.4 | 155% | Britannia Life | 545.0 | 801% |
| | | | GT | 540.4 | 57% |
| Midland | 1,524.9 | No 1990 data | Lazard | 529.4 | 337% |
| Baillie Gifford | 1,519.2 | 800% | Edinburgh | 525.8 | 227% |
| Sun Life of Canada | 1,505.3 | 5,038% | Cazenove | 514.0 | 410% |
| Scottish Amicable | 1,502.4 | 259% | | | |
| Fleming UT Man | 1,438.7 | No 1990 data | Credit Suisse | 468.4 | 969% |
| Equitable | 1,374.1 | 241% | Martin Currie | 458.5 | 231% |
| Sun Life | 1,354.8 | 406% | NPI Managers | 443.4 | 116% |
| Clerical Medical | 1,329.7 | 302% | St. James | 414.7 | 95% |
| Prolific | 1,281.5 | No 1990 data | Thornton | 413.7 | 222% |
| Invesco | 1,255.6 | 18% | Woolwich | 410.5 | No 1990 data |
| | | | National Westminster | 402.0 | No 1990 data |
| Scottish Widows | 1,225.0 | 212% | Sun Alliance | 398.6 | 80% |
| Baring | 1,159.4 | 134% | Rothschild | 382.0 | 383% |
| Lloyds Bank | 1,124.9 | 128% | Marks & Spencer | 372.8 | 195% |
| Pearl | 1,087.9 | 148% | | | |
| Scottish Life | 1,032.4 | 225% | Capel-Cure Myers | 366.2 | 114% |
| HSBC | 992.9 | No 1990 data | Dimensional | 314.2 | 105% |
| Foreign & Colonial | 856.8 | 636% | | | |

Source: The Unit Trust Year Book 1995.

**Fig 14.3 Consistent funds and their management companies**

| Fund management company | Size | Fund name |
|---|---|---|
| Allied Dunbar | Large | Allied Dunbar European Growth |
| Barclays | Large | Barclaytrust Investment |
| Baring | Large | Baring Europe Select |
| Britannia Life | Large | Britannia Higher Yield |
| BWD Rensburg | Small | BWD UK Equity Income |
| Cazenove | Large | Cazenove UK Equity |
| Commercial Union | Large | CU PPT Equity Income |
| Credit Suisse | Medium | Credit Suisse Growth Port. |
| Eagle Star | Large | Eagle Star UK High Income |
| Friends' Provident | Large | Friends' Provident Euro. Grth. |
| Gartmore | Large | Gartmore European Select Ops. |
| | Large | Gartmore UK Index |
| GT | Large | GT Income |
| Guardian | Large | Guardhill |
| Invesco | Large | INVESCO Euro Small Cos. |
| | Large | INVESCO European Growth |
| Jupiter | Medium | Jupiter European |
| | Medium | Jupiter Income |
| Lazard | Large | Lazard UK Income |
| Mercury | Large | Mercury European Growth |
| | Large | Mercury Income |
| Metropolitan | Medium | Metropolitan Eurogrowth Plus |
| Prolific | Large | Prolific High Income |
| | Large | Prolific UK Blue Chip |
| Schroders | Large | Schroder Euro Smaller Cos. |
| | Large | Schroder Income |
| | Large | Schroder UK Equity |
| Sun Alliance | Medium | Sun Alliance Equity Income |

# IFA – YOUR EAR TO THE GROUND

You employ an IFA precisely to keep abreast of developments in the unit trust world. Occasionally, there are articles in the press about various good and bad developments in the unit trust business. Your IFA should know the rumours as well as the facts. If you work with a financial advisor who works for one financial institution – a so-called tied agent – obviously you cannot rely on him or her to be unbiased.

I make the point in Chapter 17 as well as here; your IFA serves as your eyes and ears on the unit trust business. Rely on him or her for this as well. As I write this, two of the more prominent fund management companies have undergone criticism for poor performance. Whether this is justified or not, I'm not certain.

> Chapter 17, Working with an IFA, discusses choosing an IFA.

However, your IFA should know about just these kinds of matters and whether the comments are justified.

## THE AWARDS

Besides size, another hallmark of performance ability are the awards to fund managers by various investment magazines. The awards are useful in that they try to give investors a snapshot about a fund management company's success. Unfortunately, as one investor said to me, 'Everyone seems to be the best.'

The diversity of the awards reflects the diversity of fund types and the difficulty of measuring quality. *What Investment?* editor Keiron Root notes that the awards provide 'a little help to make sense of it all'.[1]

Generally, the awards fall into two categories: overall performance and particular-sector performance. You'll often see mention of Fund Management Company of the Year. It seems like there are a lot of these.

> 'The diversity of the awards reflects the diversity of fund types and the difficulty of measuring quality.'

Then there are other awards which try to capture excellence in a particular sector, say Asia or emerging markets or income-producing investments.

The awards use a technique not very different from the BRUT technique suggested previously. Essentially, the performance award adds together fund percentile rankings across all sectors or in particular sectors, tallies up the score, and sees who's got the best overall percentile ranking.

There are further refinements, such as using volatility-adjusted returns or demarcating between large and small fund management companies. What you find again is that the industry is seeking a solution for the difficulty of choosing a fund management company. You'll note that each of the award categories corresponds to some characteristic we've explored.

Keiron Root continues that 'some fund management groups do achieve a high level of consistency in their performance – which investors will find particularly attractive. It is these consistent performers that the *What Investment?* awards are intended to track down.'[2]

Figure 14.4 shows *What Investment*'s list of top performing fund-management companies.

**Fig 14.4 Unit trust fund management companies of the year**

| 1 | Perpetual | 11 | Capel-Cure Myers |
|---|---|---|---|
| 2 | Provident Mutual | 12 | Stewart Ivory |
| 3 | Credit Suisse | 13 | Prudential |
| 4 | Lazard | 14 | Gartmore |
| 5 | Jupiter | 15 | Schroders |
| 6 | Eagle Star | 16 | Baillie Gifford |
| 7 | Martin Currie | 17 | AXA Equity & Law |
| 8 | Britannia Life | 18 | Morgan Grenfell |
| 9 | Framlington | 19 | Newton |
| 10 | AIB (Grofund) | 20 | Henderson Touche Remnant |

As part of their selection process, they average results over one, three and five years. In essence, they try to collapse all the fund-ranking statistics into one number. Again, this technique will help you to limit your choices. If a fund management company receives one of these awards, this provides another positive indication that it consistently performs better than average.

*Money Management*'s ranking takes a similar approach. Mark Battersby reports that 'The aim of these awards is to recognise an investment house's depth of fund management expertise over three different time scales and across a reasonable range of products. The performance figures are calculated . . . by taking into account both the actual investment performance and adjustment to take into account the portfolio's volatility.'[3]

**Fig 14.5** *Money Management*'s fund management company winners

| Area | Position | Fund management company |
|---|---|---|
| UK/Europe | Winner | Jupiter Unit Trust Managers |
| | Runner-up: | Perpetual Unit Trust Managers |
| | Highly commended: | Credit Suisse Investment Funds |
| International | Winner | Provident Mutual Unit Trust Managers |
| | Runner-up: | Templeton Unit Trust Managers |
| | Highly commended: | Cazenove Unit Trust Management |
| Overall | Winner | Provident Mutual Unit Trust Managers |
| | Runner-up | Perpetual Unit Trust Management |
| | Highly commended: | Lazard Unit Trust Managers |

My discussions with investors suggest they have no impact. One investor said to me, 'Everyone seems to win something.' My suggestion to the industry is to eliminate all but one.

# CALL THE LAW

A final check on the fund management company might mean a quick call to the Investment Management Regulator Organisation (IMRO) or a check of the Internet, where notices of findings are published. After all, it's not a good sign if there are numerous disciplinary actions against a fund management company. Obviously, it's a good sign, if there aren't.

**IMRO Investor Helpline:**
0171–390 5777
**IMRO's Website address:**
www.imro.co.uk

You can view a list of disciplinary action press releases on IMRO's website. If you discover the firm you're considering is the subject of disciplinary action, you should call the firm or ask your IFA to look into the matter. It might not have anything to do with the unit trusts.

You'll be surprised by some of the names you'll see on the list.

In summary, there are many things you can do to investigate the fund management company. I suggest strongly that you telephone several fund management companies and ask them to send you all the brochures, the *Micropal* summary sheets, and the scheme particulars. See if they do it; see how long it takes them; can they answer your questions over the phone? Trust your intuition.

Buy one magazine with the awards listing. *What Investment*'s awarding issue is in March and *Money Management*'s is in April. See if the fund management company you're considering is on their list.

Call IMRO to ask whether there are disciplinary actions pending against any of the fund management companies you're considering.

The point of these exercises is to form an impression. After all, it's your money . . .

REFERENCES

[1] 'UT Comment' by Keiron Root, *What Investment?*, London: Charterhouse Communications Group, March 1996, p. 49.

[2] Ibid., p. 49.

[3] 'Fund management group winners', by Mark Battersby, *Money Management*, April 1996, p. 25.

# <u>SUMMARY</u>

- *What Investment?* and *Money Management* magazines rank fund management companies based on overall performance.

- IFAs know whose reputation is growing and whose is sliding.

Before you invest:

- select a unit trust at a fund management company based on the following:
  - administratively competent
  - financially strong
  - strong fund-management skills.

Trust your judgment:

- How quickly do they answer the phone?

- How quickly do they mail you information?

- Do you receive all the documents you requested?

- Do they answer your questions clearly and simply?

- Do they spell your name right?

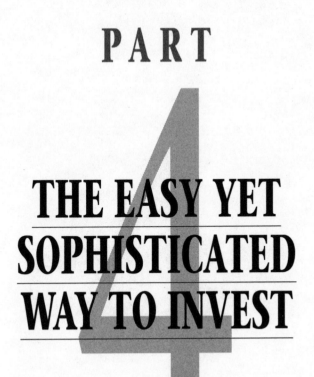

PART

# THE EASY YET SOPHISTICATED WAY TO INVEST

# TO TRACK
# OR NOT
# TO TRACK?

Tony Woods delights in taking the mickey out of the unit trust establishment. A gleeful smile creeps on to his face as he relates a story about sneaking an emissary into a Fidelity Investments press conference: 'We had one of the Virgin Atlantic flight attendants go to the press conference to read an investor's bill of rights outside the meeting. She claimed she was a journalist, and said to the receptionist, "I'm late for the press conference, where is it?" Rushing her into the meeting, they didn't check her credentials. After Fidelity was finished with the meeting, she peeled off her coat to reveal Virgin's trademark red flight attendant outfit, and read from a parchment scroll the benefits of Virgin's passive investment strategy and low costs.'

Woods, as you might realise now, is the marketing director for Virgin Direct, Sir Richard Branson's foray into the personal finance business. A press release sent out by him celebrates Virgin's Growth PEP's number one annual performance (see box).

---

### Virgin highlights severe gravity of active fund management[1]

Virgin Direct today welcomed new statistics which provide overwhelming evidence of the advantages of index-tracking over active fund management. Virgin Direct continued that 'The advantages of passive over active management – in terms of performance potential, cost, and risk diversification – have been widely understood within the investment industry, but rarely shared with the investing public.'

---

Virgin Direct introduced its Growth PEP two years ago, and, together with a bond PEP, has since grown fast. Virgin's first entry into the marketplace was with an index-tracking equity fund, easy to understand and cheap.

The decision to invest in a 'tracker', a fund which mirrors a stock market index, is altogether different from investing in an actively managed equity fund. The decision about which tracker to invest in relies on some of the same criteria as with an actively managed fund, namely, cost and performance along with deciding which index to track.

I should say upfront that I am biased in favour of tracker funds, having invested in them for the last ten years. Everyone should have a portion of their equity holdings in a tracker fund. Gary Smith, who runs Gartmore's UK Index Fund, what the *Financial Times* called the 'Rolls Royce'[2] of tracker funds recommends a core holding of up to 50 per cent in a tracker fund with the balance in actively managed funds.

Bill Mott, 17-year investment director with top-rated Credit Suisse funds, Ph.D. in quantum physics, puts his money in his own funds and tracker funds. I spent an intense one-and-a-half hours discussing the intricacies of picking the right unit trust. Mott says that investors should fully understand what investment philosophy you're using: Mott's speciality is sectoral (investing in sectors, based on their potential for growth, or income). I asked, 'Where do you have your money? His reply was, 'Credit Suisse funds for UK, Europe, emerging markets (there it is again!) and tracker funds.'

> '... the talent and raw brain power required to manage a tracker fund are far greater than you would imagine.'

Investing in a tracker is non-intuitive. That you could outperform other funds using a passive strategy goes against the grain. 'You've got to work to get ahead', 'no pain no gain' – all those idioms about effort and reward fly in the face of the passive tracking strategy. More and more pension funds are indexed because they've discovered that their highly paid investment managers cannot consistently beat the averages.

All tracker funds are not created equal, though. And the talent and raw brain power required to manage a tracker fund are far greater than you would imagine. Most importantly, the results from the various tracker funds vary considerably, depending on the index being tracked, the costs, the particular style chosen, and the skills of the manager.

In this chapter, we'll discuss how an index is constructed, what the various indices are, how a tracker fund works, how to assess whether the fund is tracking, and how to evaluate costs. Charges and costs are a key issue. We'll look at performance to discover huge performance variations. The chapter concludes with a technique for timing your investment to minimise volatility and increase the likelihood of investing right at the top of the market.

# FLIPPING COINS

Tracker funds have been one of the growth industries in the unit trust business over the past several years. There is a tremendous body of academic work which states that no one manager can, over time, consistently beat the market. Professor Burton G. Malkiel, in his classic *A Random Walk Down Wall Street*, makes an example about investment managers' prowess. His students begin the 'month' with a share valued at $50. Each 'day', they toss a coin to determine whether the share appreciated or went down by half a point ($0.50).

After a month of 'days', the student 'investment pros' charted their results on graph paper. Malkiel says, 'The chart derived from random coin tossing looked remarkably like a normal stock price chart and even appeared to display cycles.' Indeed, some of his more proficient coin tossers produced outstanding profits. Alas, he concludes, 'The cycles in the stock charts are no more true cycles than the runs of luck or misfortune of the ordinary gambler.' He summarises by saying that, 'Yes, history does tend to repeat itself in the stock market, but in an infinitely surprising variety of ways that confound any attempts to profit from a knowledge of past price patterns.'[3]

In another analogy, Malkiel hires 1,000 coin tossers. In this game, tossing a head yields a win; a tail, a loss. As expected, 500 flip heads and 'those winners advance to the next stage of the contest'. Again, 50 per cent toss heads and this 'skilled' group of 250 win. The contest continues as before and in the third round, there are 125 winners, 63 in the fourth, 31 in the fifth, 16 in the sixth, and eight in the seventh.

Malkiel livens it up: 'By this time, crowds start to gather to witness the surprising ability of these expert coin tossers. The winners are overwhelmed with adulation. They are celebrated as geniuses in the art of coin-tossing – their biographies are written and people urgently seek their advice. After all, there were 1,000 contestants and only eight could consistently flip heads. The game continues and there are even those who eventually flip heads nine and ten times in a row.'[4] The point of this analogy is not to indicate that investment fund managers can or should make their decisions by flipping coins, but that the laws of chance do operate and they can explain some amazing success stories.

> The parable of coin tossers is not all that different from the adulation poured on to those who know the secrets of the lottery.

The only discernible pattern exhibited by the market is a long, upward trend, averaging 7.8 per cent per year from 1919.[5] But this 7.8 per cent doesn't occur year after year; instead, the market went up 3 per cent and then 12 per cent and then down 5 per cent, and then back up 2 per cent, and so on. Last year, the market (FTSE All-Share) was up 16.5 per cent. The long-run average is 7.8 per cent.

Simon Bell, who works in equity information technology with investment giant Merrill Lynch, said, 'Even though I've got access to all the information, my own results with individual shares have been up and down.' Bell, who recently completed a Masters degree in Finance at the London Business School, added, 'The evidence is so much in favour of index tracking. I chose the Virgin Index PEP because it's so difficult for managers to consistently beat the Index.'

Often you'll hear the comment, tracker funds are so boring. Rightly so. The constant trudge upwards is what volatility-minimising investors seek. Further, it requires a Zen-like wisdom to invest in an index tracker; it requires patience. You won't have to worry about the thousands of countless details which go into evaluating a successful portfolio manager. You won't have to worry if the manager has changed companies; you won't have to worry about if the fund's variety, for example growth, has gone out of favour.

However, what will worry you is that when the market goes down, the value of your tracker fund will go right down with it. It's not clear if you can find the fund manager who is:

(1) capable of consistently predicting when the market is going to go down;

(2) able to sell at the right time.

If he can do both these things, then he will have, in fact, timed the market. (He or she could be just an excellent coin tosser.)

For example, the gigantic Fidelity Magellan Fund in the United States houses investors' funds totalling £32 billion ($52 billion), slightly more than half the value of all unit trusts investing in UK equities. All in one fund. Some time late in 1995, its manager believed that the US equity market was ready for a fall. He began selling equities in favour of bonds. This strategy would have paid off, had the US equity market fallen and the bond market risen. The fund manager, Jeff Vinik, obviously was no slouch, having been given the reins of the most closely watched fund in America. In his prior assignment for Fidelity, he beat the index by 85 percentage points over seven-and-a-half years. This time, though, he got it wrong. Six months later, he resigned to set up his own fund. The message is: even if you get it right seven and a half times out of seven and a half times, there's always the eighth.[6]

> 'After having made the decision to track, the next step is to decide which market to track.'

By tracking, you avoid this.

## WHAT YOU TRACK

After having made the decision to track, the next step is to decide which market to track. Today, the unit trust market allows you to track stock markets all over the world (see Figure 15.1).

The indices followed by the tracking funds in the UK were first created in the 1930s by the *Financial Times* and the London Stock

Fig 15.1 Equity markets: average return and average volatility

| Equity market | 10-year annual average return | 10-year annual average volatility |
|---|---|---|
| United Kingdom | 14.2% | 18.2% |
| United States of America | 13.7% | 19.8% |
| Europe, excluding the UK | 10.6% | 16.8% |
| Europe, including the UK | 10.9% | 16.0% |
| Japan | 1.9% | 24.5% |
| The Far East, excluding Japan | 14.9% | 28.1% |
| The Whole Wide World | 9.5% | 16.3% |

Exchange. As a group, they are referred to as the 'Footsie Indices' (*Financial Times* and *Stock Exchange*). To create the index, the total value of all shares is added together. This is called a capitalisation-weighted index. The other main type, known as a price index, is created simply by adding together the share prices: the famous Dow Jones Index in the US is simply the sum of the prices of the 30 stocks in the Index. A capitalisation-weighted index is more representative of movements in the entire market.

For a capitalisation-weighted index, the relative size of a company is important: companies with larger capitalisation have more influence on the index than companies with smaller capitalisation. For example, a 1 per cent share price increase in British Petroleum (BP), one of the larger companies, will have considerably more influence on the resulting index than if the share price of Boots moves 1 per cent because the total market value of BP is nearly seven times as large as Boots.

The broadest index is the FTSE All-Share which comprises shares in 919 companies. There are three sub-indices of the FTSE All-Share Index, which capture distinct sub-segments of the market. The FTSE 100 Share Index is the most well-known index. It contains 100 companies whose stocks have the biggest market capitalisation. These 100 stocks, the Blue Chips, make up 70 per cent of the value of the FTSE All-Share Index. When commentators speak of the Footsie, they are referring to the FTSE 100 Share Index.

A second category is the Mid-250 Index, which replicates results of the next 250 shares, representing companies with a capitalisation between the big boys and the small stocks. Not surprisingly, the next sub-category – the Small Cap Index – comprises the remaining 569 smaller stocks.

Each index represents a different market segment and a different opportunity. Broadly speaking, 'Small Cap' stocks have, over history, outperformed the 'Larger Caps'. No reward without volatility, however: the 'Small Caps' are more volatile than the FTSE 100. The 'Mid Caps' fall in between the two.

Other indices are the FT Actuaries European Index, both including and excluding the UK. For the United States, the most widely followed and replicated index is the Standard & Poor's 500, a selection of the 500 largest shares. For Japan, the main index is the Topix Index, which monitors the top section of about 1,200 Japanese companies.

For each category, there are generally two indices, one which varies only with the price, and another, called total return, which calculates the effect on the index if the dividends paid are reinvested. The total return index will be higher than the price index. You should note whether you're looking at a Total return (TR) index or a simple price index.

# IT'S SO EASY

The index fund manager has it so easy, it seems. His stocks have already been selected by the chosen index, all he need do is buy shares, sit back, and wait for the money to come pouring in.

I spent a few hours with Gary Smith who has managed Gartmore's UK Index Fund for the last six years. My headache on departure indicates the technical difficulties of running such a fund. Smith, a native of Zimbabwe, holds a Master's degree in Finance from Cambridge and is an actuary by training. Smith runs the quantitative desk for Gartmore and is responsible for a host of retail and institutional tracking funds.

There are many problems, Smith explains, associated with running a fund that aims to mirror the FTSE All-Share Index. First, there's a question of balance. The index changes every second as share prices change causing the relative weighting of each stock to change. This wouldn't be a problem if the index-tracking unit trust was fixed and no one bought or sold units. But it isn't, and money comes in and goes out all the time. The index-tracking fund manager must constantly adjust the shares in the portfolio to:

(1) reflect the index;
(2) take care of the daily inflows and outflows of cash.

David Johnson, who manages the Index Fund for Norwich Union and the Virgin Index Tracking PEP, solves this problem by the judicious use of stock-index futures. Thus, if the fund finds itself with a small amount of money, not enough to buy the 919 shares in sufficient size, he'll use futures to capture movements in the index without buying the shares. Then, when he has sufficient funds, he sells the futures and buys the shares. Funds such as Virgin and Norwich Union's are full replicators, as they try to replicate the index fully. Because of the complications of owning the correct proportions of all 919 shares, the index fund manager have devised various methods to help meet their tracking objectives.

The larger capitalisation stocks can be freely bought and sold almost any hour of the day in any size. For the smaller stocks, it can be downright difficult to find the shares at a reasonable price.

To solve this problem, some indexers purchase only a sample of the full number of shares; this is called 'sampling'. Here's where Smith's actuarial background comes in. With the growth in index funds, and as the problems of acquiring smaller shares became familiar, somebody observed that by holding only a selection of those shares, you could largely achieve the same movements as the index. A similar concept holds with life assurance; you can bet that everyone's not going to pass on at once, thus you assess how many people will die in a given year, and then set up funds for this likelihood; you don't need the funds all at once.

With the index trackers, if the fund manager buys all the shares in the FTSE 100 Index, he captures 71 per cent of the FTSE All-Share Index; by buying a large sample of the FTSE 250 Mid Caps, he picks up a reflection of another 21 per cent, which, *Money Management* says, gives him 92 per cent of the market's moves. The index fund manager then buys a selected sample of the remaining 8 per cent of the Small Caps, and lo and behold, he has the FTSE All-Share without having to buy all 919 shares.[7]

This proves a more cost-effective means of running an index fund, since you're not always buying and selling 919 shares; it's cheaper to buy or sell the larger capitalisation stocks.

The trade-off is that maybe you don't get it right, and your one 'Small Cap' stock takes off or plummets out of line with the index. The likelihood is small, but explains in part why an index fund won't always match the index.

Another issue: when a stock goes into or out of the index. Again, to me, it sounds so simple; you just buy or sell the stock. Gartmore's Smith explains that once the FTSE International Committee decides to include a new stock in the index, the particular market-makers for that stock push up the offer price for those shares, because they know that the index fund managers must buy those shares – and a lot of them – for their funds. The reverse is true as well, when a stock is dropped from the index list; the market-makers drop their bid price on those shares because they know the indexers must soon sell those shares.

A third complicating issue is dividends. The FTSE indices are updated the minute a company's shares go ex-dividend, meaning the holders no longer have the right to receive the company's previously announced dividend. However, the fund manager won't receive the cash for days or weeks. Yet, he must take into account the payment of the dividend, and its effect on the index.

Finally, most unit trust funds are valued at some point during the day, 12:00 or 14:00, while the index is always reported at day's end. This last point seemed minor to me, until Smith explained. 'If the market moves up 1 per cent or 2 per cent in the afternoon on the last day of the month, then we'll appear to be off by 1 per cent or 2 per cent, when in fact the difference is not real. You would be surprised how many phone calls we get about this.'

## WHY THE FUNDS DON'T EQUAL THE INDEX

These are some technical difficulties associated with running an index fund, which give rise to 'tracking error'. Tracking error refers to how closely the unit trust tracker fund tracks its chosen index. Sometimes you'll see articles in the press about how well this or that fund did in replicating the index.

There are two main reasons why your fund value won't equal the index. The first is that an index is just the addition of numbers. Indices don't pay brokerage, safekeeping fees, and index-fund manager's salaries.

A more serious reason why your investment in a tracker fund won't equal the growth in the index is, once again, the initial charge levied on your entrance to the fund and the continued, on-going, relentless annual management charge. Indexing fees should be a lot less than for an actively managed fund. It's criminal that in some cases they aren't. Marketplace competition is driving down the costs of investing in tracker funds.

Let's look at the charges levied by the tracker funds – again – the same general types: initial charge, initial 'extra bit', and annual management charges (see Figure 15.2).

As you can see, there is quite a wide variation in expenses. The range varies from an initial spread of 6.5 per cent to a low spread of 0 per cent. Note some funds have exit charges, which are included in the 'flat earth' calculations. Also note that even though the fund may have a 0 per cent initial charge, the actual spread can be 50 basis points. Secondly, the estimated exit charges need to be considered. Finally, take note of the annual management fees, which range from 1.0 per cent to 0.20 per cent.

If the performances were identical, then all you would need to focus on would be the fees. Alas, investment is not so simple.

The performance varies considerably as well, a function of the expenses, the type of index, full or partial replication, and the skill of the manager in dealing with all the minutiae.

A wide variation in one-year performance is shown among index funds that have been operational for at least a year (Figure 15.3). This stems from the skills of the tracker fund managers and, as always, the charges.

The first thing to note in Figure 15.3 is that the top performer is the index itself. Secondly, and most important, the high performers have in common low charges. The third point is the variation in returns. The top performer over the last year, the Virgin Tracker, returned 16.0 per cent while the lowest tracker, Old Mutual, returned 7.3 per cent, though both purport to mirror the same index.

In an article entitled 'Why Passive has become Massive', the *Financial Times* called Gartmore's fund, managed by Smith, the 'Rolls-Royce of trackers with top quartile performance in the UK

**Fig 15.2 Index-tracking funds by region, ordered by total five year charges**

| Area | Tracker fund | Index tracked | Flat earth 5-year PV | Flat earth 1-year PV | Charge | Initial 'extra bit' +Initial | =Spread | Mgmt. ann. charge | Exit charge* |
|---|---|---|---|---|---|---|---|---|---|
| UK | Govett FTSE Mid-250 Index | FTSE MidCap | −£105 | −£74 | 5.50% | 1.00% | 6.50% | 1.00% | |
| UK | Lloyds Bank FTSE 100 | FTSE 100 | −£100 | −£69 | 6.00% | 0.05% | 6.05% | 1.00% | |
| UK | Sovereign FTSE 100 | FTSE 100 | −£95 | −£64 | 5.00% | 0.49% | 5.49% | 1.00% | |
| UK | Govett UK Index | FTSE 100 | −£93 | −£62 | 5.50% | −0.22% | 5.28% | 1.00% | |
| UK | Royal Life UK Index Tracking | FTSE All-Share | −£71 | −£62 | 5.25% | 0.67% | 5.92% | 0.30% | |
| UK | Equitable UK Index Tracking | FTSE 100 | −£70 | −£55 | 5.00% | 0.00% | 5.00% | 0.50% | |
| UK | Norwich Union UK Index Track | FTSE All-Share | −£61 | −£54 | 5.00% | 0.25% | 5.25% | 0.20% | |
| UK | Old Mutual UK All Share Mirror | FTSE All-Share | −£48 | −£23 | 0.00% | 1.63% | 1.63% | 0.75% | |
| UK | Virgin UK Index Tracking | FTSE All-Share | −£42 | −£14 | 0.00% | 0.00% | 0.00% | 1.00% | 0.50% |
| UK | Direct Line FTSE 100 Tracker | FTSE 100 | −£42 | −£10 | 0.00% | 0.00% | 0.00% | 1.00% | |
| UK | Fidelity MoneyBuilder Index | FTSE 100 | −£37 | −£14 | 0.00% | 0.70% | 0.70% | 0.70% | |
| UK | BG British 350 | FTSE 100 & 250 | −£35 | −£19 | 0.00% | 1.43% | 1.43% | 0.50% | |
| UK | Gartmore UK Index | FTSE All-Share | −£26 | −£10 | 0.00% | 0.50% | 0.50% | 0.50% | |
| UK | Kleinwort Benson UK Index | FTSE All-Share | −£26 | −£10 | 0.00% | 0.49% | 0.49% | 0.50% | |
| UK | HKSB UK Index | FTSE All-Share | −£26 | −£9 | 0.00% | 0.47% | 0.47% | 0.50% | |
| UK | River & Mercantile Top 100 | FTSE 100 | −£19 | −£8 | 0.00% | 0.43% | 0.43% | 0.35% | |
| E Asia | HSBC Tiger Index | Capel E. Asia | −£47 | −£14 | 0.00% | 0.48% | 0.48% | 1.00% | |
| Eur-Ex UK | HSBC Eurotrak 100 | FTSE Eurotrak 100 | −£47 | −£14 | 5.25% | −4.75% | 0.50% | 1.00% | |
| Eur-Ex UK | Legal & General Euro Index | FTA Europe (ex UK) | −£39 | −£34 | 0.00% | 0.00% | 0.00% | 0.75% | 3-2-1% |
| France | Govett French Index | CAC-40 | −£93 | −£62 | 5.50% | −0.18% | 5.32% | 1.00% | |
| Germany | Govett German Index | DAX | −£93 | −£62 | 5.50% | −0.18% | 5.32% | 1.00% | |
| Japan | Govett Japan Index | Nikkei 225 | −£94 | −£63 | 5.50% | −0.15% | 5.35% | 1.00% | |
| Japan | Morgan Grenfell Japan Tracker | FTA Japan | −£72 | −£56 | 5.00% | 0.17% | 5.17% | 0.50% | |
| Japan | Legal & General Japan Tracker | FTA Japan | −£39 | −£34 | 0.00% | 0.00% | 0.00% | 0.75% | 3-2-1% |
| US | Govett US Index | S&P 500 | −£93 | −£62 | 5.50% | −0.19% | 5.31% | 1.00% | |
| US | Morgan Grenfell US Eq Index | S&P 500 | −£76 | −£60 | 5.00% | 0.57% | 5.57% | 0.50% | |
| US | John Govett US Index | S&P 500-fut/opt | −£71 | −£55 | 5.25% | −0.16% | 5.09% | 0.50% | |
| US | HSBC American Index | S&P 500-sampling | −£47 | −£14 | 0.00% | 0.49% | 0.49% | 1.00% | |
| US | Legal & General US Index | FTA World Index US | −£39 | −£34 | 0.00% | 0.00% | 0.00% | 0.75% | 3-2-1% |

*Source: Micropal Expert, October 1996, author's calculations.*

* No exit fee after the fifth year; exit fees are as percentage of investment at time of sale; 3-2-1% is sliding scale, depending on length of investment.

Fig 15.3 Performance and charges: Above and below average UK trackers

| Tracker fund | Index tracked | 12 month return* | Flat earth 5-year PV | Flat earth 1-year PV | Initial charge+ | 'Extra bit' | =Spread | Mgmt. ann. charge | Exit charge** | Launch date |
|---|---|---|---|---|---|---|---|---|---|---|
| FTSE All-Share | The Index itself | 16.5% | £0.00 | £0.00 | 0.00% | 0.00% | 0.00% | 0.00% | | 1930s |
| | | | | | | | | | | |
| Virgin UK Index Tracking | FTSE All-Share | 16.0% | -£42.48 | -£14.24 | 0.00% | 0.00% | 0.00% | 1.00% | 0.50% | Mar-95 |
| Gartmore UK Index | FTSE All-Share | 15.4% | -£26.34 | -£9.74 | 0.00% | 0.50% | 0.50% | 0.50% | | Jan-89 |
| Kleinwort Benson UK Index | FTSE All-Share | 15.3% | -£26.24 | -£9.64 | 0.00% | 0.49% | 0.49% | 0.50% | | Apr-95 |
| BG British 350 | FTSE 100 & Mid Cap 250 | 13.1% | -£35.44 | -£18.99 | 0.00% | 1.43% | 1.43% | 0.50% | | Apr-95 |
| River & Mercantile Top 100 | FTSE 100 | 12.9% | -£19.29 | -£7.62 | 0.00% | 0.43% | 0.43% | 0.35% | | Jul-95 |
| Legal & General UK Stockmkt | FTSE 100 | 11.2% | -£83.36 | -£19.05 | 0.00% | 0.00% | 0.00% | 2.00% | | May-93 |
| Legal & General UK Index | FTSE 100 | 10.4% | -£21.44 | -£33.19 | 0.00% | 0.00% | 0.00% | 0.50% | 3-2-1% | Sep-92 |
| average, high performers | | 13.5% | -£36.37 | -£16.07 | 0.00% | 0.41% | 0.41% | 0.76% | | |
| | | | | | | | | | | |
| Govett UK Index | FTSE 100 | 10.1% | -£93.04 | -£61.82 | 5.50% | -0.22% | 5.28% | 1.00% | | Dec-91 |
| HKSB UK Index | FTSE All-Share | 10.0% | -£26.04 | -£9.44 | 0.00% | 0.47% | 0.47% | 0.50% | | Mar-90 |
| Norwich Union UK Index Track | FTSE All-Share | 9.7% | -£60.67 | -£54.30 | 5.00% | 0.25% | 5.25% | 0.20% | | Oct-89 |
| Sovereign FTSE 100 | FTSE 100 | 9.3% | -£95.05 | -£63.90 | 5.00% | 0.49% | 5.49% | 1.00% | | Jul-94 |
| Lloyds Bank FTSE 100 | FTSE 100 | 8.8% | -£100.41 | -£69.45 | 6.00% | 0.05% | 6.05% | 1.00% | | Nov-94 |
| Royal Life UK Index Tracking | FTSE All-Share | 8.6% | -£71.35 | -£61.89 | 5.25% | 0.67% | 5.92% | 0.30% | | Sep-88 |
| Govett FTSE Mid-250 Index | FTSE Mid Cap 250 | 7.5% | -£104.72 | -£73.90 | 5.50% | 1.00% | 6.50% | 1.00% | | Aug-92 |
| Old Mutual UK All Share Mirror | FTSE All-Share | 7.3% | -£47.79 | -£22.33 | 0.00% | 1.63% | 1.63% | 0.75% | | Apr-92 |
| average, low performers | | 8.9% | -£74.88 | -£52.25 | 4.03% | 0.54% | 4.57% | 0.72% | | |

Source: Micropal Expert, 30 September 1996, author's calculations.

* Performance takes into account spread; offer to bid.

** No exit fee after the fifth year; exit fees are as percentage of investment at time of sale; 3-2-1% is sliding scale depending on length of investment.

growth and income sector over one and five years with gross income

> '... choose an index tracker that tracks close to the index and that charges low fees.'

reinvested'[8] (see Figure 15.4) while others were in the second quartile.

The message: choose an index tracker that tracks close to the index and that charges low fees.

Besides tracking funds, the other means of simplifying your decision is to let a professional choose on your behalf. In Chapter 16, we turn to the fund of funds.

## REFERENCES

[1] 'Virgin highlights severe gravity of active fund management,' Virgin Direct Press Release, 6 November 1996.

[2] 'Why passive has become massive' by Anthony Bailey, *Financial Times*, 14 September 1996, *FT Guide*, p. 14.

[3] *A Random Walk Down Wall Street* by Burton G. Malkiel (New York: WW Norton & Company, 1981).

[4] Ibid., pp. 169–170.

[5] *The BZW Equity-Gilt Study – 41st edition*, Barclays de Zoete Wedd, January 1996, pp. 3–4.

[6] 'The Real Story at Fidelity Magellan,' by John Rekenhaler, Chicago: *Morningstar Investor*, June 1996, V. 4, #10, pp. 1–2.

[7] 'On Course,' by Howard Goldring, *Money Management*, March 1995, p. 50.

[8] 'Why passive has become massive' by Anthony Bailey, *Financial Times*, 14 September 1996, *FT Guide*, p. 14.

## Fig 15.4  Gartmore UK Index Fund

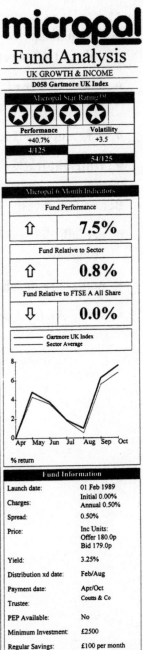

### Gartmore UK Index

Gartmore Broker Unit Trusts, Gartmore House, PO Box 65, 16-18 Monument Street, London EC3R 8QQ.

Information: Telephone - 0171 782 2000   Dealing - 01277 264 421

**Fund Objective:**
To track the capital performance of the FTSE All share index and to maintain a gross income yield equal to that of the index.

**micropal**
**Fund Analysis**

UK GROWTH & INCOME
D058 Gartmore UK Index

Micropal Star Rating™

| Performance | Volatility |
|---|---|
| +40.7% | +3.5 |
| 4/125 | |
| | 54/125 |

#### Micropal Cumulative Performance - to 30th September 1996

| Performance Period | 6 Months | 1 Year | 3 Years | 5 Years | 10 Years |
|---|---|---|---|---|---|
| Fund Performance | +7.0% | +15.4% | +40.7% | +81.1% | |
| Sector Average | +1.3% | +8.3% | +27.4% | +61.6% | +189.5% |
| Best Performing Fund | +8.6% | +17.2% | +44.9% | +95.2% | +431.0% |
| Fund Performance | | | | | |
| Sector Average Performance | | | | | |
| Worst Performing Fund | -10.7% | -7.7% | +6.8% | +27.1% | +111.7% |

(Offer-bid, net income reinvested)

| | | | | |
|---|---|---|---|---|
| Top Quartile | 4/151 | 3/141 | 4/125 | 8/112 |
| Second Quartile | | | | |
| Third Quartile | | | | |
| Bottom Quartile | | | | |

Micropal 6 Month Indicators

Fund Performance
⇧ **7.5%**

Fund Relative to Sector
⇧ **0.8%**

Fund Relative to FTSE A All Share
⇩ **0.0%**

#### Fund Size

| | |
|---|---|
| Fund Size | £216.4m |
| Sector Average | £137.2m |
| Largest Fund: | £1108.6m |
| Smallest Fund: | £0.8m |
| No. of Funds: | 152 |

■ Fund Size
□ Average Fund Size in Sector

#### Micropal Consistency of Performance Analysis

— Gartmore UK Index
— Sector Average

% indexed accumulated return (1986 = 0%)

87  88  89  90  91  92  93  94  95  96

150 100 50 0 -50

— Gartmore UK Index
— Sector Average

8- 6- 4- 2- 0
Apr May Jun Jul Aug Sep Oct
% return

**Year Ending 30 September (offer-offer, net income reinvested)**

| | 1987 | 1988 | 1989 | 1990 | 1991 | 1992 | 1993 | 1994 | 1995 | 1996 |
|---|---|---|---|---|---|---|---|---|---|---|
| Performance of Fund (%) | | | | -13.8 | 34.4 | 0.2 | 28.4 | 3.0 | 18.4 | 15.9 |
| Performance of Sector (%) | 62.9 | -17.1 | 24.0 | -17.2 | 30.9 | -4.1 | 32.3 | 1.1 | 16.3 | 14.3 |
| Perf. of Micropal UT Total (%) | 46.8 | -18.1 | 27.6 | -20.7 | 26.8 | -3.9 | 40.8 | 4.2 | 10.0 | 12.8 |
| FTSE A All Share (%) | 61.3 | -19.1 | 27.5 | -14.6 | 37.3 | -1.2 | 29.0 | 3.4 | 18.8 | 16.5 |
| UK Retail Price Index (%) | 4.2 | 5.9 | 7.6 | 10.9 | 4.1 | 3.6 | 1.8 | 2.2 | 3.9 | 1.2 |

| | 1987 | 1988 | 1989 | 1990 | 1991 | 1992 | 1993 | 1994 | 1995 | 1996 |
|---|---|---|---|---|---|---|---|---|---|---|
| Top Quartile | | | | | | | 26/142 | 21/125 | 31/131 | |
| Second Quartile | | | | | 26/161 | 29/108 | | | | 46/143 |
| Third Quartile | | | | | | | 78/120 | | | |
| Bottom Quartile | | | | | | | | | | |

#### Micropal Rolling Period Analysis

| | 1987 | 1988 | 1989 | 1990 | 1991 | 1992 | 1993 | 1994 | 1995 | 1996 |
|---|---|---|---|---|---|---|---|---|---|---|

| | |
|---|---|
| Highest 12 monthly return: | 34.4% |
| Lowest 12 monthly return: | -13.8% |
| Average 12 monthly return: | 12.2% |

% return
40 30 20 10 0 -10 -20

offer-offer, net income reinvested

#### Fund Information

| | |
|---|---|
| Launch date: | 01 Feb 1989 |
| Charges: | Initial 0.00% Annual 0.50% |
| Spread: | 0.50% |
| Price: | Inc Units: Offer 180.0p Bid 179.0p |
| Yield: | 3.25% |
| Distribution xd date: | Feb/Aug |
| Payment date: | Apr/Oct |
| Trustee: | Coutts & Co |
| PEP Available: | No |
| Minimum Investment: | £2500 |
| Regular Savings: | £100 per month |

**To subscribe: Micropal Publications / Micropal Ltd  Tel: 0181 741 4100  Fax: 0181 741 0939**

© Micropal Publications / Micropal Ltd 1996

The contents of Funds in View have been approved for the purpose of Section 57 of the Financial Services Act 1986 by a person authorised by the Law Society of England and Wales. Funds in View is available only by subscription and application to Micropal. It is issued subject to the risk factors and disclaimers set out on page(I) of Volume 1 of Funds in View - Sector and Fund Performances and the Explanatory Guide and should be read in conjunction with the Explanatory Guide (available free of charge from Micropal) which also contains important information regarding the Micropal Star Rating™. The Micropal Star Rating is a trademark of Micropal Ltd.

*Source: Micropal.*

# SUMMARY

- The manager of a tracking or indexing fund (a 'tracker') invests only in the shares of companies comprising the index.

- The manager of a tracker makes no judgements about the potential of shares to increase.

- The aim of a tracking fund is to follow the index: up or down.

- Different trackers following different indices around the world.

Before you invest:

- get all the available documents from the fund management company

- make sure the charges are low

- verify the fund performs like the index.

# Chapter 16

# GET THE BALANCE RIGHT

Tim Miller, chairman of fund of funds company, Portfolio, and former director of M&G and managing director of Framlington, suggests the following analogy between football predictions and picking the right unit trust.

'If you're trying to pick who will win the Premiership, it's likely to be Man United, Liverpool, or Arsenal. You can't predict the future. But it's more likely a consistent performer will win the Premiership than a team that has consistently been at the bottom.'

> 'Academic and practical studies confirm the inconsistency of consistency.'

And so it is with unit trusts. In Parts 1 to 3, we outlined the technique for isolating the consistent top performers. But the bad news is that today's five-year consistent performers won't be the same in five years. Academic and practical studies confirm the inconsistency of consistency.

But there is hope: the fund of funds. A fund of funds is a unit trust comprised of other unit trusts. The managers of these funds face the same challenge that you do: picking a consistently top-performing unit trust. This chapter summarises some of the techniques used by professional fund selectors to manage their funds. We'll look at how two professionals pick their funds – which is remarkably similar to the technique I outlined in Chapter 13. Next we'll look at evaluating a group of fund of funds in the international growth sector.

## THE TWO CRITERIA

Funds of funds are great for the individual investor – provided they meet the criteria – higher return with lower volatility than individual funds. The fund managers must develop an expertise in choosing funds. They stake their livelihood on the success of their approach.

Funds of funds fall into the same general categories as the rest of the unit trust universe: income-oriented, growth-oriented, equity and bond, Asia, Europe, and so on. The other major distinction is whether the fund-of-fund manager is free to choose among the universe of unit trusts or whether the fund-of-fund manager chooses only from his firm's stable of unit trusts.

If the manager has free rein to choose internal or external unit trusts, this is better for you than if the manager is forced to pick and choose among his firm's funds. Of course, some fund management houses have developed reputations in certain sectors (for example, M&G for income-producing funds, or Schroders for Asian-based funds) in which case it might not be such a bad thing. Yet, given the choice, I'd rather my fund-of-fund manager were able to choose from all companies.

There are several good arguments in favour of a fund of funds and one major argument against funds of funds. On the positive side first: unlike you, if this fund sells out of one fund to buy another fund, it is not liable for capital gains tax. The second major benefit is that because they buy in volume, they are able to get larger discounts off the initial charge and possibly a reduction in the annual management fee.

The other side of the coin, however, is that the fund charges a healthy annual fee on top of each fund's annual fee. Thus, if a fund has an annual management charge of say, 1.25 per cent, and the fund of fund charges 1.00 per cent on top of this, that's 2.25 per cent in charges which the choice of funds must overcome in terms of returns. But the record has been surprisingly good. Offsetting this huge charge is the possibility that they may get a volume discount from the initial charge. And if the fund of funds chooses only in-house unit trusts, it's likely that there will not be a double charging of annual and initial fees. The key is to look very closely at the fees.

## A TALE OF THREE FUNDS

After ten years running Fidelity Investments and, before that, running Schlesingers (Invesco), Richard Timberlake finally ran out of steam. 'I'm an entrepreneurial butterfly,' he says, 'and I found myself more and more involved in business administration. I wanted a multiplicity of venture,' he added, handing me three different current business cards with his name on them.

On leaving Fidelity, he took his pension fund with him. Unlike ordinary mortals who would have simply moved their pension, Timberlake decided to turn his pension into a unit trust, which was a collection of unit trusts, enlisting several colleagues and family members to invest in it. Because of his experience and expertise at selecting fund managers, others knowledgeable in the industry poured more money into his fund of funds, which is now known as Portfolio Fund of Funds.

He wanted to build a successful fund of funds built on a solid base of research. He believed that the available analyses of unit trusts were dismal. He set up Fund Research with a colleague from Fidelity, Peter Jeffries. Fund Research provides four-page summary sheets of both qualitative and quantitative analysis on chosen funds. Of the 1,600-strong unit trust fund universe, Fund Research selects the top 250 for thorough analysis.

'I needed a system to narrow down the 1,600 to 250. We needed an army of unit trust analysts. We then would go and interview the top 20 per cent of managers to develop a rating system.'

He said, 'We looked at all the academic studies. We found that past performance has no correlation with the future. [A warning we've seen before.] But,' he says, looking up with a smile, 'if we looked at discrete annual periods' and rank funds on a decile basis, 'then we could find some funds which would consistently perform well.'

> A decile basis ranks funds as top 10 per cent, top 20 per cent, and so on.

And this is the basis of the first screen. Basically, he looks to see how well the fund has performed in each of the prior five-year periods, and then calculates an average decile performance. Thus, if over five years a firm ranks in the top 10 per cent, top 20 per cent, top 30 per cent, top 40 per cent and top 50 per cent respectively, the average of these figures is 30 per cent. This is what he calls the 'consistency ratio'.

He says of the cumulative performance statistics reported in magazines, 'Cumulative is meaningless', because if the fund performs exceedingly well in the most recent year, this will influence the other four-year performance figures.

Thus, the top 250 funds ranked on an average decile basis, with their consistency ratios, are included in Fund Research's analysis.

Timberlake then chooses funds for investment by geographic diversity and by the qualitative report from Fund Research.

If a fund falls out of favour on the consistency measure, Timberlake will ring up the portfolio manager to determine what the problem is: the familiar bad patch or whether the fund manager is preoccupied with other matters.

I asked him for how long he would be willing to put up with poor performance.

He said, 'I can't wait if the guy's got out of gear – three months, six months at the most.'

The performance of his fund? Very good indeed.

On a cumulative basis, Portfolio Fund of Funds ranks first out of 27 over five years. But we know that cumulative basis is 'meaningless'. Let's look at the performance record on a discrete, offer-to-offer basis as shown in Figure 16.1. Figure 16.2 shows the *Micropal* chart for Portfolio Fund of Funds.

**Fig 16.1 Portfolio Fund of Funds: 1992–96 performance on a discrete and cumulative basis**

|  | *1992* | *1993* | *1994* | *1995* | *1996* | *Cumulative* |
|---|---|---|---|---|---|---|
| Portfolio Fund of Funds | 3.0% | 40.3% | 19.4% | 11.4% | 13.5% | 118.2% |
| FTSE All-Share | −1.2% | 29.0% | 3.4% | 18.8% | 16.5% | 82.4% |
| Better/(worse) FTSE | 4.2% | 11.3% | 16.0% | −7.4% | −3.0% | 35.8% |
| MSCI World Index | −2.3% | 42.7% | 2.1% | 14.0% | 15.1% | 86.8% |
| Better/(worse) World Index | 5.3% | −2.4% | 17.3% | −2.6% | −1.6% | 31.4% |
| Fund of funds sector | −2.7% | 37.6% | 6.2% | 8.0% | 11.3% | 70.9% |
| Better/(worse) sector | 5.7% | 2.7% | 13.2% | 3.4% | 2.2% | 47.2% |
| Quartile | 1 | 2 | 1 | 2 | 2 |  |

*Source: Micropal, 30 September 1996.*

The performance summary for Portfolio Fund of Funds includes comparisons with the FTSE All-Share Index and the Morgan Stanley World Index as well as other funds of funds. In comparing a fund of funds, the investor should make comparisons with the appropriate benchmark because these types of unit trusts can be comprised of lower-volatility, lower-return gilt and fixed interest funds to higher-volatility, higher-return emerging markets funds.

## Fig 16.2 *Micropal* chart for Portfolio Fund of Funds

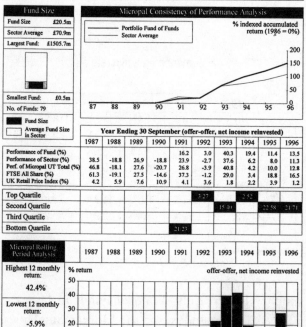
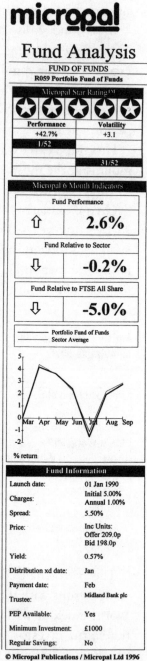

### Portfolio Fund of Funds

Portfolio Trust Managers, Walbrook House, 23 Walbrook, London EC4N 8LD.

Information: Telephone - 0171 280 3700    Dealing - 0800 262 443

**Fund Objective:**
To achieve maximum total return (mixture of capital growth & income) from a low risk very diversified portfolio.

## micropal

### Fund Analysis

FUND OF FUNDS

R059 Portfolio Fund of Funds

#### Micropal Cumulative Performance - to 30th September 1996

| Performance Period | 6 Months | 1 Year | 3 Years | 5 Years | 10 Years |
|---|---|---|---|---|---|
| Fund Performance | -3.1% | +7.3% | +42.7% | +106.3% | |
| Sector Average | -2.8% | +5.1% | +20.2% | +67.1% | |
| Best Performing Fund | +2.8% | +13.5% | +42.7% | +106.3% | |
| Fund Performance | | | | | |
| Sector Average Performance | | | | | |
| Worst Performing Fund | -10.2% | -7.7% | -4.1% | +29.2% | |

(Offer-bid, net income reinvested)

#### Micropal Star Rating™

| Performance | Volatility |
|---|---|
| +42.7% | +3.1 |
| 1/52 | |
| | 31/52 |

| | 6 Months | 1 Year | 3 Years | 5 Years |
|---|---|---|---|---|
| Top Quartile | | | 1/52 | 1/27 |
| Second Quartile | | 21/71 | | |
| Third Quartile | 44/75 | | | |
| Bottom Quartile | | | | |

#### Micropal 6 Month Indicators

**Fund Performance**

⇧ **2.6%**

**Fund Relative to Sector**

⇩ **-0.2%**

**Fund Relative to FTSE All Share**

⇩ **-5.0%**

#### Fund Size

| | |
|---|---|
| Fund Size | £20.5m |
| Sector Average | £70.9m |
| Largest Fund: | £1505.7m |
| Smallest Fund: | £0.5m |
| No. of Funds: | 79 |

■ Fund Size
□ Average Fund Size in Sector

#### Micropal Consistency of Performance Analysis

— Portfolio Fund of Funds
— Sector Average

% indexed accumulated return (1986 = 0%)

#### Year Ending 30 September (offer-offer, net income reinvested)

| | 1987 | 1988 | 1989 | 1990 | 1991 | 1992 | 1993 | 1994 | 1995 | 1996 |
|---|---|---|---|---|---|---|---|---|---|---|
| Performance of Fund (%) | | | | | 16.2 | 3.0 | 40.3 | 19.4 | 11.4 | 13.5 |
| Performance of Sector (%) | 38.5 | -18.8 | 26.9 | -18.8 | 23.9 | -2.7 | 37.6 | 6.2 | 8.0 | 11.3 |
| Perf. of Micropal UT Total (%) | 46.8 | -18.1 | 27.6 | -20.7 | 26.8 | -3.9 | 40.8 | 4.2 | 10.0 | 12.8 |
| FTSE All Share (%) | 61.3 | -19.1 | 27.5 | -14.6 | 37.3 | -1.2 | 29.0 | 3.4 | 18.8 | 16.5 |
| UK Retail Price Index (%) | 4.2 | 5.9 | 7.6 | 10.9 | 4.1 | 3.6 | 1.8 | 2.2 | 3.9 | 1.2 |

| | 1987 | 1988 | 1989 | 1990 | 1991 | 1992 | 1993 | 1994 | 1995 | 1996 |
|---|---|---|---|---|---|---|---|---|---|---|
| Top Quartile | | | | | | 3.27 | | 2.52 | | |
| Second Quartile | | | | | | 15.40 | | | 22.58 | 21.71 |
| Third Quartile | | | | | | | | | | |
| Bottom Quartile | | | | | | 21.23 | | | | |

| Micropal Rolling Period Analysis | 1987 | 1988 | 1989 | 1990 | 1991 | 1992 | 1993 | 1994 | 1995 | 1996 |
|---|---|---|---|---|---|---|---|---|---|---|
| Highest 12 monthly return: **42.4%** | | | | | | | | | | |
| Lowest 12 monthly return: **-5.9%** | | | | | | | | | | |
| Average 12 monthly return: **16.4%** | | | | | | | | | | |

% return — offer-offer, net income reinvested

— Portfolio Fund of Funds
— Sector Average

% return

#### Fund Information

| | |
|---|---|
| Launch date: | 01 Jan 1990 |
| Charges: | Initial 5.00% |
| | Annual 1.00% |
| Spread: | 5.50% |
| Price: | Inc Units: |
| | Offer 209.0p |
| | Bid 198.0p |
| Yield: | 0.57% |
| Distribution xd date: | Jan |
| Payment date: | Feb |
| Trustee: | Midland Bank plc |
| PEP Available: | Yes |
| Minimum Investment: | £1000 |
| Regular Savings: | No |

*Source: Micropal.*

# A TALE OF SUCCESS

Unfortunately, consistency is a moving target. Consistently strong-performing funds do not stay that way. Why consistency is impossible to maintain is the subject of fierce debate. Bill Mott, who runs Credit Suisse's funds, put it best: 'There are no rules. People who try to get investment advice expect it to be like accountacy. But the investment world is constantly changing.' He gives an example: 'Anybody who bought a house between 1955 and 1987 thought that owning a house was the best investment possible. Yet, if you took that view from 1988 onwards, you'd find that it was no longer true.' Mott and Timberlake used the same analogy: 'It's like driving looking only in the rear-view mirror.'

The conclusion I reached from my analysis is that unit trust fund holdings need to be reviewed periodically, and eventually changed. The world moves forward.

With this in mind, we look at how Jonathan Fry, an investment director at Premier Investments of Guildford, approaches fund selection. Fry and a colleague, Mike O'Shea, have established several Premier Selector fund of funds, which takes the consistent inconsistency of fund managers to heart. The funds are administered by Scottish Widows, though Premier's Fry and O'Shea are the investment managers. Their first step is to select only funds above £10 million, with at least a one-year track record, and sponsored by a reputable name.

They review all available unit trusts with the aim of choosing less well-known ones who may show exceptional risk-adjusted performance.

The investment managers insist on at least 20 different holdings, with no one holding exceeding 6 per cent. Thus, if one of the funds in the Selector runs into a bad patch, its performance will not overly influence the results.

The funds are growth, income, or globally oriented.

The three key points are:

1 fixed global weighting
2 discrete top-quartile fund performance/volatility rating within geographic region
3 rebalancing of funds every 90 days.

The Growth Fund invests 55 per cent in the UK and 45 per cent internationally while the Global Fund is worldwide. For the global portions of a fund, Fry first fixes the geographical weighting to mirror the world market capitalisation, e.g., if Europe makes up 20 per cent of the world's stock markets, then 20 per cent of his fund is allocated towards Europe. This view goes with the momentum of the world markets: if European markets are growing, its allocation moves up. Each quarter, fund returns and absolute volatility in each sector are reviewed against their peers.

Every 90 days, Fry recalculates the return/volatility balance indicators, the Sharpe ratio, for every fund in the unit trust universe, divided up by geographical sector. If the fund is no longer performing up to standard, it goes on his 'watchlist'. He'll call the fund managers to find out what's going wrong. If, after the next 90 days, he finds the same underperformance/volatility combination for the fund, out it goes.

The final stage results in 'judgement call'. The mechanistic screen filters down several excellent funds. It is then a matter of choosing the best among the best, and he makes a selection based on his own judgement. Fry and O'Shea's technique is similar to the BRUT technique described in Chapter 13.

In the last year, his fund returned investors 14.6 per cent. While the fund has only been around for about two years, its consistent approach is solid.

## PICKING A FUND OF FUNDS

We've seen two funds of funds which have adopted many of the principles described to you in this book: search for strong discrete performance, coupled with lower volatility. The fund of funds approach solves three problems you face: consistent selection techniques, constant monitoring, and an ear to the ground. Fund of fund managers are experts at choosing the best unit trusts. They stake their own livelihoods on their abilities. Will they always get it right? Probably not. But that's your responsibility to monitor.

All funds of funds are not created equal. Indeed, not even all fund of funds appear on the fund of funds list. Some funds of funds are income-oriented, some growth-oriented, some comprise only gilt and fixed interest funds, and

> 'If you are considering a fund of funds, find out immediately what sector it purports to choose funds from.'

so on. Hence, when comparing a fund of funds versus the average of fund of funds, it is a clear issue of apples and oranges. It's better to compare like with like: for example, for Premier's Growth fund of funds described above, an appropriate comparison would be with UK growth and international growth unit trusts.

If you are considering a fund of funds, find out immediately what sector it purports to choose funds from. The box gives a list of general and specific funds of funds in terms of the various categories, which offer a blend of investment area, investment style, and equities and fixed-interest instruments.

As an example of analysing a fund of funds, I chose one of the larger fund of funds available for investment: TSB Selector, which holds £407 million in clients' funds. According to its brochure, 'The

| **Fund of fund categories** | | |
|---|---|---|
| *Area* | International | Europe including UK |
| | North America | Far East including Japan |
| | United Kingdom | Japan |
| | Emerging markets | |
| *Style* | Growth | Growth and income |
| | Income (or value) | |
| *Instruments* | Fixed-interest | Mixed: fixed interst and equities |
| | Equities | |

fund seeks to obtain long-term capital growth from investment in the range of TSB Funds.' We also learn that 'from 1.4.91 to 29.4.96, income units with income reinvested have increased 60.56 per cent on an offer-to-bid basis'.

Later the Manager's Report states that 'the TSB Selector Fund grew 11.6 per cent as compared with a rise of 10.7 per cent in the FTSE All-Share Index during the six prior months'.

Digging into the small print, we learn in the Management Charges section that the initial charge is 5.5 per cent while the annual management charge is 1.5 per cent. No mention is made about whether or not this is on top of the management charges made by the funds included in TSB's fund of funds. The information provided to investors in TSB's Selector Fund manager's report is scant, and an investor desiring more information might ring up TSB to find out further details.

Or you could request the *Micropal* fact sheet to be sent to you (see Figure 16.4).

Your main question: what are the performance and volatility like?

First off, you can't compare the return and volatility with the average for fund of funds. We saw in the box how many different flavours of fund of funds there are. It would be inappropriate to compare these returns with, say, an emerging markets or Japanese fund of funds.

My suggestion is to compare it with two indices: the FTSE All-Share Index and the average for the UK equity growth sector whose primary aim is achieving capital growth (see Figure 16.3).

**Fig 16.3  TSB Selector Fund of Funds vs average UK equity growth and FTSE All-Share Index**

| Returns, net of tax and charges | TSB Selector | Average UK equity growth | FTSE All-Share |
|---|---|---|---|
| Last 12 months | 6.9% | 10.7% | 16.5% |
| Last three years | 22.3% | 32.3% | 43.1% |
| Volatility | 3.3% | 3.6% | 3.5% |

*Source: Micropal Expert*, 30 September 1996.

## Fig 16.4 TSB Selector

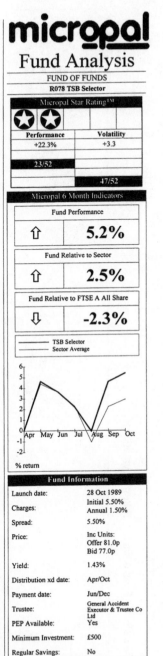

# TSB Selector

TSB Unit Trusts, Charlotte Place, Andover, Hants SP10 1RE.

Information: Telephone - 01264 345 678   Dealing - 01264 346 794

**Fund Objective:**
To provide long term capital growth from investment in the range of TSB funds.

### Micropal Cumulative Performance - to 30th September 1996

| Performance Period | 6 Months | 1 Year | 3 Years | 5 Years | 10 Years |
|---|---|---|---|---|---|
| Fund Performance | -0.6% | +6.9% | +22.3% | +54.9% | |
| Sector Average | -2.8% | +5.1% | +20.2% | +67.1% | |
| Best Performing Fund | +2.8% | +13.5% | +42.7% | +106.3% | |

| | | | | | |
|---|---|---|---|---|---|
| Fund Performance | | | | | |
| Sector Average Performance | | | | | |
| Worst Performing Fund | -10.2% | -7.7% | -4.1% | +29.2% | |

(Offer-bid, net income reinvested)

| | | | | |
|---|---|---|---|---|
| Top Quartile | 17/75 | | | |
| Second Quartile | | 28/71 | 23/52 | |
| Third Quartile | | | | |
| Bottom Quartile | | | | 23/27 |

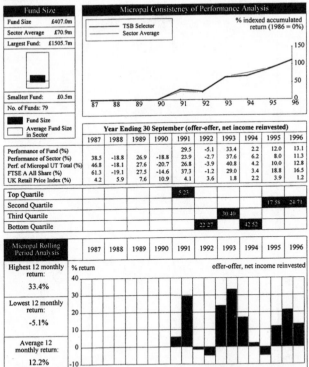

### Fund Size

| | |
|---|---|
| Fund Size | £407.0m |
| Sector Average | £70.9m |
| Largest Fund: | £1505.7m |
| Smallest Fund: | £0.5m |
| No. of Funds: | 79 |

Fund Size
Average Fund Size in Sector

### Micropal Consistency of Performance Analysis

TSB Selector
Sector Average

% indexed accumulated return (1986 = 0%)

### Year Ending 30 September (offer-offer, net income reinvested)

| | 1987 | 1988 | 1989 | 1990 | 1991 | 1992 | 1993 | 1994 | 1995 | 1996 |
|---|---|---|---|---|---|---|---|---|---|---|
| Performance of Fund (%) | | | | | 29.5 | -5.1 | 33.4 | 2.2 | 12.0 | 13.1 |
| Performance of Sector (%) | 38.5 | -18.8 | 26.9 | -18.8 | 23.9 | -2.7 | 37.6 | 6.2 | 8.0 | 11.3 |
| Perf. of Micropal UT Total (%) | 46.8 | -18.1 | 27.6 | -20.7 | 26.8 | -3.9 | 40.8 | 4.2 | 10.0 | 12.8 |
| FTSE A All Share (%) | 61.3 | -19.1 | 27.5 | -14.6 | 37.3 | -1.2 | 29.0 | 3.4 | 18.8 | 16.5 |
| UK Retail Price Index (%) | 4.2 | 5.9 | 7.6 | 10.9 | 4.1 | 3.6 | 1.8 | 2.2 | 3.9 | 1.2 |
| Top Quartile | | | | | 5.23 | | | | | |
| Second Quartile | | | | | | | | | 17.58 | 24.71 |
| Third Quartile | | | | | | | 30.40 | | | |
| Bottom Quartile | | | | | 22.27 | | 42.52 | | | |

### Micropal Rolling Period Analysis

| | 1987 | 1988 | 1989 | 1990 | 1991 | 1992 | 1993 | 1994 | 1995 | 1996 |
|---|---|---|---|---|---|---|---|---|---|---|
| Highest 12 monthly return: 33.4% | | | | | | | | | | |
| Lowest 12 monthly return: -5.1% | | | | | | | | | | |
| Average 12 monthly return: 12.2% | | | | | | | | | | |

offer-offer, net income reinvested

---

*Source: Micropal.*

---

**From image 1 (right column):**

# micropal
## Fund Analysis
### FUND OF FUNDS
**R078 TSB Selector**

#### Micropal Star Rating™

| Performance | Volatility |
|---|---|
| +22.3% | +3.3 |
| 23/52 | |
| | 47/52 |

#### Micropal 6 Month Indicators

**Fund Performance**
⇧ **5.2%**

**Fund Relative to Sector**
⇧ **2.5%**

**Fund Relative to FTSE A All Share**
⇩ **-2.3%**

TSB Selector
Sector Average

% return

#### Fund Information

| | |
|---|---|
| Launch date: | 28 Oct 1989 |
| Charges: | Initial 5.50% Annual 1.50% |
| Spread: | 5.50% |
| Price: | Inc Units: Offer 81.0p Bid 77.0p |
| Yield: | 1.43% |
| Distribution xd date: | Apr/Oct |
| Payment date: | Jun/Dec |
| Trustee: | General Accident Executor & Trustee Co Ltd |
| PEP Available: | Yes |
| Minimum Investment: | £500 |
| Regular Savings: | No |

**Fig 16.5 TSB Selector Fund of Funds: return vs volatility**

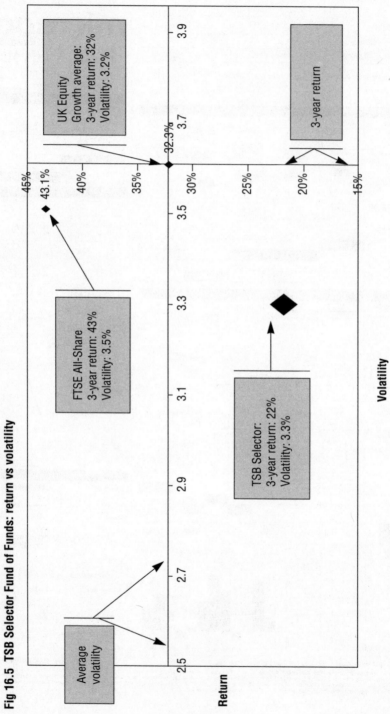

*Source: Micropal Expert, 30 September 1996.*

For the TSB Selector, we find that the return over three years is less than the average, as is the volatility (see Figures 16.4 and 16.5). Thus, while you would enjoy lower volatility than the average for this fund, the trade-off is the lower return. A preferable fund of funds to invest in would have greater than average returns coupled with lower than average volatility.

# INTERNATIONAL FUNDS OF FUNDS

I've chosen 11 funds of funds which are internationally growth-oriented and have at least three years of data.

Most funds met the criteria for lower than average volatility; however, only a few of the funds had higher returns than average for the sector. These high-return, low-volatility funds are then candidates for investment (see Figure 16.6).

The fund of funds offers investment expertise along with an ear to the ground about the goings-on in the unit trust business. Given the higher expense associated with a fund of funds, you should very carefully scrutinise the performance before investing.

**Fig 16.6  Internationally growth-oriented funds of funds: data for volatility and returns over three years**

|  | Lower volatility | Higher volatility |
|---|---|---|
| **Higher return** | Invesco Managed: 29.3% & 3.3%<br>Royal Life Managed: 26.5% & 2.8%<br>Matheson Select Portfolio: 25.3% & 3.2%<br>HTR Independent Portfolio: 25.0% & 2.9% |  |

International growth sector average: 24.6% & 3.5%

|  | Lower volatility | Higher volatility |
|---|---|---|
| **Lower return** | TSB Selector: 22.3% & 3.3%<br>Friends' Provident Capital Growth: 19.7% & 3.0%<br>Sun All Pygmalion Internat. Equity: 18.2% & 3.2%<br>Friends' Provident Open Cap. Growth: 17.6% & 3.0%<br>OM Roxborough Strategic Growth: 12.5% & 2.6%<br>OM International Growth: 8.05% & 2.3% | City Financial Buckley World Growth: 11.5% & 4.2% |

*Source: Micropal Expert*, 30 September 1996.

# BOILING IT DOWN

This brings us to the close of our analysis of particular funds. The techniques necessary to evaluate all aspects of a fund have been discussed. The summary of the BRUT technique is shown in Figure 16.7.

Knowing what's going on is crucial. Rumours fly around the fund management companies. It takes a skilled manager to detect the difference between a rumour that is nonsense and one that is worth heeding. Hiring an IFA who is aware of activity in the unit trust business can be a form of insurance. How to select an IFA is discussed in Chapter 17, Working with an IFA.

**Fig 16.7  Buying the right unit trust, the BRUT technique**

1 **Choose a sector,** e.g. UK Growth or Europe

2 **Picking funds:**\* Select only those funds with first quartile performance in each of the last five years; this is your consistent funds list.

3 **Reduce risk:** Note the volatility of each of the Consistent Funds for use in final determination.
 *Short-cut:* you can rely on *Micropal*\*\* four or five stars to point you towards high-returning, low-volatility consistent performers.

4 **Get information:** Ring up the fund management companies for those funds on the consistent list to request information[†].

5 **Evaluate fund management companies:** From the consistent funds list, pick reliable and financially strong fund management companies.

6 **Pay the least:** From the consistent list of funds run by financially strong and reliable fund management companies, invest in the fund with the lowest combined five-year expenses: bid-offer spread percentage, five years of management charges, and exit fees, if any, and volatility.

**Sources of information:**

\* You can conduct the sector and fund analysis by using *Money Management* magazine or *What Investment?* magazine, which both include extensive fund listings. These magazines highlight top quartile performers for each sector in **bold face**.

\*\* *Micropal Expert* software and data were used extensively for this book and are available for purchase through *Micropal* 0181-741 4100. You can conduct the above analysis with this software. Otherwise, *Micropal* might be willing to photocopy a page or two for you if you ask them.

[†] Request all brochures for fund, including Manager's Report and Scheme Particulars; also make sure to request application for investment.

# SUMMARY

- A fund of funds invests, not in shares or bonds, but in other unit trusts.

- The investor acquires the skills of a manager to assess other unit trusts.

- Fund of funds come in the same varieties as most unit trust categories; growth, income, international, and so on.

Before you invest:

- get all the available documents from the fund management company

- check to see whether the fund of funds invests only in other funds from the same management company or whether it can invest in any company's unit trusts

- compare performance, not with other funds of funds, but with other like unit trusts in the same category

- verify the fund of funds reports of higher performance coupled with lower volatility than an ordinary unit trust in the category.

PART

5

# GETTING IT RIGHT

# WORKING WITH
# AN IFA

Most people turn to untrained family members for financial advice, surveys show, because they 'believe financial advisors to be rogues and charlatans'.[1] Only a small proportion turn to professionally trained financial advisors. That's too bad.

> Market research suggests that 10 per cent of men and 7 per cent of women use financial advisors.

My own instincts and experience tell me why people choose family members over financial advisors for advice. They trust them, as opposed to financial advisors, who are financially motivated. That financial motivation cannot be denied. However, there's a very simple technique for eliminating the financial motivation and ensuring you're given the best advice. Before getting to that, let's see what a few financial advisors say. You'll find there are many different kinds of financial advisors with differing specialities.

Fiona Price, founder and namesake of Fiona Price & Partners, says, 'Risk is different for everyone. Most people don't want to take much risk,' she continues. 'But clearly, they want to get better results than what the building societies offer. We try to help people understand the risks attached to different savings and investments. Not even the building societies are free of risk because of inflation.'

Jamie Berry, founder and namesake of Berry Asset Management, is solely dedicated to professional investment management. He says 'You should understand and be comfortable with the fees. You should be prepared to ask for a discount. If you don't ask, you won't get it.'

David Brennan, of Swire Fraser Investment Management, says, 'Cut me in half and you'll find "unit trusts" inscribed.'

Pascal Matic, owner of UNITAS, launched into an assessment of my portfolio and recommended his choice of unit trusts that would fit into my portfolio. 'We are solely a *Unit* trust *Advisory Service*' – whence comes the name, UNITAS – 'A small firm cannot cover all specialities. The worst is to be a jack of all trades and specialists in none. We score highly by offering a narrow range of products.'

Affable Mark Hynes with Quay Associates doesn't like chasing clients. 'Clients,' he adds, 'don't like to be chased.'

Trevor Howard with M.D.H Hughes: ' "Risk" is such a funny word. We hear whether our clients want high risk or low risk. People feel that if they invest solely in the UK, somehow that's a low-risk fund, which I don't agree with. It has always made sense to spread investments around the world; that's the point of investing in unit trusts in the first place, they spread the risk around.'

There have been a few bad apples, such as emerged with the Knight Williams fiasco, which attracted a vast amount of press coverage. Be aware of this possibility, and guard against it by asking the right questions and by recognising that anything that sounds too good to be true probably is. However, the actions of a few have tarred an institution created out of an excellent premise: people require independent financial advice.

In this chapter, we'll discuss seeking professional financial advice. We'll hear IFAs describe their work. Unlike unit trusts themselves, there are not scores of statistics to pore over in choosing a good financial advisor. There are several classes of financial advisors about which you need to make a decision, such as tied or untied. Armed with the information in this book, you can make as good a decision as your advisor's recommendations about worthy unit trusts.

Earlier, I discussed the execution-only IFA, whose only job is to get you a discount on your unit trust investment and who will not provide advice. Occasionally, you might get a little bit of advice in terms of choosing one unit trust over another. However, this chapter will focus entirely on full-service IFAs.

> '... people require independent financial advice.'

A financial advisor is likely to have his or her ear to the ground though, and this can prove valuable. Finding the name of a financial advisor is easy enough; finding one you want to work with for the rest of your investing life is a bit more difficult.

## JUST THE FACTS

The facts about financial advisors are quite simple. The Financial Services Act of 1986 established two types of financial advisors: tied and independent. Independent financial advisors are free to offer products of any company, while tied agents only represent products of the company to which they are tied. Obviously, you need to find out whether the agent you're dealing with is truly independent to give you independent advice or whether the agent describes and sells only one firm's products. Tied agents receive salary plus some performance-related compensation.

> '... financial advisors must maintain a breadth of knowledge about all potential client financial requirements ...'

Independent financial advisors work for themselves or groups of IFAs. They are compensated solely by you through fees, commissions from products you purchase, or a combination of both.

Both varieties of financial advisors are regulated by the Personal Investment Authority (PIA) or Investment Management Regulatory Organisation (IMRO). They must pass a certifying exam, which enables them to be certified as an authorised financial planner. Usually, they'll have printed on their business card that they are a member of the PIA or FIMBRA, a predecessor organisation.

Like GPs with their patients, financial advisors must maintain a breadth of knowledge about all potential client financial requirements; they know a little about a lot, such as life assurance, pensions, investments, mortgages, and savings. Typically, financial advisors develop a speciality, born either of interest or the organisation where they were originally trained. In my research, I have focused on unit trust-oriented financial advisors. Let's meet Jamie Berry.

## THE ANALYTIC APPROACH

Jamie Berry began his career as a trainee at the age of 17 working for GT Global Fund Management in 1973. Four years later, aged 21, he was the unit trust department manager, where he oversaw two funds valued at £3 million. By the time he was 25, he knew he wanted to be on his own and founded Berry Asset Management. Today, at 40, he has built up a reputation as a thorough investment manager.

He says, 'Most IFAs tend to give life and pensions advice. That's not our scene, we're solely investment managers.' He says of his firm, 'It's more akin to the financial firms, which are heavily involved in unit trusts.' His clients hold roughly 60 per cent of their assets in unit trusts, whereas the balance is spread across investment trusts and private stock holdings.

He clearly prizes and sells his independence. The first lines of his brochure include the following:

> We also believe that our independent status is vital: we have no general financial planning interests and we manage no unit or investment trusts of our own. This means that we have no conflicts of interest and can make investment decisions for you which are impartial and which only have your best interests at heart.

Sounds good to me.

I asked him, 'How do you pick a unit trust?'

'Based on our discussions with the client, we choose different selection criteria for the screening process. We run our asset allocation model. For one client of some size, we might structure a portfolio consisting of a fund or funds from the UK equity sectors, the UK smaller companies sector, and Asian companies.'

> Asset allocation models allocate investments around the globe and investment types and aim to achieve a portfolio with desired volatility and return characteristics suitable for the goals of the client.

'What about PEP's?' I asked him.

'Out of 170 unit trust PEPs, we already know those that we want to deal with; we stay away from those that are too small. And we might feel uncomfortable with those PEPs offered by life assurance companies or stockbrokers.'

I asked him what he preferred then.

He said, 'We don't like large groups that are struggling', and went on to name a few, well-known, large unit trust houses whose funds were not performing very well. He told me that he suggested that his clients sell their investment in Morgan Grenfell's European Fund nine months prior to the eruption of the scandal. 'We were unhappy with Morgan Grenfell's European Fund because it relied too much for its success on one stock.'

He explained that once they had narrowed down the list of houses he was comfortable with, then they began to look at performance. 'We look at discrete, five-year periods. We screen for funds which are discretely consistent.'

Once again, we see the reliance on consistent performers, year after year. This is similar to the consistency technique outlined in Chapter 13, based on the top quartile criteria (see page 215).

'We make sure that the chosen fund is the right sort of size in relation to its marketplace. For example, a small cap [smaller companies] fund at £300 million is too large – £100 million might be the right size.'

After screening and narrowing-down the funds to a handful, he elaborated on the choice of fund management company, something we've seen before: 'One fund may adopt a house view, like Schroders, which works very well. Perpetual, on the other hand [with its independent managers] works very well as well.'

I asked him what characteristics in particular he looked for.

'We look at the turnover of the portfolio': that is, how many stocks the fund manager is buying and selling. 'We also look at the number of stocks held in the unit trust. We look at volatility, and then we check the Fund Research rating.' (Fund Research is a unit-trust-rating service for the industry.)

'Then we want to meet the fund manager to find out whether we feel comfortable with him. We want to understand whether the manager is a stock-picker or whether he takes a sector approach', meaning whether the fund manager just chooses stocks he or she believes are good buys, or whether he or she methodically narrows down choices based on his or her views on the direction of the economy and which areas of the economy will do well.

I asked him how he could make sure he wasn't being taken in by a charismatic fund manager.

'It's very much a seat-of-the-pants approach. It's difficult to do,' he allowed. He maintained it was the final screen, of meeting the fund manager personally, which ensured quality investment selections for his clients. He added that, 'Post-Barings, we also look at the financial strength of the parent company.'

On the subject of fees, touchy for IFAs, he had strong feelings. 'Charges matter more than a few years ago,' he said. 'People don't want to get ripped off. Potential IFA customers,' he explained, 'should be satisfied that they're paying a competitive fee.' And as I said earlier, Berry suggests 'be prepared to ask for a discount. If you don't ask, you won't get it.' He said that the fund charges 'depend on the type of fund you're investing in.' For example, bond fund fees should be less than an actively managed equity portfolio.

And he said of high spreads, which we dissected earlier, 'It's more important to get the unit trust at the right price. If there's a 7 per cent spread, that's a rocky road to climb out of,' implying that the fund must do well just for you to break even. And here's a man who's been monitoring equity fund managers for 24 years.

## TRUSTING UNIT TRUSTS

Clive Scott-Hopkins has been investing in unit trusts both personally and for his clients for over 35 years, after joining the Towry Law Group in 1960, one of the largest IFA groups in the country.

He says he's 'wedded to the [unit trust] concept'. His philosophy is born of someone who's seen it all. 'For me, anything less than 20 years is short-term.'

He has learned several rules over the years. 'You've got to make a reasonable selection at the start. Get a good fund manager. To make some money, you've got to stay invested over 20 years.' (In my research, I've generally found the younger the speaker, the shorter the investment term outlook.) He describes an investment in M&G's Special Situations, where £500 turned into roughly £25,000. He explained that for many years it didn't move, and then it did quite well. 'You must be patient,' he advises.

He gives another example. 'The M&G Recovery Fund – we called it the Dustbin Fund, because it aimed to buy undervalued situations. This was very forward thinking in 1967. The portfolio managers average two failures out of 100 investments. Over 25 years, this is the most successful fund. In 1966, M&G launched the M&G Special, which is called today, M&G Smaller Companies.' He estimated that £500 roughly turned into some £10,000. 'What I've learned over the years is if you sit on something long enough, eventually you'll get results.'

Condemning the short-term view, he comments, 'The average person wants to make a quick turn.' He noticed that 'more people today are aware of markets, especially when they're high.' He cautions investors, 'Timing is all important.' He laments that 'the difficult bit is to get people to buy when the markets are down'. It's the old saw about buying low and selling high, which is exactly the opposite of what people's natural tendencies are.

'The other thing I've learned is to buy cheap,' he adds.

Scott-Hopkins continues, 'The great thing about unit trusts is that managers can move shares around without paying out capital gains tax (CGT), while the individual must always look over his shoulder [to the Inland Revenue] when playing the stock market.'

He describes that 'over the years, unit trusts have become an acceptable way of diversifying a portfolio', and he believes it's the perfect way to get exposure to America and the Far East. He is especially encouraged by the positive changes in the last decade. 'The new entrants have livened it up and focused managers' minds, so you get better performance.' He said, in addition, that 'typically the banks do poorly'. This is a comment I've heard over and over again: that bank and life assurers are underperformers. A study by fund management company Framlington found that banks' PEP returns were 'consistently below average' and 'weak'. Not surprisingly, Framlington recommends switching to top investment houses. The basic message is to review your investments regularly by comparing the performance you receive versus other similar investments. Some bank funds have done well however.

Speaking of unit trusts in general, he said, 'Of the 1,600 unit trust funds, the sad fact is that an awful lot are underperforming. If you make a reasonable choice, you've got to sit on it a long time,' he says.

'I'm not a great believer in moving things around. I try not to react because there's the cost of buying something else. Inevitably, you'll get the timing of a switch wrong.' His view is that it's very important to choose the fund management company carefully, and then to have faith.

The only time to switch, he believes, is when the group has

consistent underperformance. 'If you've got someone like Perpetual, you have a fair amount of confidence that their investment philosophy is right.'

I asked him the number one question: 'How long do you wait, how long do you endure underperformance?'

He pondered this question and responded, 'two to three years', adding that, 'unit trusts by their nature are a core holding and are long-term in nature'. He highlights his discussion with a Perpetual brochure: £1,000 invested in the Perpetual International Growth Fund in 1974 has grown to £73,875 today.

Like many others, he says the investor should look to the fund management companies' strengths. 'The great thing about Perpetual is their stock-picking skills. Then there is a group like M&G, which has a reputation for high-yielding stocks, small stocks, and recovery stocks.'

He likes unit trust portfolio management services, such as Rothschilds, which offer to select a combination of internationally diversified unit trusts: 'because there are so many unit trusts with so much performance variation'. He says that 'a typical portfolio has to have a core holding, comprising an internationally diversified fund and then a predominantly high-income UK fund'. He advocates what he called 'a satellite holding', a fund with the opportunity for greater gain, tied of course to higher volatility. To justify the fund selection service, they need to outperform the benchmark by 1 per cent or 1½ per cent.

As for corporate bond PEPs, he says, 'I'm not sure the unit trust providers are as experienced at managing fixed-interest investments.'

'I think bond funds are fairly boring. We're coming into a scenario where they might make sense. We sell a lot of corporate bond PEPs to retirees because they want the jam today, not the cream tomorrow. For these types of funds, you can't expect an increase [in capital value]. Investors must be careful not to go for too high yields.' He also points out correctly that 'buying gilts is pretty cheap. You don't need to pay expenses. If you expect a manager to justify his charges, they've got to actively manage the fund, instead of holding gilts like a national monument.'

# TARGETING

Women invest in unit trusts because they provide good value for their money. Aiming to provide women with good advice for their money is Fiona Price & Partners. Price established her firm to fill a market void; namely, that business and professional women who had begun earning higher salaries wanted a better understanding of the financial world, which is still male-dominated. Her firm is geared towards providing financial advice for women.

She believes a lot of men don't understand the financial world, but they're afraid to admit their lack of knowledge. 'Women find the financial world full of jargon.' Providing advice and information in plain English 'empowers women' to make decisions that they might not otherwise make.

She is very vocal about the financial advice industry. Her articles and her comments regularly find their way into newspapers. She's produced *The Shark-Free Guide to Financial Advice*,[2] which we'll look at later (see page 286). She is concerned that 'the cumulative results of all the recent scandals is that many people are finding they made investment decisions which were of higher risk than they thought'. She says, the results of these scandals means that 'we, as an industry, need to do a better job of assessing risk in a broader sense'. As suggested at the beginning of the chapter, her most important first stop is a risk assessment. She says, 'most people pick between three and five' on a scale of one to ten, with ten being the highest.

She says that a financial planner must 'look at everything the client has already done, to determine whether it fits in with their objectives. We look at investments, pension funds, life assurance cover, school fees.'

'What's unusual about us is that we keep time-sheets on time spent with clients and we know how much time we've spent working with a particular client.' Price knows that 'the impartiality factor is tied up with how you're paid'. She estimates that 40 per cent of her clients pay straight fees while 60 per cent pay the costs through commissions.

This is an important point. There are two ways you can pay an IFA: either through straight fees on an hourly basis or through the commissions paid by the fund management company to the financial advisor. The difference is important. When you visit a financial planner, most will say that you don't pay for their services directly, but that they receive their compensation through a rebate from the fund management companies from the products you buy.

This argument is circular; of course you pay their commissions, it just goes through a third party. And for this reason, I suggest working from the start from an understanding of the basis of the fees by using a time-sheet or some other mechanism. The problem with the 'commission is my payment' route is two-fold. First, whether your portfolio is, say, £100,000 or £120,000, it is likely the financial advisor's efforts will be the same. In the latter instance, you're paying 20 per cent more in fees.

The second problem is more dramatic: if the advisor is faced with two investments with basically equal prospects and a higher versus a lower commission, which do you think he or she will recommend? In addition, the fund management companies are always running specials and incentive programmes to encourage the sale of their products, which you may or may not know about.

The financial advisor is required to give you a summary sheet of commissions he or she will earn if you follow the recommendations. Accordingly, you'll be able to calculate the rate of commission charged, but typically, it will not be a comparison with charges on other similar products. And this isn't to say anything about the non-cash perks that grease the wheels of business and which could affect (probably) the recommendations of your advisor.

How to stay out of this mess? Fee-only. Some advisors are strictly fee only, and you can find a list of such advisors in the back of *Money Management* each month. It may cost you a bit more, but probably not. You should request that the financial advisor rebate to you all commissions he or she is paid. This one simple move erases all the conflict-of-interest issues inherent in the advisor/advisee relationship.

Price generally does not recommend individual unit trusts. Her firm 'tends to use specialist investment managers and stockbrokers, who are expert in this area with the right research and monitoring facilities, to select and manage portfolios of unit trusts for clients'.

Her firm's job is 'to pick the right investment manager and to keep a watchful eye'.

Many IFAs I spoke to say if a client's portfolio exceeds some threshold, usually £100,000, £500,000 or more, they'll recommend the services of a stockbroker for individual share selection, because they say the overall costs will be lower. I recommend reviewing this suggestion very closely. Unit trusts provide the same professional management services, and it is not clear which method is cheaper. With a unit trust, however, all capital gains made by the unit trust are free of tax to the unit holder. Only when the unit holder sells out is tax incurred.

## THE SHARKS AND CHARLATANS

Price provides *The Shark-Free Guide to Financial Advice* which I recommend to those considering hiring a financial advisor. A simple, easy-to-read guide highlighting your considerations. Among the highlights are an overview of what financial advice is, a simple guide to sorting out your financial affairs and the protection afforded to investors against the 'sharks and charlatans'.

She outlines means of finding an advisor:

> IFA Promotion Limited,
> 4th Floor, 28 Greville
> Street, London
> EC1N 8SU
> telephone:
> 0171-831 4027.

- Personal recommendation from a friend or colleague
- IFA-run seminars
- Independent Financial Advisor Promotion will give you the names of three independent financial advisors nearest you.

She suggests ensuring that the financial advisor is properly oriented towards your special requirements, e.g., pension, life assurance, or investments.

Typically, the financial advisor meets with you to learn about your circumstances, completing what's called a 'Fact-Find'. Price suggests visiting the advisor's office to get a feel of 'how the organisation works and presents itself'. Usually, having analysed your situation prior to the second meeting, the financial advisor will then recommend an investment, savings, and tax-reducing strategy.

If you follow the strategy and continue to work with a particular financial advisor, Price recommends annual reviews.

She makes the same point about advisors that I made about fund management companies: do they return your phone calls? Price says, 'Good service is hard to define, but you know it when you see it. The hallmark of good service is good business practice.' The indicators she suggests you should look for are:

- how quickly your advisor responds to queries;
- written confirmation of applications made on your behalf;
- efficient office administration;
- friendly telephone manners.

Price, like me, is worried about the effects of remuneration on financial advice. 'In the past, most financial advisors have been paid solely from commission earned from arranging pensions, assurances, and investments,' she says. This means the advisor may be biased towards the products and providers which pay the highest level of commission. Price concludes that, 'It is better to use someone who will charge a fee when all you need is advice, and who can be paid by commission if he or she arranges an investment for you and this is appropriate.' She urges your advisors 'to explain their charges to you clearly so that you understand exactly what you are paying for and when charges are likely to be incurred.'

## HOW MUCH WILL YOU PAY?

In Chapter 7, we discussed at length the initial charge levied upon unit trust investments. The initial charge partly compensates the IFA for his or her work. The IFA typically receives three percentage points of your 4 per cent to 7 per cent initial fee payment, as a commission. If you're working on a pre-arranged fee/hourly type basis, the commission can be used to pay for your advisor's charges. No VAT is due on this commission as opposed to straight fees. However, that doesn't change our basic premise that the level of the fee should not be related to the size of the commission. Indeed, if the commission is less than the agreed-upon fee, you should come up with the funds out of pocket. Alternatively, if the commission exceeds the fee for the IFA's services, this should be rebated to you.

On a PEP and other unit trust investments, the IFA sometimes receives back 0.50 per cent of the annual management fee from the unit trust sponsor as a renewal or trailing commission. You should be made aware of this. For as long as you have a PEP or unit trust investment with a particular fund management company and you purchased it through an IFA, the IFA may receive a continuing yearly commission. For a £6,000 annual PEP, this amounts to £30 – not much money. If you multiply this by, say, 500 clients, you're talking about a more substantial amount of money; and, all of a sudden, the IFA's interest in moving you from a fund management company paying renewal commissions to one which doesn't will be very, very small.

The IFA can and should serve as your eyes and ears on the unit trust marketplace. As in any business proposition, it pays to pay for professional advice. Everything you need to know about industry developments will be in the newspapers. Eventually. But it may be too late by that point. An IFA can serve as another form of insurance against making a mistake. The unit trust investor does not look to the unit trust as a speculative investment; indeed, there are many volatility-reducing techniques (paying the right price, buying at the right time, spreading your investments, considering short versus medium versus long-term investments) we've discussed. You should view your use of an IFA as just another building block to making informed decisions.

### REFERENCES

[1] 'Points to bear in mind' by Hazel Spink, *What Investment?*, January 1995, p. 10.
[2] *The Shark-Free Guide to Financial Advice*, available free of charge from Fiona Price & Partners, 33 Great Queen Street, Covent Garden, London WC2B 5AA, 0171–430 0366.

# SUMMARY

- Financial advisors come in two varieties: tied and independent.

- A tied agent sells only one fund management company's investments.

- An independent financial advisor (IFA) is legally required to be independent and can freely recommend products from any fund management company.

- An IFA provides a good ear to the ground about the goings on in the unit trust industry.

- IFAs typically earn 3 per cent from your purchase of a unit trust, paid by the fund management company out of the initial charge you paid.

- The financial advisor is legally required to detail the charges and commissions before you invest.

- Like any professional, such as a lawyer or accountant, an IFA deserves to be paid for research and analysis provided.

- It is unfair to take his or her advice, and then invest in a unit trust directly or through an execution-only dealer.

- Expect a once-a-year annual financial check up.

Before you invest:

- verify whether the agent is tied or independent

- look over the charges

- ask for a discount.

# Chapter 18

# WHEN TO
# INVEST

# WHEN DO YOU INVEST?

You decide to invest in the equity market with a fund you've picked. Then, the investor's dilemma presents itself: when to invest? Two scenarios:

**(1) Each day the Footsie hits a record high.**
Pundits in the newspapers say, 'The correction is coming', or 'There's still a lot of steam left in corporate earnings, interest rates are . . . blah, blah.' You think, 'Don't want to invest now, the market's at a record . . . too much uncertainty. I'll wait until it settles down, and then I'll go in.'
*Result: You never invest.*

**(2) Each day, the Footsie trundles lower.**
You read the papers, and the pundits say that it will get better (a) in the New Year, (b) after the budget is released, (c) something equally optimistic. You think, 'Don't want to invest now, the market's falling . . . too much uncertainty. I'll wait until it starts going up, and then I'll go in.'
*Result: You never invest.*

**The solution:** don't force yourself to make a decision about when the market's going to go up or go down. The decision about when to invest can and should be put on automatic pilot. Monthly investments of equal size solves several problems at once.

This is known by the smart name of 'pound-cost averaging'. It's beguiling in its simplicity. You establish a monthly standing order with your bank to transfer the same amount to your unit trust/PEP account. Your order at the fund management company is to buy as many units as your funds will allow at the current market price.

You will buy more units when the price is low and fewer units when the price is high. The benefit is unbelievable: You don't have to time the market.

If you are hesitant that this is exactly the right time to buy, and you're not sure when you will need the money, and if you're not sure if tomorrow will be the right time, pound-cost average: dripfeed your investment. The potential gain is indeed reduced, but so is the volatility.

Let's look at some numbers. Assume you have a £36,000 lump sum to invest. Three scenarios:

(1) **You invest it all today.**

(2) **You invest £500 monthly with the balance earning interest in the bank, until it's all invested (six years of PEP allowance).**

(3) **Store it in the bank and earn interest until you think it's time to go into the market** (mid-point in the chart in Figure 18.1).

The summary statistics in Figure 18.2 say it all. The greatest advantage – and the greatest volatility – come from investing all at once, at the beginning. The second-best return and the least volatility come from investing monthly and earning the interest with the funds in the bank in the meantime. The worst scenario comes from letting the money sit in the bank until you think the time is right, mid-way through our experiment.

Please look at the last row in the summary statistics, the annualised volatility range. I have changed the monthly volatility statistics to an annualised basis. This shows the possible swings on a more understandable basis.

Jamie Campbell of Jupiter Fund Management doesn't believe that pound-cost averaging is the right approach. His view for the greatest possible gain regardless of volatility: invest today. You never know what the market will do tomorrow, but you can bet that in five to ten years' time, the market will be higher than it is today.

The other benefit of the monthly investing is the convenience. You place a standing order with your bank to transfer money to the fund management company, once a month, right after you are paid. It's convenient. The investment is made automatically. Usually, the fund management companies provide this option on their investment application form.

## TIME, BUT NOT TIMING

The returns from the market vary considerably from year to year, as shown in the 35 year history from 1960 through to 1995 (see Figure

**Fig 18.1  Three scenarios: lump sum at beginning; monthly investment; bank until midpoint, then lump sum**

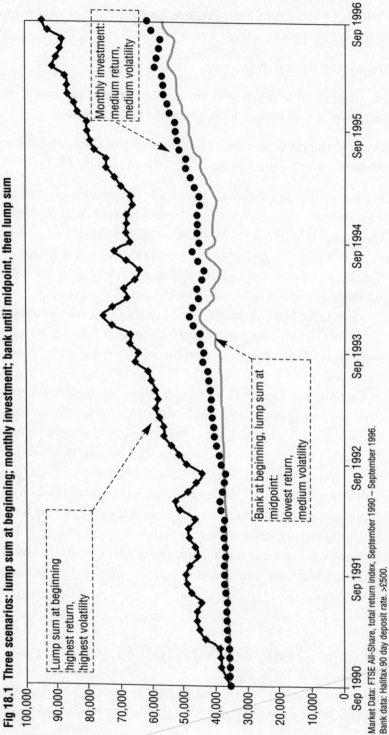

Market Data: FTSE All-Share, total return index, September 1990 – September 1996.
Bank data: Halifax 90 day deposit rate. >£500.

**Fig 18.2 Three investment timing possibilities: 1990–96**

|  | All at once | Monthly investment | Bank until time is right |
|---|---|---|---|
| Monthly average return | 1.4% | 0.8% | 0.7% |
| Monthly volatility | 3.9% | 1.9% | 2.4% |
| Best month | 11.3% | 5.1% | 8.3% |
| Worst month | −6.8% | −4.7% | −6.7% |
| Total return | 164.4% | 72.9% | 60.3% |
| Annual return | 16.32% | 9.16% | 7.89% |
| Total £ gain | £59,192 | £26,391 | £21,849 |
| Annualised volatility range | 63% to −29% | 33% to −14% | 37% to −21% |

18.2). The jumps can be quite dramatic, like in 1974, when the market plummeted 59 per cent in real terms or when it shot to the sky in the next year, up 96 per cent.

Tom Seale, head of Citibank's Luxembourg mutual fund operations, implores investors to give their investments time. He says, 'successful investors understand that most stockmarket gains occur at unpredictable intervals. Trying to time the market, to move in and out based on forecasts about peaks and troughs, is a sure recipe for investment disaster.' You may get it right once or twice or, if you're lucky, even three times, but not over a lifetime.

Seale says if you are out of the market, 'just a fraction of the time, you could miss out on all the gains. Let's say you were inept at forecasting and missed out on the five best years. All your gains evaporate.' Seale was right: Under this scenario, even though you had money in the market for 20 of the 25 years, you would have been better off keeping your money in the building society, as depicted in Figure 18.3.

I conducted another test: assume the investor again misses every up year, but gets out in time to avoid the five worst years: the return equals 7.4 per cent, slightly less than remaining fully invested over the entire period. And these scenarios didn't consider the charges you'd face in buying and selling.

If you are clairvoyant, though, you'll do just fine.

Elaine Garzarelli, formerly of Lehman Bros., made a big name for herself by predicting the 1987 US stockmarket crash. During her stint managing Lehman's Sector Analysis Fund, though, her fund

**Fig 18.3  UK stocks: real returns, after basic tax and inflation, 1960–1995**

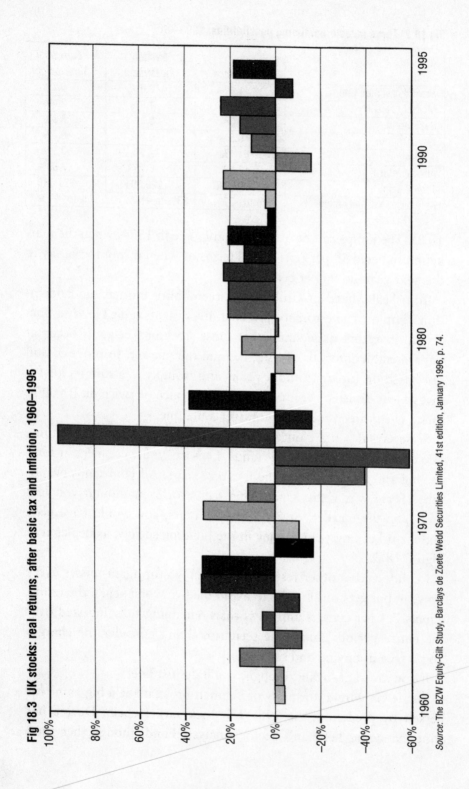

*Source:* The BZW Equity-Gilt Study, Barclays de Zoete Wedd Securities Limited, 41st edition, January 1996, p. 74.

**Fig 18.4 Staying in the market vs missing the peaks**

|                                               | Average annual return |
|-----------------------------------------------|-----------------------|
| Fully Invested: 1960–1995                     | 7.7%                  |
| Inept market timer: missed five best years    | 1.3%                  |

returned an annualised 4.8 per cent versus the 8.4 per cent by Standard & Poor's US stock index.[1]

Patience is rewarded. Evaluate your financial requirements, buy the right unit trusts, and then let your funds grow by themselves.

## REFERENCE

[1] 'Leaving Las Vegas as wise, if not richer, investors' by Anthony Cook, *Money Magazine*, July 1996, retrieved from Internet on 19 January 1997 @ http://www.compuserve.com/money/magazine/9606/027.htm

# SUMMARY

- Because stockmarkets have always eventually gone up, today is the best time to invest.

- If you wait until the time is right, you may never invest.

- Moving in and out of the market according to forecasts has proven a losing strategy – no one can predict the future.

- Constant amount monthly investing (pound-cost averaging): results in:

  - the lowest volatility

  - an easy way to build up your investment

  - removing the worry about the best time to invest.

# TOMORROW?

'**E**veryone knows,' says Chris Poll, chairman of *Micropal*, 'that past performance is not necessarily a guide to the future. Poll, whose firm keeps score of unit trust funds' performance, believes, 'There are only two ways of making a decision on investing in a fund. One is to believe implicitly that what the investment manager forecasts is going to happen. The other is to analyse past fund statistics, principally performance.'[1]

Jeff Prestridge, personal finance editor of the *Financial Mail on Sunday*, says, of picking the right unit trust, 'Bloody hell, it's a nightmare.'

In this book, we have focused on the details you need to know. We have considered all the pieces of the jigsaw. In this last chapter, we discuss a longer-range view of unit trusts, and how they can help you to reach your financial, and therefore your life, goals.

> 'If you open the newspaper at the section on markets, you'll always find some pundit saying what the market will do over the coming weeks.'

Before summarising, let me bring up a subject I've touched on throughout the book.

Most of the people I spoke to – the people who really know what's going on in the unit trust business – have invested a portion of their financial resources in one or two of the riskiest sectors – technology and emerging markets. It was uncanny that so many chose emerging markets. These people are all very concerned with their money. And we find that they invest for the long-term.

If I ask you to tell me the weather a week from now, there's probably a 50/50 chance you'll get it right. But if I ask you the weather in six months, you're probably able to predict it with more certainty. It's winter now, and six months from now, it'll be summer, and will probably be warmer and sunnier and so on.

It's the same with the markets, though they don't run on seasonal patterns. But their pattern is upward. If you open the newspaper at the section on markets, you'll always find some pundit saying what the market will do over the coming weeks. If you methodically analysed their comments, you'd find the same pattern with the weather; 50/50 they get it right; 50/50 they get it wrong. But if you ask me whether or not the market will be up five years from now, I

# Constructing your portfolio

In Parts 2 and 3, we built a portfolio for you based on your financial and timing needs. The emergency and medium-term funds should be invested in cash funds, if the rates are good enough, and in gilt and fixed-interest funds – those with a redemption yield near their simple yield. But the last timing class of investments, your long-term growth-oriented funds, should be in equities.

My suggestion for a portfolio is shown in Figure 19.1

**Fig 19.1 Unit trusts for your personal Timing Class of Investments:**

| Term | Investment | PEP? |
|---|---|---|
| Day-to-day | Bank or building society | No |
| Emergency | Cash unit trust | No |
| Medium-term or for Income | Gilt and fixed-interest fund | PEPable |
| Long-term | Core: UK tracker | PEPable |
| | UK growth or value fund | PEPable |
| | European growth or value fund | PEPable |
| | International growth or value fund | PEPable* |
| | Emerging markets, Far East | PEPable* |

* Allowed in non-qualifying portion of PEP – £1,500

I've seen asset allocation models that are very complex, that optimise equity investments across various volatility and return classes. Their aim is to maximise return while minimising volatility and depend on the correlation across markets. The value at the end of the day of these fancy techniques remains to be seen.

Life is better simple, and a simple allocation across the equity categories is probably the best bet: something like 40 per cent to 50 per cent UK index tracker, 40 per cent to 50 per cent UK, European and international equities, and 10 per cent emerging markets. A hypothetical portfolio constructed as suggested above would have returned 12 per cent per year over the last five years and yielded gross 2.5 per cent (see Figure 19.2)

**Fig 19.2 Equity portfolio returns**

| Average fund in sector | Per cent of portfolio | Five-year average annual return | Annual volatility | Gross yield |
|---|---|---|---|---|
| Core: UK tracker | 40% | 13.1% | ±12% | 3.2% |
| UK value fund | 20% | 10.5% | ±12% | 4.7% |
| European fund | 15% | 13.5% | ±11% | 0.9% |
| International growth fund | 15% | 10.7% | ±12% | 0.8% |
| Emerging markets, Far East ex Japan | 10% | 9.8% | ±25% | 0.3% |
| Total portfolio | 100% | 12.0% | ±13% | 2.5% |

Source: Data: *Money Management*, December 1996; author's calculations.

can answer with 80 per cent certainty that it will be. If you ask me what it will be like ten years from now, I can with 100 per cent certainty say that it will be up.

The key principle of investing in equities is that fast growth drives fast appreciation. As Alan Torry, investment manager for Prolific's Technology Fund said, technology is going to be one of the fastest-growing sectors in the next 20 years. Tomorrow it'll be bumpy. Next week, probably just as bumpy. Ten years from now, it'll be up. Twenty years from now, it most certainly will be ahead of the gain in the FTSE 100 Index over that time.

> 'Even though a unit trust may be stellar when you invested, the investment world changes.'

I have tried to give you a sense of what a good unit trust is, what are mediocre ones. There are far more of the mediocre ones. If you want to succeed in making a wise choice, you need to put in a little effort. Once or twice a year. Look at how your investments are doing. Buy *Money Management, What Investment?*, or *Money Observer*, and review how your investments are faring.

Write your finding down on a sheet of paper or enter the data on your computer. Don't make it too complex or you'll give up. Print it out. Save it in your files. Next year, review it once again. There is quite a bit of inertia on the part of investors. Even though a unit trust may be stellar when you invested, the investment world changes. If there are problems, be patient, read the manager's reports, ring the fund management company, and, if you're not satisfied, invest elsewhere.

And, by the way, don't pay the full charges.

## REFERENCE

[1] 'Practical Implementation of Modern Portfolio Theory', paper presented at Schwab Institutional annual conference, Impact 96 by Christopher Poll, November 1996, p. 1.

# SUMMARY

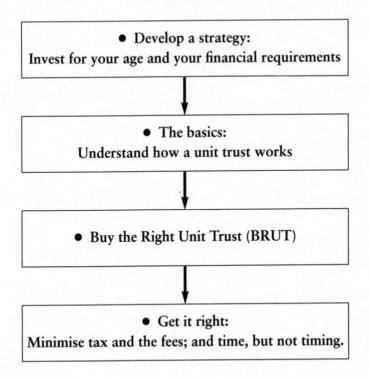

● Develop a strategy:
Invest for your age and your financial requirements

● The basics:
Understand how a unit trust works

● Buy the Right Unit Trust (BRUT)

● Get it right:
Minimise tax and the fees; and time, but not timing.

- For equities:

    - invest 40 per cent to 50 per cent in tracking funds
    - invest 40 per cent to 50 per cent in UK, European, or international actively-managed funds
    - invest the balance in a high volatility, high-return category.

- Make sure you have a PEP.

# GLOSSARY

This glossary is adapted from *The 1997 Chase de Vere PEPGUIDE* (Chase de Vere: 0800 526 091), *The Good PEP Guide, Unit Trusts: A user's handbook from AUTIF, AUTIF Performance Categories* (Unit Trust Information Service: 0181 207 1361), and author's additions.

**Note:** The official Association of Unit Trust and Investment Fund (AUTIF) definition for unit trust sectors is indicated by the designation (AUTIF sector) after the heading.

**Active Portfolio Management**   Refers to a style of unit trust investment management, where the investment manager chooses to buy and sell shares based on potential for growth of shares or lack thereof. The opposite is passive portfolio management, where the investment manager simply buys shares comprising an index without regard to the future potential of shares.

**Advisory PEP**   Similar to a Self-Select PEP although the plan manager will offer advice about what to buy and sell.

**Accumulation unit**   One of two types of unit trust units (the other is called 'income') whereby dividends are received through increased units or a higher price for the units, not through the payment of a cash dividend.

**Annual management charge**   Levied by the fund management company to the unit trust fund. It is paid out of the funds assets, thereby reducing the performance by a like amount.

**Association of Unit Trusts and Investment Funds (AUTIF)**   Trade group, represents member fund management companies; primary objective is to improve regulations, tax, and other rules affecting the sale of unit trusts in the UK.

**Authorised unit trust**   A unit trust which meets the rules governing the industry set by the Securities and Investment Board (SIB).

**AUTIF**   See *Association of Unit Trusts and Investment Funds*.

**AUTIF sector**   Demarcation of funds by type of investments held within fund, which is established by the Association of Unit Trusts and Investment Funds.

**Investment Management Regulatory Organisation (IMRO)**   Unit trust industry watchdog.

**Bed and breakfast**   Selling a share or unit trust one day and buying it back the next, usually to establish a profit to be used against individuals' £6,300 annual capital gains allowance.

**Bid basis**   When a fund has more sellers than buyers and the fund management company is forced to reduce the number of outstanding units, the bid price is at the cancellation price (the lowest possible price) and the offer price is usually less than the creation price.

**Bid/offer spread**   The difference between the bid and offer price. Usually quoted as a percentage of the offer price, not the bid price.

**Bid-to-bid**   Unit trusts' performance is sometimes reported as the bid price to sell today as compared with the bid price from an earlier period. This method can be used to evaluate performance alone, without regard to the initial spread. The more common basis is offer-to-bid, which does take into account charges.

**Bid price**   The price you receive when you sell stocks, shares, or unit trusts. It is always lower than the offer price at which you invest.

**Cancellation price**   The lowest price at which the fund management company will buy back units. It is the actual value of the underlying securities if they were all to be sold back to the market plus the other assets in the fund itself, such as cash.

**Capital growth**   An increase in the value of the unit trusts or the underlying assets.

**Capital gains tax**   Tax on the profit earnt on the sale of a unit trust or other asset. Tax is not paid on the first £6,300 of capital gains each year.

**Cash**   Short-term or non-interest-bearing deposit. May not be held in a PEP for more than 42 days.

**Cash Trust (AUTIF sector)**   Unit trust holding with at least 80 per cent of its assets in bank deposits or money market securities, which usually come due within the next six months though it can be as little as overnight. May not be held in a PEP for more than 42 days. Cash funds enjoy a negligible risk of capital loss, though the interest rate will change as market interest rates change. Referred to by AUTIF and in the United States as money market funds.

**Commodity and energy (AUTIF sector)**   Trusts which invest at least 80 per cent of their assets in commodity or energy securities.

**Convertibles**   Bonds or preference shares which can be converted into ordinary shares either at a particular date or on a range of dates over a set period. They usually provide greater income than ordinary shares of a company, but less than a bond from that same company.

**Coupon**   The interest payment made from a bond; the term comes from when holders redeemed paper coupons to receive periodic interest payment.

**Corporate Bond**   An IOU issued by a public company. Typically, the purchaser receives a fixed set of interest payments with a promise to repay the capital at a known price at a certain date in the future.

**Corporate Bond PEP**   Launched in July 1995, a general PEP allowing investment in corporate bonds, convertibles, preference shares and Euro-Sterling bonds.

**Creation price**   The highest possible price to invest. The actual investing price (offer) may be less.

**Dealing charge**   Cost incurred for buying and selling shares and investment trusts within a unit trust.

**Debenture**   Loan made by a company secured by assets of the company.

**Diversification**   Refers to the ownership of a variety of shares within or across industries or geographic regions. Reduces volatility – or risk – of an investment.

**Dividend**   A payment made to holders of shares and unit trusts out of the underlying companies' earnings for which the plan manager reclaims income tax. Dividends may be distributed (by owning 'income units') or reinvested (by owning 'accumulation units').

**Dividend collection fee**   Charge levied by the plan manager to collect and distribute dividends.

**Dow Jones Industrial Average**   A US index measuring the average share price of 30 major US industrial companies.

**Early encashment fee**   This may be payable if you encash or transfer out of the PEP within the first few years (usually five). The charge will often decrease the longer the investment is maintained.

**Emerging markets funds (AUTIF sector)**   Funds which invest 80 per cent or more of their assets directly or indirectly in emerging markets as defined by the World Bank, without geographical restriction. Indirect investment, e.g. China shares listed in Hong Kong, should not exceed 50 per cent of the portfolio.

**Equity**   The ordinary share capital of a company, as distinct from its preference or loan capital.

**Equity and bond (AUTIF sector)**   At least 80 per cent of portfolio must be invested in fixed-interest securities or shares with neither shares or fixed-interest securities making up more than 80 per cent of the fund. For the UK sector, the fund should strive to provide a yield of up to 120 per cent of the yield on the FTSE All-Share Index and 80 per cent must be invested in UK securities. International funds may invest internationally.

**Equity and bond income (AUTIF sector)**   Same as equity and bond sector for UK funds, except fund yield should exceed 120 per cent of the yield on the FTSE All-Share index. No international counterpart.

**Equity income**   For the UK sector, trusts with at least 80 per cent of their assets in UK equities which aim to yield in excess of 110 per cent of the FTSE All-Share Index yield. For the international sector, the same guidelines except equities are worldwide and the index for yield comparison is the FT Actuaries World Index.

**Europe funds (AUTIF sector)**   Trusts which invest at least 80 per cent of their assets in European securities, which may include UK securities so long as the UK component does not exceed 80 per cent.

**Euro-Sterling bond**   A corporate, sterling-denominated bond issued by a company wanting to borrow money on the international markets, rather than in the UK.

**Ex-dividend date**   The date after which new investors will not receive the previously-announced dividend.

**Execution-only**   Instructions to buy or sell, given directly by the investor to the firm/manager/advisor without receiving any advice.

**Exit charge**   A charge sometimes imposed by fund management company for selling before a certain time period has passed. Typically, exit charge disappears after holding the investment for five years. In newspapers' price quote section, the existence of an exit fee is noted by an 'E' adjacent to the initial charge. For PEPs, a charge which is sometimes imposed for withdrawing completely from the PEP, whether by encashment or transfer to another manager.

**Far East including and excluding Japan (AUTIF sector)**   Trusts which invest at least 80 per cent of their assets in Far Eastern securities. Those with Japan must include Japanese securities which may not exceed 80 per cent of the portfolio.

**Financial and property (AUTIF sector)**   Trusts which invest at least 80 per cent of their assets in financial or property securities.

**Fixed Interest (AUTIF sector)**   Trusts which invest at least 80 per cent of their assets in fixed-interest stocks internationally. UK fixed-interest funds are classified as gilt and fixed interest.

**FT A All-Share Index**   The Financial Times [London] Stock Exchange measure of all companies listed on the UK stockmarket.

**FTSE Index**   The Financial Times [London] Stock Exchange 100 Index, commonly known as 'Footsie' – an index combining the UK's 100 leading companies.

**Fund of funds (AUTIF sector)**   Unit trusts which are able to invest only in other authorised unit trust schemes.

**General PEP**   Shares, unit trust, investment trust or fixed-interest securities may be invested in such a PEP, up to the annual individual allowance of £6,000 per year.

**Gilts**   Stock issued by the government. Both the capital at maturity and interest are guaranteed. Although PEPs can invest in unit trusts which themselves invest in gilts, over 50 per cent of the unit trust must be invested in equities.

**Gilt and fixed-interest trusts (AUTIF sector)**   Unit trusts holding 80 per cent of their assets in UK fixed-interest securities, such as gilts, debentures, loan stock, convertible bonds, or preference shares.

**Gross yield**   The return on an investment before tax has been deducted.

**Growth funds (AUTIF sector)**   Trusts with at least 80 per cent of their assets in equities (UK equities for UK growth) that aims to achieve capital growth.

**Growth and income funds (AUTIF sector)**   Trusts with at least 80 per cent of their assets in UK equities, which aim to yield 80 per cent – 110 per cent of the FTSE All-Share Index – and which aim to provide gains through both growth and income.

**Income units**   Generic unit trust type which pays out dividends in cash, as opposed to accumulation units whose payout is either in additional units or a higher price for existing units.

**Index**   A measure of stockmarket performance which typically contains largest companies or some other section of the market. Indices exist for most markets in the world and are created through a mathematical calculation.

**Index bear funds (AUTIF sector)**   Funds designed to inversely track the performance of an index by using derivatives.

**Index fund**   A unit trust which aims to match the performance of a specific index; also called a 'tracker' because it aims to track a certain market index.

**Investment trusts**   A company, usually listed on The Stock Exchange, which invests in other companies or financial instruments. The price of investment trusts rises and falls depending on demand for shares of the investment trust itself. Also referred to as a 'closed-end fund'.

**Investment trusts units (AUTIF sector)**   Trusts which are only able to invest in shares of investment trust companies.

**Japan funds (AUTIF sector)**   Trusts which invest at least 80 per cent of their assets in Japanese securities.

**Loan stocks**   Loans made by companies which are not secured by company's assets as opposed to debentures, which are loans secured by company's assets.

**Managed PEP**   May contain shares, unit trusts, investment trusts, or combinations of the three. While the managers decide what assets to hold within the pooled investments, the investor often has the choice of selecting the trusts.

**Market-maker**   A dealer who quotes both a buying and a selling price for stocks and shares.

**Meeting charge**   A charge levied to attend shareholders' meetings.

**Middle (Mid) price**   The price halfway between the bid and offer share prices shown in the Stock Exchange Daily Official List. Newspapers usually show the Mid Price.

**Money market fund**   See *Cash fund*.

**Moody's**   An independent credit rating agency scrutinising the financial health of companies, awarding them a rating according to their ability to withstand volatile market conditions. The ratings range from AAA at the top to CCC at the bottom. Other well-known rating agencies include: Standard & Poor's and IBCA.

**Net yield**   The return on an investment after tax has been deducted.

**North American funds (AUTIF sector)**   Trusts which invest at least 80 per cent of their assets in North American securities.

**Non-qualifying**   Unit trusts or investment trusts with more than 50 per cent of the underlying assets invested outside the UK or other European

Union Member countries. A maximum of £1,500 may be invested in such funds if they are held within a PEP.

**OEICS**   See *Open-Ended Investment Company.*

**Offer price**   The price an investor pays to buy a unit trust or share.

**Offer to bid**   Compares the original purchase cost or offer price – usually of a unit trust – with its bid price, the price at which it may be sold. This measure is useful for determining performance taking into account charges.

**Open-Ended Investment Company**   Recently approved type of managed fund, compatible with European Union requirements. Authorised in January 1997. Meets UCITS requirements. (see *UCITS.*)

**Passive Portfolio Management**   Investment manager is required to achieve results as close to index as possible, even if index goes down; synonymous with 'indexing' or 'tracking'.

**PEP**   Widely accepted abbreviation for Personal Equity Plan, even though now the regulations permit corporate bonds to be included.

**PEP allowances**   For an individual, £6,000 per year general PEP plus £3,000 per year single-company PEP.

**PEP-able funds**   Shares, unit trusts, or investment trusts which may be placed in the PEP.

**PEP switch**   To move invested assets from one fund to another within the same fund management company. With unit trust and investment trust PEP, a selection of funds are often offered from the same fund management company's list of unit trusts.

**PEP transfer**   To move the underlying assets or cash value from one PEP Manager to another. This does not affect current tax year allowances because the PEP remains relevant to the year in which it was originally purchased.

**Personal pension and FSAVC unit trusts (AUTIF sector)**   Trusts which are only available for use by investors in a unit trust personal pension plan or FSAVC scheme.

**Plan manager**   A PEP must be managed and administered by a Registered Scheme Manager approved by the Inland Revenue and authorised under the Financial Services Act.

**Pooled investments**   Unit trusts and investment trusts are examples of where investors pool their money together to make investments.

**Preference shares**   Issued by companies to pay a fixed dividend each year. Preference shares rank ahead of ordinary shares for receipt of dividends and the distribution of the company's assets. They may be redeemed at a certain date, be irredeemable or be convertible into ordinary stock. All preference shares issued by UK and EU companies are PEP-able with the exception of those issued by banks and building societies.

**Qualifying funds**   Funds containing at least 50 per cent of the underlying assets invested in the UK or other European Union Member countries. The maximum general allowance of £6,000 per year may be invested in such funds.

**Recognised stockmarket**   A stockmarket approved by the Inland Revenue for PEP investments.

**Redemption**   Refers to a date or a range of dates when a loan, for example, a government stock or corporate bond becomes payable. The government or company concerned has an obligation to redeem the stock at the nominal or par value. This may often be at £100.

**Redemption yield**   The current dividend or interest rate yield increased or decreased to take into account the capital value of the asset if held to redemption.

**Replication**   Describes technique used by index fund managers, whereby all shares in relevant index are held. The other technique is called sampling, whereby index fund managers invest in only a representative sample of shares from the index.

**Running yield**   Typically, the current dividend or interest payment per unit from a fund divided by the bid price.

**Sampling**   A technique used by index tracking managers where a selection of shares thought to be representative of the index, as opposed to all shares of an index, are held.

**Self-select PEP**   The investor makes all the decisions as to what is bought and sold with the PEP. A plan manager is still required and would usually be a stockbroker.

**Share exchange**   A facility offered by plan managers to sell existing share holdings. The proceeds may then be used to invest in a PEP.

**Single company PEP**   A PEP with a £3,000 allowance investing in the shares of one company only.

**Smaller companies (AUTIF sector)**   Trusts which invest at least 80 per cent of their assets in the UK equities of companies which form part of the Hoare Govett UK Smaller Companies Extended Index.

**Stamp tax or duty**   An indirect tax payable on buying shares. It currently stands at one-half of one per cent.

**Standard & Poor's**   An independent credit rating agency scrutinising the financial health of companies, awarding them a rating according to their ability to withstand volatile market conditions. The ratings range from AAA at the top to CCC at the bottom. Other well-known rating agencies include: Moody's and IBCA.

**Tax year**   Runs from 6th April to the following 5th April.

**Tracker fund**   A unit trust which follows a stockmarket index, such as the FTSE 100 or the FTSE All-Share. Tracker funds are said to be passively managed because the manager simply tries to replicate the index, without regard to the potential for growth or loss of the individual shares.

**Unit trust**   A portfolio of shares or bonds, managed by professional investment managers, created by trust deed; generically, called an 'open-ended' fund because outstanding units can increased or decreased by the fund management company depending on investor demand. An investment trust, by comparison, has a fixed number of shares and so is called a 'closed-ended' fund. Price of unit trust rises or falls depending on value of underlying securities, not on demand for units themselves.

**UCITS**   Undertakings for Collective Investment in Transferable Securities. Describes fund which meets regulatory requirements such as allowing it to be sold within the European Union.

**Withdrawal fee**   Similar to exit fee, although, in addition, there may be a charge levied to withdraw capital sums from the PEP, whilst retaining the investment.

**Yield**   The dividend return on an investment expressed as a percentage of the purchase price. Yields for PEPs are quoted gross (i.e., without deduction of tax at source).

# INDEX